The Duty to Act

Tort Law, Power, & Public Policy

The Duty to Act
Tort Law, Power, & Public Policy

by Marshall S. Shapo

University of Texas Press, Austin & London

To the memory of

My Father

MITCHELL SHAPO

and My Mother

NORMA S. SHAPO

Library of Congress Cataloging in Publication Data

Shapo, Marshall S., 1936–
    The duty to act.

    Includes bibliographical references and index.
    1. Torts–United States. 2. Personal injuries–
United States. 3. Assistance in emergencies–United
States. 4. Public policy (Law)–United States.
I. Title.
KF1250.S47   346'.73'03   78-3576
ISBN 0-292-78025-7

Printed in the United States of America

Contents

Acknowledgments

I owe much to many persons who have contributed to the ideas in this book and to its production.

Many colleagues have provided criticism and helpful encouragement. I am particularly grateful to Harvey Perlman, John Jeffries, and Harry Pratter, each of whom read and criticized the entire manuscript at various stages in its development. I appreciate also the criticism and supportiveness of Tom Bergin and Larry Walker. Monrad Paulsen, a dean whose capacious personality matches his talent for encouraging scholarship, provided an atmosphere of respect for learning and writing that enabled the principal work on this book to proceed. For continued decanal support in the final stages of work, I am grateful to Emerson G. Spies, who has continued the tradition of fostering scholarship at Virginia.

It is particularly fitting in a book published by the University of Texas Press to affirm again my continuing obligation, both professional and personal, to Page Keeton and Leon Green. It is in the nature of scholarship that this kind of debt grows with each acknowledgment of it by the debtor.

A dozen years of classroom give-and-take in Austin and Charlottesville have contributed to my thinking about this subject. Out of the more than one thousand students who have been involved in that process, I must mention at least the two who participated in the final labor of assuring the accuracy of my scholarship: Bill Austin and James K. Hammond.

Many librarians have provided me with indispensable aid to research. The University of Virginia Law Library funneled thousands of books and documents to me under the dedicated administrations of Frances Farmer and Larry Wenger. Roy Mersky originally showed me the frontiers of the librarian's art, instructing me on a scholar's bibliographic privileges as well as obligations. Among the platoons of library staff members who have aided my work, the foremost is Hazel Key.

The members of the Publications Office at the University of Virginia have cheerfully and promptly produced manuscript in several stages. For this assistance, always generously rendered, I am grateful to Diane Moss and her band of secretarial warriors. Those who helped the most on this book include Gail Branch, Madeline

Branch, Kathy Burton, Gloria Kelarakis, Virginia Trenka, and Sandy Harris.

An academic haven in which I did a substantial amount of the writing and thinking on this book is the Centre for Socio-Legal Studies, Wolfson College, Oxford. I am very grateful to the Centre's director, Donald Harris, for his hospitality.

In the end, it is people who make books, but institutions have done much to make this volume possible. Vital to this undertaking was the support of the National Endowment for the Humanities, of which I was a Senior Fellow in 1974–1975, and the University of Virginia, which provided me a Sesquicentennial Associateship during the same period.

As always, my greatest gratitude is to my closest comrade, Helene S. Shapo. Her affection and her demanding intellect are my primary inspiration. And an author could not ask better filial support than that of Benjamin Mitchell Shapo and Nathaniel Saul Shapo—solid fellows, keen dinner table analysts of hypothetical tort puzzles, and great readers who know what it means to write.

Introduction

Tort law is an important social mediator, reflecting a rough consensus of the way the legal system should respond to personal injuries which one person attributes to another. Polar cases that one typically thinks of as tort cases are reflected in the image of the automobile injuring a pedestrian and the deliberate assault in the street. Tort law in fact reaches far beyond cases of simple bodily injury to property damage and many kinds of economic loss and, in doing so, impinges on property law on one perimeter and contract law on another, as well as maintaining a border with the vast body of public and private regulation effected through the antitrust laws. At the same time, tort law has become entwined with the Constitution, with the development of an expanding body of law under civil rights legislation dating back to the nineteenth century. These varied missions of tort law make it a mirror for complexity, in terms of the areas of human endeavor to which it responds and the political and social as well as economic tensions and biases that it reflects in society at large.

Much of the story of tort law has been the development of doctrines of culpability, ranging from intentional tort and categories of reckless conduct through negligence and into the broad category of strict liability. In the conventional lexicon, conduct that is at least substantially certain to produce a harmful or offensive contact qualifies for the label of intentional tort, whereas negligence applies to behavior that falls below the standard of reasonable prudent persons so situated. Strict liability has come to be defined in various ways, but generally requires that the defendant conduct himself in a way that is at least unreasonably dangerous as it affects the plaintiff, even though it cannot be shown that the defendant was careless, let alone substantially certain that he would produce a harmful contact.

Linked with these theories of culpability are various notions of duty. A classic English definition from the late nineteenth century holds that, when circumstances place one individual in such a position with regard to another that thinking persons of ordinary sense would recognize the danger of injury to the other if ordinary skill and care were not used, a duty arises to use ordinary skill and care to avoid the injury.[1] A much quoted American judicial definition of duty emphasizes its relational aspects, with a focus on the foreseeability of risk to those "within the range of apprehension."[2] At about the same time, one of the most creative of American law teachers defined duty as a complex of factors, including administrative, economic, and moral ones, to be applied by judges in their analyses of the legal strength of personal injury cases.[3]

Within the ground covered by these alternative theories of duty, there exist numerous doctrines that relate to many kinds of fact situations and varied patterns of functional activity. They deal with questions of when to require compensation for conduct that has gone awry in some way, as in the case of a vehicle driven too fast for conditions; they embrace cases of inadequate oversight of situations in which the exertion of more control would have avoided injury, as in many cases of substandard product manufacture; and they have been fashioned to respond to the failure to react to hazards that befall others whose peril becomes known to the one who could have averted it.

The analysis I offer here thrusts toward an alternative definition of duty, specifically stated with reference to cases that generally are known as failures to act. From these cases and across these pages come many persons whose plights touch us at a level so deep that we must either help them or turn away, aware of our own vulnerability. Victims of accidents or sudden medical problems lie on the workplace floor, on the athletic field, or in the road, and bystanders are reluctant to react. Hotel guests and casual patrons in business establishments appeal in vain for aid against threatened criminal assault. A woman terrified by the threats of a jilted suitor is denied police protection. In each of these cases we are torn by competing social and individual concerns. Examining such problems, I suggest solutions founded primarily on a concept of power which will be outlined with reference to a number of factual and functional categories.

My analysis will include the duties of both private persons and governments within this framework of power. In the first part, which focuses on the obligation of private persons, I shall examine a series of continuing relationships, including employment and commercial relations and those stemming from educational environments, and then relationships more fortuitously growing from emergency circumstances. In the course of this analysis, I shall advance the thesis that persons who can use energy, ability, or information to aid others in serious peril without significant inconvenience or harm to themselves should do so. Then, in the second part, I shall explore the issue of when governments have a duty to act to save citizens from various kinds of injury. First, I shall analyze this question with reference to rather conventional applications of tort doctrine to several functional contexts, ranging from traffic control and highway design to police duties in varied situations, and, finally, I shall deal with frontiers of tort possibilities in matters of health, education, and welfare. In this part, I shall compare the law respecting governmental duties with that applicable to private obligation, arguing that various considerations of public policy support an expanded view of public duty.

In the course of this discussion, I shall be presenting a structural framework of tort duty that is partly doctrinal and partly functional, which I think provides a persuasive alternative casting of the central issue related to that subject. Together with this reading of tort topography, with attendant efforts at explanation and criticism of judicial performance in that area, I shall set forth views, involving primarily normative concerns, regarding the kinds of questions that should receive more articulate attention from judges. And I shall venture some answers which reflect my own notions of how cases should be decided, at the same time making clear that those holding differing views of questions that have substantial ethical or political components can reasonably disagree on results while accepting the analytical model. Thus, I will hope to persuade readers in two different modes of thought. Rather neutrally, I will argue that an analysis based on power provides a most satisfactory framework for tort questions of duty, particularly of duties to act, and that this analysis requires a substantial component of moral judgment; more normatively, I will seek to convince readers about the desirable vector for judicial approach.

Power in tort law. This study has grown from the conviction, developed during my study of tort law and related areas, that much of that body of doctrine can best be understood as a manifestation of the law's concern with exercises and defaults in the use of power. Power in the sense I use it here includes physical force and the ability to use various forms of energy in ways that exercise effective control of people's destinies in particular transactions or circumstances. I undertake here to begin an investigation of the effect of various forms of power on a large body of cases in the field of torts and neighboring areas. The principal hypothesis is that power relationships provide meaningful explanations of desirable results in these cases—not an exclusive analytical vehicle but one that enables us to understand the goals of the legal system more clearly, particularly with reference to the relation of this area of law to considerations of public policy.

It is useful first to set out certain premises that guide this study. Tort law involves considerable tension between various personal rights and freedoms, to which is added competition between diverse social notions of what is appropriate legal relief for the consequences of injurious fortuitous occurrences. Basically, this area of the law involves clashes between rights of locomotion and action and rights to be free from injury caused by forces unleashed by other persons. To take a simple exaggerated example, a possessor of land has a right to use his power lawnmower on his grass, but his visitor standing nearby has a right not to have the mower run over his feet. This is surely so with respect to deliberate acts by the landowner and to acts that community representatives, sitting in judgment, would later deem careless according to the standard of prudent persons. Indeed, the physical energies of the device are such that as a practical matter this may be so with respect to any accidental occurrence concerning which it cannot be shown that the visitor chose to encounter the risk.

One important element in the mixture of compensation law is that of fortuity. In many cases of personal injury, the harm is one relatively unpredictable in advance. Although risk is known in a general way to exist, conditions of considerable uncertainty may surround it. The more fortuitous the harm, the stronger the theoretical case becomes, generally, for socialized compensation. There is a strong element of equity in this, a notion that more generalized risks of living should fall on society generally, if not on the injured party, rather than on one whose act or default caused an event that is in common parlance an accident. Yet, so long as common law liability may stimulate actors to take more precautions, even harms properly labeled fortuitous will call forth judgments against those who cause injury. Since the personal injuries that occasion litigation involve the unleashing of or failure to expend physical force, or the use of other forms of energy or failure to communicate the information in which power resides, the award of damages manifests a clear judgment that exercises or defaults in the use of power entail liabilities. Similarly, when harm is quite fortuitous, the law's refusal to demand compensation from the defendant takes account of the fact that both parties lacked ability to control the event. Yet, most significantly in the analysis I develop in this book, when there is control and transactional superiority in one party, liability may be imposed for reasons that often blend elements of humanitarian concern with efficiency factors. The notions of control and submission and of power and dependence which are developed here will reflect my belief that in the area of tort law and associated doctrine that I will particularly analyze—principally involving duties to act—considerations of fairness and humanity deserve special though not exclusive emphasis, and that judges are well situated to articulate the views of the community with respect to cases of this kind. Given the guessing and estimating of social benefits and costs that are necessary to achieve efficiency-biased judgments of liability, an analysis centered on humanitarian elements and considerations of fairness may often produce results that are more persuasive to the community, whose judgment is the ultimate one on matters of law as well as politics.

The elements of power that affect the imposition of liability for personal injury are several. As the example of the lawnmower illustrates, the manipulation of physical power by voluntary action is an obvious classification. In this area alone, the subcategories are as various as human existence. One may inflict injury by the direct application of physical power through means that vary from the fist and the wielding of a hatchet[4] to the radiations of a nuclear machine.[5] Quite as directly affecting personality and freedom, those who have lawful custody of persons wield significant control over the lives of their charges and exercise power in ways dispositive of physical security. Moreover, one may use words or pictures to achieve the same lacerative or searing effects of fists, guns, and radiation and the same brutalization as maltreatment of prisoners. The law of defamation and some aspects of liability for "invasion of privacy" have developed because of the "explosive power resident in words."[6] And the way in which products are represented, either directly or indirectly, will often prove dispositive in the assignment of liability when their failure or subpar performance causes injury.[7] Apart from that, those who control financial power in various forms have faced legal constraints on the ability to exercise it to the detriment of particular individuals, as in the case of insurers who find courts taking an expansive view of their duties to defend claims advanced against policyholders,[8] as well as limiting their right to cancel policies.[9]

The factual settings of these cases range broadly across modern commercial and industrial activity, as well as the more directly personal relationships. But a thread that runs significantly through all of them is the theme of power, of control of the circumstances of life for private individuals in particular transactional settings.

One who strikes another without warning, or before the other can get his guard up, effectively takes advantage of the other's physical insecurity, wielding his physical power to inflict injury. By analogy, the defamer always strikes the one who is libeled when, figuratively, his guard is down. One who unleashes atomic radiation into the community acts to the detriment of those who cannot defend themselves; he impinges on their physical security even though he does not come physically within a hundred yards of them. In these and the other categories mentioned, distinguishing features of the cases lie in the ability to use force or constraints of a physical nature, or other effective means of personal control, in a way that injures another who is not in a practical position to resist the use of that force or the exercise of that control.

Besides referring to the concept of power in the way I have described, I shall use some broad definitions concerning the activities of power holders. I originally began this study as an investigation of tort remedies for the "abuse of power," a concept that during the course of the study gained the official linguistic sanction of congressional charges in the presidential impeachment proceeding, as well as growing usage among various commentators in law and politics. Granted the rather imprecise nature of this phrase, I think it has meaning in the legal context on which I focus here: I use it to signify situations in which power holders employ their superiority over others in such a way as to be offensive to prevailing community standards of decent conduct, seriously disruptive of the social bonds in the relevant community, and presumptively productive of justifiably overwhelming feelings of frustration or fear in those whose interests are damaged.

I shall also utilize various terms to refer to uses of or failures to use power that are less socially repugnant than the actions I have called abuse. The general concept on which I rely here is the relatively neutral one of mismanagement, which would include both acts and omissions as conventionally defined. This concept signifies a community judgment that the way in which a power holder has behaved merits legal relief in favor of the person in the inferior position, for reasons that may include those of economy or justice or both. In this vein, I shall refer to "misuse" or "mishandling" of power to encompass a range of behavior that now is categorized under various tort headings, principally classified under headings of negligence and strict liability, as well as activities of governmental officers that are often litigated directly or by derivation under certain constitutional provisions. I shall use "default in the use of power" to refer to a range of occasions which include what traditionally would be called "omissions" or "failures to act," but which shade off into circumstances in which a power holder actively engaged in a course of conduct does not exercise a given precaution, or otherwise take certain steps within the course of that overall activity, that would prevent harm to someone who lacks the power to avert it.

Although this book is directed principally to people who do not have a professional interest in the literature of tort law, it is appropriate to note that, in the development of this system of definitions and the analysis which uses them, I have been aware of the development of a substantial body of recent and contemporaneous scholarship in the field of torts. All workers in this area are indebted to Guido Calabresi and his associates, both for defining an economic perspective on tort law[10] and for pushing forward the effort to distinguish considerations of wealth distribution from those of efficiency.[11] References in this study to factors of cost avoidance and the role of information about risk in deciding tort cases manifest the fact that scholars in this area today stand on the shoulders of Calabresi, as well as deriving continuing help from the efficiency-centered studies of Ronald Coase[12] and Richard Posner.[13] On parallel tracks, the work of George Fletcher[14] and Richard Epstein[15] has provided stimulating alternative analyses based, respectively, on notions of fairness and causation. Calabresi has presented a model bifurcated into "specific deterrence," emphasizing cost avoidance through positive regulation, and "general deterrence," a system that seeks to establish optimal accident levels through the market with the aid of judicial determinations of liability, overlaid on a threefold framework of costs—those associated with the happenings of accidents themselves, those incurred in the aftermath of accidents, and the administrative costs of dealing with accidents. Contemporaneously with Calabresi's early work, Coase focused attention on the costs of acquisition of information and negotiation by theorizing that there is no difference in resource allocation whichever way the liability determination is made between parties in a position to bargain costlessly about an externality. Later, Posner asserted, after a study of thirty years of appellate decisions beginning in 1876, that negligence law is primarily a response to efficiency considerations. By contrast, Fletcher argued for a "paradigm of reciprocity," as contrasted with a utility-centered "paradigm of reasonableness," as an explanation for modern liability theory. Through a different lens,

Epstein found causation his polestar and emphasized individual liberty as a limitation on tort liability with particular reference to an area explored in this book.

Although I make rather little specific reference to this body of literature in this work, this does not denigrate my debt to these and other authors who have enriched my thinking about tort law, but rather reflects the absorption of their ideas in the common currency of torts scholarship. It will also, however, imply a belief on my part that the analyses and usages of these scholars may be improved by the articulation of a framework centered on considerations of power relationships. Moreover, the analysis offered here is not bound so closely to the terminology of conventional legal doctrine, particularly that of the label "strict liability," which recently has taken on meanings perhaps too various for one term.[16] Further by contrast with some of these analyses, I have not taken as my province in this book the field of tort or accident law generally. It is rather my intention to send a shaft of light across one substantial corner of tort law, where elements of control and dependence are principally at issue, at the same time believing that the analysis developed here may prove useful in other realms of tort. Within the more limited field I have defined, I have tried to provide a formula alternative to those I have encapsuled above.

It is well here to advert to the nature of choice that is involved in various kinds of compensation law. The terminology of "accident" law tends to denote occurrences that are principally fortuitous. However, there often is a significant element of choice in events leading to injuries. Many times this basically is a social choice,[17] but often there is a component of personal choice on the part of the injured party. This clearly would be the case when a stunt rider is injured in the pursuit of his business. To take a classic hypothetical from the torts literature, it is also so when someone accepts a ride with an obviously drunk driver in order to save his family from a burning house.[18] I should note in this connection that there are a number of choices that the law will not permit individuals to make. For example, legislatures may constitutionally prohibit certain dangerous practices, such as snake handling, even in the name of religion,[19] and may enforce the wearing of crash helmets for motorcyclists.[20] Moreover, the legal system may refuse to enforce written statements that one will accept certain risks, either when there is a coercive element of circumstance involved or when the risk is not brought home effectively to the party who is injured. Mixtures of these elements probably appear in such instances as the refusal to enforce an exclusionary clause against the child of a tenant in a building run by a public housing authority.[21] In many cases involving defective products, courts may ignore disclaimers that are placed inconspicuously in small type.[22] In situations of this kind the law recognizes that power, in the sense of actual or potential situational control by one person over the destiny of another, including control through the possession of information, should influence the placement of liability. Often, however, the law does allow bargains that involve choices of risk, by refusing to permit personal injury actions by those who take certain risks against those who create them.

A related point is that parties who injure others themselves engage in bargain and choice. This observation leads us into the complicated question of tortious intent. The categories of "intentional tort," "negligence," and "strict liability" are hardly airtight, and in many cases it is wise to avoid complete judgmental reliance on the characteristics of the injurer's conduct to which these terms refer. This is a subject for a substantial separate study and here I wish only to note that the degree of choice made by the injuring party may well affect the nature of his liability. This is so both viewing the injured party's situation independently and regarding it in its relation to choices made by him with which the injurer's choice is necessarily intertwined.

With respect to a parallel definitional problem, I should further emphasize that there is much twining and overlapping between traditional notions of action and inaction. For example, when one drives an automobile and collides with another vehicle at a time when he momentarily takes his eyes off the road, it may be described both as action in the sense that he was pressing the accelerator and inaction in the sense that he was inadvertent in relation to the particular circumstances. Thus, although this particular study deals principally with the imposition of liability for defaults in the use of power—"failures to act"—it is important to note that the categories blend into each other quite freely. It is also worth noting that there is a considerable difference in practical terms between the highly repetitive kind of act that is involved in the routine driving of an automobile and the kind of decision that more generally involves awareness, judgment, and conscious choice—a description applicable to the types of cases principally involved in questions of "duty to act."

At this juncture, it is useful to mention a related conceptual distinction that I shall be making, one between "planning" and "maneuvering." This distinction is one that is partly congruent with the difference between deliberation and inadvertence. In the realm of public duties, it has an analogue in the effort to separate "discretionary" from "operational" or "ministerial" functions. The parallels are not exact, but I believe that a distinction between planning and maneuvering meaningfully captures a reality that is related to the nature of choice that power holders have, both in relation to time periods and as a matter of the ability to consider the implications of one's transactional superiority as well as to respond rationally to given circumstances.

Generally, I shall suggest here that it is well to begin the analysis of such personal injury cases by discovering where the locus of power lies and estimating the consequences of that social geography. One should then proceed to examination of the overlapping conceptualisms and realities of fortuity, culpability, and choice, as well as the social infrastructure of ethical concern, which produce results in individual cases that reflect the complex relationships these factors bear among themselves and with the facts of power.

Before proceeding to a particular investigation of when the law requires power holders to use their abilities and energies, I may indicate with a further set of examples the variety of configurations of control, reliance, and uncertainty to which the broad power-centered analysis outlined here would generally apply. In the case of prisoners, and to a somewhat lesser extent in instances involving employees and school children, the circumstances in effect impose a substantial obligation on the controlling party. And in certain cases in which control is surrendered voluntarily over the body or affairs of the injured person, it is done only with the understanding that the controlling party will exercise his power with special regard for the interests of the other. This is the case with contracts of insurance, for example. It is also the case as a practical matter when people entrust part of their personal lives to the care of a professional.[23] Indeed, courts may use the language of fiduciary obligation to characterize legal liabilities in situations of this kind.[24]

Striking a conceptual tangent, on one side, to situations in which reliance on safe conduct is fostered by legally imposed custody and, on another, to those in which it is a feature bargained for or created by law in particular transactions are cases in which the reliance interest is rather more attenuated. That interest is still significant in cases of visitors to land. It is less so in the case of most vehicular accidents, in which there is little or no personal relationship involved between the injuring party and the one who is harmed. In these cases the only reliance is one constructed by law;

it is loosely divined from the existence of both individuals in society, in the sense that each of us implicitly tends to assume that his fellows in the vicinity are not acting in a way that will harm him, else defenses would be mustered and much higher levels of caution exercised.

Thus, power is wielded in a web of intersecting threads of rights of action and rights to security, as well as varied milieus of bargain, and in differential environments of uncertainty with consequently differing levels of the fortuity inherent in injurious consequences. It is against this background that we turn to specific questions of when power confers obligations and engenders liability. The principal inquiry in the study that follows is one of how duties arise from the control and exercise of power.

PART ONE

Private Duties to Act:
Legal Affirmation of the
Obligations of Personal Power

Introduction

The focus of this study is the general question of whether one person must act to protect another. In legal terminology, the core question is whether there is a "duty to act," but this inquiry is rather broader. It is an attempt to explore a number of issues packed around that core, as instances of the development of citizen remedies for abuse and default in the use of power. In this part, I shall deal with problems that arise from relations between private individuals, reserving for the second part questions involving the relations between individual citizens and governments. As I have suggested above, the law must respond to many diverse forms of the control of power, of which only the simplest form that generates everyday tort law is that involving the release of physical forces. I shall deal here more with default through control rather than misuse by release–control not only of physical energy but also of other forms of power by private individuals–and I shall ask when legal obligations arise to use power in particular ways. Among other questions of policy, I shall refer specifically to the possible derivation of obligation from the fact that a power holder derives his power principally from social nourishment.

Basic to this analysis is the idea that duties arise from power, which is a central fact in relationships created both primarily by bargain and principally in a fortuitous way. Thus, this study deals in large part with the nature of relationships between individuals, including those created by explicit bargains, those that rest in well-defined tradition, and those that the law recognizes to exist through a synthesis of external reality and inarticulate social consensus. At the end of this scale is the question of the pure duty to act–whether, for instance, one must rescue another in imminent peril with whom he has no relation of bargain or tradition, and when the sources of obligation lie alone in power, policy, and humanity. Many times situations of the kind discussed here involve someone who has come into a perilous situation because of a combination of circumstances that may include some preliminary carelessness or even choice on his part. Typically, however, any contributory conduct on the part of the imperiled party has not entailed full appreciation of the risk involved, a factor which militates against application of the view that that person is in the position to avoid injury at the least cost. In the moment of maximum danger there is usually only one cost avoider, practically speaking, and the question of whether he should expend resources is often one which depends at the margin on the judge's view of humanitarian obligation. Emphasizing judicial articulation of basic notions of respect for human life and personal security, the view advanced here sometimes embodies a practical judgment that it is just to spread occasional losses whose occurrence would not be deemed inefficient when compared with the social gains from the activity that produced them.

In most situations in which the law imposes an obligation to act, it will itself arise from some kind of action.[1] Often the solution for a particular case will depend principally on the fact that a power holder already has done something in a way that engenders reliance on the part of the injured party or has created a generalized sense of security with reference to the latter's physical integrity. Many times the question of whether the party with the control of power was negligent will seem crucial. But it will be useful at the outset to dissociate ourselves from traditional theories of culpability, in order to examine how the law imposes obligations when the central issue of social policy concerns the duties that the control of power entails. This is so because culpability theories are so tangled together that in many cases an inquiry into power relationships will supply a more effective instrument for analysis, a better focus on the salient elements of cases—and perhaps ultimately will point the way to a superior definition of culpability. I should stress also that action and inaction are categories with considerable overlap.

The analysis will follow a structure that moves in a general way from the law's tendency to base duties on established relationships, principally defined by an economic nexus, to its historic reluctance to require action when there is no conventionally defined relationship which exists before the moment when the potential obligor recognizes the other person's peril. First, I shall examine a series of common relationships with reference to the obligations they create.[2] As an offshoot of this analysis in terms of relationships, I shall note how representations and other undertakings give rise to obligations to act. Then, applying and elaborating the ideas thus developed, I shall ask what obligation falls on individuals to protect others against injuries caused by third persons and, briefly, what duties there are to protect a person against the consequences of his own acts. Finally, I shall deal with the question of whether the law ever should impose duties on persons whose relation to one in peril is quite fortuitous. As I examine these questions, I shall refer recurrently to the way they tie into the power relationships between individuals and to the sources of the power that is entwined with these relationships. It will become clear that, whether duty is primarily tied with a pre-existing relationship or a humanitarian rationale seems predominant, it is the possession of power that provides a reliable signpost to the creation of obligation and usually appears to occasion it. Even in those cases in which there is an established reliance factor, there is generally an underlying sense that, when one party holds a significant superiority over the other in particular circumstances or transactions, practical requirements of humanity dictate that the power holder must act to save the other from serious injury if he can do so at minimal cost.

Besides the primary focuses I have mentioned, I shall also consider interstitially a variety of fact patterns that may themselves provide organizing categories, classifications closely connected with the ability of one party to control individual destinies. For example, it will tend to make a difference in the formulation of liability rules whether the imperiled party's danger is due to the conduct of the defendant, of others, or of himself or is the result of circumstances that cannot be ascribed meaningfully to the conduct of any person. In each of these cases, the assignment of liability depends importantly on the locus of control.

i. Primarily Economic Relationships That Give Rise to Duties

BUSINESSES, PROFESSIONS, AND ACTIVITIES

Employment Relations

It is appropriate to begin the search for the roots of obligation in power at a point of great social tension, in the employment relation. *Szabo v. Pennsylvania R.R.*[3] exposes such a pressure point, in an action under the Federal Employers Liability Act (FELA) for failure to render necessary medical care to a track maintenance laborer who died after being rendered "powerless to help and care for himself" by heat prostration. After the plaintiff's decedent collapsed, his experienced foreman told him to stop work and ordered two fellow employees to take him home. The co-workers did transport Szabo to his house, but, as the lower appeals court's summary of the facts indicates, there was no one home.[4] They left him seated in the kitchen and departed when he "motioned with his hands" that they should leave. Within the hour, Szabo's son returned to find his father lying on the bedroom floor. Although the trial court gave a verdict for the plaintiff, the intermediate court reversed on grounds that there was no evidence that the employer had knowledge that Szabo was in mortal danger.

The Court of Errors and Appeals then reversed the intermediate court, saying there was enough evidence to raise a jury question of whether the foreman had exercised due care in aiding the plaintiff's decedent. The theory, evidently, was alternative—"whether there was an initial duty resting upon the respondent or one voluntarily assumed." The latter alternative is a version of the familiar principle, discussed below, that one who undertakes to help another must do so carefully. But the court found a starker obligation to rest on the employer: "[W]here one engaged in the work of his master receives injuries, whether or not due to the negligence of the master, rendering him helpless to provide for his own care, dictates of humanity, duty and fair dealing require that the master put in the reach of such stricken employee such medical care and other assistance as the emergency, thus created, may in reason require."[5]

This definition of the required response, typically described in the language of negligence, relies basically on the element of control that resides in the master. That control is a creature of the bargain that led to the employment relation, and thus the obligation stems at least in part from the bargain. However, I would submit that the setting of the standard also partakes of a social judgment concerning the minimum obligation owed by any person who knows that another's physical security is effectively in his hands. Thus, power gives control, which in turn confers duty, the breach of which is conventionally described as negligence and in a case like *Szabo* entails a finding of employer liability. It seems most helpful to view the issue in terms of its roots in power relationships because this fixes on the practical source of the liability in various forms of control over personal dignity and security. To fix on power rather than negligence theory is revealing, incidentally, because it demonstrates that even deliberate action, in a situation that does not demand the split-second response and is in a nonpejorative sense willful, may well be "negligent." In sum, the use of the negligence label in such a case stands for a judgment that there has been a compensable default in the control of power.

Precedent on shipboard. The court's creation in *Szabo* of an obligation resting on "dictates of humanity, duty and fair dealing," which the decision said probably had its inception in the code of moral conduct, called on several bases in precedent. Among these was a decision by the United States Supreme Court in a seaman's case under the Jones Act, *Cortes v. Baltimore Insular Line*,[6] in which Justice Benjamin Cardozo's opinion for the court exposes clearly the roots of personal injury law in power relationships. The plaintiff was the administrator of a seaman who died from pneumonia in a hospital at his home port, claiming that better care on board ship would have saved his decedent's life. Replying to the defendant's argument that the action must be viewed as one on an implied contract term, Cardozo wrote that "the origin of the duty is consistent with a remedy in tort." The duty, he said, was "one annexed by law to a relation, and annexed as an inseparable incident without heed to any expression of the will of the contracting parties."[7] Cardozo found some room for argument as to the breadth of the duties of railroad employers to give aid; but he declared the duty to be clear and well understood in the case of seamen, pinned to the necessity of placing a "despotic" authority in the master. Beyond this, we find broad and general language that recognizes the importance of power and control: "Out of this relation of dependence and submission there emerges for the stronger party a corresponding standard or obligation of fostering protection."[8] It should be stressed here—a point that will be reiterated later—that this view is not one founded in a search for cheaper cost avoidance. Indeed, it might have been that the wrongful death damages for a seaman in the nineteen thirties would have been outweighed by the requirements of providing the necessary care on a seagoing vessel. The standard articulated by Cardozo is one that recognizes that certain relationships require a response to imperiled individuals simply because of their humanity. This moral sense—the articulation of which is necessarily abstract but has captured generations of torts scholars[9]—blends with more economic considerations, including the uncertain character of valuations of life and personal integrity[10] and the imperfections of information relating to risk.[11]

In this connection, and before further analysis of *Szabo*, it is well to emphasize the broad panoply of obligations that has emerged from employment at sea.[12] There is a strong correlation between the theories of recovery well known to lawyers who deal with seamen's injuries and the conventional lore of land-based tort law. Illustrating the capacious concept of duty associated with the ancient doctrine of maintenance and cure is a case in which a seaman's eye was injured in an attack by hoodlums, during shore leave in Inchon. On facts that included the appearance of swelling and profile bleeding around the eye, the court held that the seaman's employer had breached a duty in not taking him to an available English-speaking eye specialist, but rather having him treated by a general practitioner who spoke only Korean.[13] The breadth of the court's approach appears not only in its insistence on this standard of conduct but also in its threshold finding that "even a layman could have recognized the possibility of internal eye damage," a conclusion that effectively subsumes the controversy over expert testimony in the analogous area of medical malpractice. By parity, it may be pointed out that, when the problem was reversed in terms of the employment relation, a court held that there was no negligence in the failure of ship's personnel to act more quickly to aid a stricken captain who insisted on carrying on; and further by comparison with the case of the seaman's injured eye, the court in the captain's case noted sympathetically that his subordinates did not possess the "discernment of a surgeon."[14]

To turn about the perspective in the maritime context once more, the way in which obligation flows from power is exemplified by a decision rejecting an action for damages for being placed in a leg iron, brought by a seaman who had a history of emotional illness and who became severely agitated on board ship.[15] This holding demonstrates that the power of a master may occasionally create obligations to impose physical restrictions. Yet the problem in this case at once points up the rigorous character of the obligations that power confers. For, although too much use of the physical power given by rank would be tortious,[16] presumably if a master does not use physical restraint when the situation calls for it, this could support a negligence action by someone hurt by a tantrum of a raving sailor—perhaps even by the seaman himself for the consequences of self-destructive behavior. The power of physical control therefore provides a primary explanation for assignment of liability in cases of injured seamen under a variety of theories.[17] More broadly, it will become evident that an analysis based on power gives us a structure that supports analogies across a wide band of the field of personal injury compensation.

Power and efficiency. This brief exploration of maritime analogs puts the case of Szabo in a more revealing light. Although the authority of Szabo's foreman may not have had the attributes of despotism possessed by a ship's master, obviously the court believed that he bore a relation to Szabo that required a high standard of response to the decedent's plight. What are the components of the obligation that the court imposed? I think we may find a significant basis for that duty in the foreman's power, in his ability to dictate the movements not only of Szabo—who he insisted must sit down when he wished to resume work—but also of the employees whom he ordered to take their debilitated co-worker home.[18] And, from at least one of the court's alternative statements of the law, it appears that no more than an employee's helplessness in the face of emergent peril will require that his employer exercise the physical power at his command to respond to that peril. Why, after all, should this be? Why should the employee not be required to accept the risk that he will be left to fend for himself after the sudden heart attack or the slip into a hazardous position?

One may posit certain reasons related to the efficient conduct of business. First, when someone signs on to do a particular kind of work, the situation may be said to be instinct with understandings about reciprocal duties. The obligation to save an employee in imminent danger may be deemed part of the original bargain in order to save the haggling that would take place over such questions in a world in which perfectly knowledgeable parties negotiated about wage rates and working conditions.[19] Moreover, the understanding among employees that they would be aided in times of peril presumably would encourage them to work more energetically and rather less risk-aversely. Certainly, morale will be higher when the employee knows that he will get careful first aid when the unforeseen danger arises or when the statistically expectable peril occurs suddenly and despite appropriate precaution. But consider Szabo, who a fellow employee testified was "ashamed" to go home;[20] does the imposition of employer obligation respond to a perceived need to affect his incentives, or is the proper source of the duty a deeper normative judgment?

"Humanity . . . and fair dealing." There are special elements of poignancy as one sees the roles played out in this tragedy on the Pennsylvania line. Here it is the worker who drives himself on, protesting orders to cease work, later bidding his comrades take their leave so he can stagger to the bedroom to die unattended. And the foreman at least tries to do the decent thing, as well as take what probably in his view was the efficient course, compelling Szabo to stop work and arranging for him to be driven home. In this emotionally charged setting, it is the court that settles that the railroad's response has no overriding justification in efficiency and that it does not comport with the broader "dictates of humanity . . . and fair dealing." Does not "fair dealing" in this situation arise from a "relation of dependence and submission"? Certainly there is dependence, for work and the living it brings; and surely there is submission to the orders of the foreman—even reluctant obedience to an enforced furlough. In this case one finds himself in the very heart of tort tensions, in the world in which the tentative, halting feeling that something is not quite right contends with the feeling that one should carry on. The drive to go on is complex, deriving doubtless in part from the lash of economic circumstance, but one may also hypothesize that in Szabo's case it welled up from an in-bred Puritanism as well as a built-in *machismo*. Against the background of such subtle psychological mechanisms, the law places obligations on the employer within a radiating web of power—both the power to give orders to the employee and the physical power to aid him in trouble. It responds, I think, to a deep-rooted belief that when situations of this kind occur the very humanity of the imperiled party creates an obligation to help.

This obligation goes beyond one of weighing expected gains and losses in the endeavor; indeed, within certain broad limits, it places a value on the single endangered life higher than that which would be derived by any averaging device for working lives.[21] Part of the reason for this formulation of duty may lie in a judicial attempt to elevate social morale, which in turn may have a basis in the trembling sense that "there but for the Grace of God go I," as well as a hope in the ordinary citizen that such decisions will influence conduct to his future benefit. Part of it may derive from a sense that, in justice, special duties should attach to entrepreneurs whose activities cause harm, in a society that often confers privileges on them and at once maintains broad freedom of action. I shall probe further the roots of this obligation. For the moment, it should be pointed out that, at least in *Szabo*, the problem did not arise from callous disregard of the employee's plight. At base, that decision deals with a choice of the uses of existing power that was impermissibly improvident in the eyes of the community.[22] The jury in Szabo's case was to determine the molecular question of whether there was an appropriate selection of methods for dealing with his collapse on the job. But there also is the larger issue of what generally should be done in such circumstances, and this begins and ends as a question for the court. It should further be stressed that this question is one of obligation imposed by the law, not only by contractual undertaking.[23]

It may be contended that the imposition of liability in *Szabo*, in the setting of a very personalized misdirection of power in a direct human relationship, is one that is deprived of its compassionate elements by its placement of the burden on the employer on the basis of respondeat superior. Yet the genesis of the liability simply emphasizes that its humanitarian thrust is so powerful that it pushes beyond the direct personal relation of worker and foreman to that of the employee and the employer with whom he first contracted; and by imposition of a tort kind of duty the law achieves a pluralistic aim, effectively fleshing out the original bargain of the parties as well as enforcing obligations of justice.

Sufficient work force. The duty of employers extends well beyond the obligation to provide medical aid and, indeed, relates to working conditions generally. A significant instance involves the duty to employ enough persons to do a particular job. The Supreme Court defined this obligation liberally in a recent maritime case, holding that a vessel became unseaworthy by the assignment of two crewmen to carry rope so heavy that it required the heft of three or four.[24] Justice Hugo Black's opinion for the court found that the assignment of too few men to the job "caused both the men and the rope to be misused," an analysis explicitly based in recognition "of the needs of the seaman for protection from dangerous conditions beyond his control."[25] Thus it appears that the shipowner has a duty to acquire information about working conditions and to act on knowledge thereby secured of hazards in need of remedy. Although other fact situations involving similar questions may produce proper judgments for employers, as when a worker does not ask for help that usually is given routinely, the principle has been applied to employment generally.[26] To this extent, even before the advent of occupational safety and health legislation, the common law properly restricted the theoretical freedom of choice of employees to assent to especially risky working conditions whose level of danger is within the control of the employer.

There arises in this connection the question of how broadly the doctrine of assumption of risk should be applied. The approach taken in this study generally imposes considerable constraints on the use of that defense. The possession of power, either in the rawest physical sense of ability to rescue or in that of control customarily attendant on a relation, saps arguments based on consent to exceptionally dangerous risks that arise in the course of the relation. When those risks are part of the very fabric of the job, as in the case of stunt riding, the doctrine properly would retain its savage vitality. But, for example, when the problem is one of deliberate use of too few employees to do a job that can be accomplished in a much safer way with more workers, the defense should not be usable except in the case of the most informed, particularized, and explicit agreement to the hazards involved.

Medical Relations

The doctor-patient relation is also fraught with legal tension. Illustratively, that tension is at a high point when the question arises as to whether a physician must give bad news to his patient. In such a situation a practical analysis of power relationships reveals great dependence on the part of the patient, owing to his ignorance of medical knowledge generally and of how it applies to the facts that have been developed in his particular case. One court couches a physician's obligation in fiduciary terms while overruling the defense that a wrongful death claim is time-barred, in a case in which the plaintiff claimed that false assurances to his decedent prevented timely discovery after her death of the doctor's negligence.[27] The "fiduciary" obligation was one to "reveal all pertinent information" to the patient; moreover, if the patient died while under the care of doctor and hospital, "the spouse has a right to know the cause of death." In a case of this kind power resides in information practically available only to one trained at a social premium – today with considerable infusions of public money – and publicly licensed. And although it is an element hard to quantify, power derives also from dependence, rooted in a mystique, which in turn is fostered by an aura of competence and reliability that is inculcated partly by cultural tradition and partly by trade association propaganda. Applying a view I have put forth in another context, I would suggest that a broad-gauged representational analysis would provide an important sidelight on this case.[28] But, beyond that, control over information in the medical situation is a function of power socially conferred on physicians, and a holding that reliance on a doctor's word will excuse a failure to sue within a limitations period is a reflection of the law's sensitivity to that power.

Medical knowledge as legal power. Confirming the value of a power-centered analysis is a hideous case[29] involving injury in a radiation treatment. This case also partly involved a statute of limitations question, with the plaintiff alleging that she was not aware of negligence which was known to the doctor who referred her for the radiation treatment, and who with the other defendants cared for her in the intense pain she experienced afterward. The court refused to allow summary judgment on the limitations defense and also held that there were enough factual questions to go to the jury on fraud and conspiracy. In addition to its receptiveness to the plaintiff's claim of fraud in the sense of intentional misrepresentation, the court referred to a doctrine of "constructive misrepresentation," arising from silence. It mentioned in this regard the "confidential and vital nature" of the doctor-patient relationship and the resultant "affirmative duty requiring the doctor to disclose to his patient fully the facts of the medical case."[30] It referred also, citing a precedent dictum, to "continuing neglect to advise a proper course of treatment" as a "continuing tort."

Thus, several doctrines cluster here around a relational pole, based in the power that resides in knowledge – here knowledge of the facts of a particular case which affects its legal as well as medical implications.[31] The possession of that knowledge effectively controls the patient's legal rights, and the application of the rule that the statute of limitations does not run in malpractice cases unless the patient discovered or should have discovered the culpable conduct in time simply provides recognition of that fact. This is so whether one employs a theory of "negligence," "fraud" because one is "intentionally" misled, "equitable fraud," or "constructive misrepresentation," to name four characterizations used at different times by counsel and the court in this case. Indeed, courts will impose a duty to communicate facts about a threatening medical condition even when the physician has not found out about it but should have done so; for otherwise, the law would "reward the doctor for failing to discover that which a finder of fact may determine was within his professional duty to discover and, therefore, was his duty to discover."[32]

It should be added that there will be some circumstances in which it is desirable to withhold knowledge for the patient's well-being, as in the case of a highly neurotic patient who would only be made miserable by a disclosure of the nature of an illness when only one course of treatment is indicated. In such instances the appropriate conclusion in terms of a power-based analysis is that there is no prejudice to the patient's rights and therefore no damage. When a case is classified in this way, it indicates that there is no room for meaningful choice on the patient's part; and if reasonable persons acting with humanitarian concern would opt not to reveal the information, justice does not require disclosure.

Fusion of employment and medical relations. Having dealt separately with the employment relation and the relationship of doctor and patient, I shall now turn to the extraordinary fusion of duties in both categories that appears in *Coffee v. McDonnell Douglas Corp.*[33] In this case, the plaintiff applied for a job as a pilot with the defendant aircraft manufacturer. As part of the defendant's required physical examination, the plaintiff took a blood test, a report of which was received by a secretary at the defendant's medical clinic, time-stamped, and filed. Although the supervising doctor of the clinic testified that blood tests were necessary for the protection of the employer, the pilot, and the public, evidently no physician reviewed the test results—which would have led to a diagnosis of cancer of the bone marrow. Treatment after later discovery of that condition resulted in a remission, but the plaintiff alleged that he suffered injuries beyond those that would have afflicted him had earlier diagnosis been made. The court found that the company was negligent in its failure to establish a proper procedure for evaluation of blood test reports, rejecting the defendant's argument that it had no duty to "discover" diseases.[34] The duty held to exist in this case seems founded in a blend of the control that employers exercise over the testing of job applicants and the deference, even awe, that laymen accord medical examinations. Arguably, it is rather fortuitous that the defendant decided that it was essential to take a blood sample, which is not a part of every routine physical examination. The court therefore sets the standard for this case within a mold established by the defendant in its rationalization of its own business; but even so it must be noted that the shape of this mold depends partly on the firm's legal duties to the public with respect to the physical condition of its pilots.

Humanitarian rationale. But how does one leap from a test voluntarily taken to the creation of a duty, when the principal and well-understood purpose of the test was not to aid the plaintiff in any positive fashion but rather corporate self-protection? The case for imposing a duty would be somewhat more obvious in the instance of a physician who conducts an insurance examination and finds evidence of a disease which he does not report to the patient. Because of the professional status of the doctor, the patient would have an expectation and, I should think, a right to be told. By comparison, the case of the corporation, although it deals in this setting with information of a medical nature, is rather a different one; but apart from distinctions between the cases, certain aspects of the firm's social position argue that it should compensate one to whom it fails to give such vital information. We may characterize the situation this way: the corporation is a private party which, in the course of business involving another, has come upon information of vital importance about the health of the other, information that it could process and disgorge in a relatively costless way with a resultant substantial saving in social costs. Thus it might be reasoned that the corporation, by virtue of its license to conduct business and the power that thereby accrues to it, owes it to the community to take the path that entails the least cost to public welfare.

However, I think there is another rationale that at least partly explains this case. It is one founded in the requirements of humanity, as the law has come to interpret them, as a basis for legal obligation. Broadly stated, the effect of that obligation is to require that persons who at very little cost have the power to give aid to others, fortuitously thrown into a relation with them in a situation in which the need for aid is clear and emergent, must act in a way that shows the respect for the others required by their common humanity and by the relation into which events have placed them. In the pilot's case, of course, the duty arises from the radiations of two well-established categories of obligation that impinge on its facts. But the case lies close enough to the boundary of each of these classifications that it is useful to state the duty in more general terms, presenting a vehicle for application not only to those facts but also to diverse other situations in which a duty is sought to be enforced. I should emphasize at this point that the basis for imposing the duty is a pluralistic one, evolved partly from requirements of respect for the humanity of others, in some measure from established categories of relationships and in part from the social interest in reduction of welfare costs. Most importantly from the perspective offered here, whatever mix of rationales is used to support liability, it is the possession of power that occasions the obligation.

Lifeguarding and elemental power. A Louisiana decision involving a municipal lifeguard[35] presents an interesting analogue to the duties of doctors and employers, in a nonprofessional service area where rescue is an ordinary function of the job. It may be said generally that a lifeguard's employment in that capacity by the municipal owner of a swimming pool effectively confers power on him, and the aura of that power is heightened by the fact that the facility is public. Thus, when he ignores the plea for help of a drowning youth's friend, thinking it a prank, he operates in that framework of power, and his failure to direct his own physical energy toward rescue would be a dereliction of legal duty. The helplessness of the plaintiff, even when a product of his own horseplay, creates a situation in which the control of physical energy is elemental, and the relationship that temporarily evolves dictates action. The court reserves by implication the question of competing demands on resource allocation, noting that the pool was not crowded. Putting aside more complex problems of that kind, in this simple context there appears an escalating set of duties, some made explicit by the court, some made clear by implication: to investigate, to observe, to pull from the water, and to give first aid. The court cites a secondary authority to the effect that tort rules "represent that conduct below which a man cannot act in the community without becoming responsible for resultant damage."[36] The language clearly covers sloth as well as action, imposes duties to expend energy as well as to harness it. And the duty is a function of power, which derives from a relationship.

Businessmen, Customers, and Other Visitors

Carriers and passengers. I shall consider now the question of when an entrepreneur owes duties to customers and others with whom he has a direct relationship stemming from his provision of goods or services. The law often may demand that enterprisers either expend physical energy to help customers when they cannot navigate by themselves, or compensate for injuries that occur in default of aid. Indeed, in the realm of common carriers, this obligation may be codified in company rules, although their applicability in particular cases may be cause for dispute.[37] Some passengers will seek to establish duties that go beyond physical assistance, and it is concerning such a claim that especially interesting issues arise in *Stupka v. People's Cab Co.*[38] In that case the plaintiff was riding in the defendant's cab, which was hit in the rear by another car. The cab driver got out and talked to the other motorist but did not secure his name or license number. Writing for the court, Justice Herbert Cohen rejected a claim that the defendant had been negligent in failing to collect facts that would have helped the plaintiff in a personal injury action. In an opinion originally printed as a concurrence,[39] Justice Cohen drew the line at financial interest as opposed to the interest in physical security, at least when the defendant was "not responsible for placing the passenger in the original position of peril." Concurring, Justice Benjamin Jones found it unnecessary to face the bedrock duty question, since he thought there was "no causal relationship" between the defendant's failure to act and the plaintiff's alleged injury in not being able to sue the unknown driver. Justice Henry O'Brien's dissent seems closer to the mark with his common sense insistence that the determination of damages would not be hopelessly speculative and his rejection of the financial loss–physical harm distinction, joined with the argument that the cab driver failed to fulfill a statutory duty to make an accident report. Replying on the latter point, Justice Cohen noted the relatively light penalty imposed by the reporting statute and argued that to create a duty would place on the defendant "a much more serious sanction for failure to act than the statute imposes."

But a holding of "no causal relationship" avoids the main question of policy, and the determination of whether the statute directly creates a duty does not settle the issue. The statute is simply part of a context of expectation on an occasion when the cab driver has effective control of the situation. Particularly in the case of a common carrier, an entrustment factor intrudes into the psychological background. The passenger is practically in the driver's care, and the law should respond to the reality of the relationship. It should enforce on the carrier the obligation to protect the passenger's interests against impingements on them expectably caused by the ride, when the driver can safeguard those interests with relatively little effort. In situations like that in *Stupka*, one would find it rather unusual if an injured passenger came forth to demand the name of the offending driver.[40] Were Ms. Stupka injured riding in a Greyhound bus that had a collision, the weakness of the argument that this is an unprotected interest becomes apparent. It will not wash, I think, to argue (as does Justice Cohen) that the complexity and variety of a person's financial interests militate against imposing an obligation. One doubts that the cab driver would have failed to identify the other motorist if he himself had been hurt but remained mobile and articulate. When a passenger is hurt, the common carrier relation casts the driver as a surrogate. Indeed, it seems clear that he would have had to take his passenger to a hospital or call for rescue aid if her physical injuries demanded that; this duty has been imposed even on the operator of a private automobile.[41] And given the driver's role, his license, his meter, and the profit it represents, it requires no stretching of principle to say that the circumstances create an atmosphere of trust in his competence and in his will to protect all the interests of his passengers that he would be quick to protect of his own. It should be stressed that the entrustment factor involved here is not easily cabined by references to cost considerations on a market model. The question is not what the effects on consumer behavior would be in a world of perfect information and substantial competition, in which all intending taxi passengers knew that such an incident had occurred with People's Cab Company. Nor is the core of the case to be found in a measurement of welfare benefits from cab transportation compared with the negative economic consequences of occasional reporting failures. It lies rather in a community sense of what is fair in the psychological context of trust and dependence involved. Judicial views of fairness will of course differ, as indeed will judicial and economic estimates of comparative benefits and costs. It might be defensible to sustain a dismissal in *Stupka*, as it would be reasonable to overrule one. But it would be better to include a specific determination of the fairness of the result rather than to mask this judgment with a highly arguable characterization of noncausation. One may visualize variations on this fact pattern that are more difficult from the claimant's standpoint, but, given the nature of the relationship and the circumstances, *Stupka* seems wrongly decided.

Airports and ditched pilots. At a conceptual as well as physical border of the area of enterprisers' duties is the problem of whether an airport on a lake must maintain rescue facilities for pilots who crash in the water. Within a period of two years, two Illinois appellate courts gave negative answers to this question in cases involving emergency ditchings in Lake Michigan waters that adjoined a public airport.[42] The reasoning in one decision was that airport "ingress or egress" was not "involved in the occurrence."[43] The other court agreed, invoking the technical spatial point that invitors have no duty to persons outside their premises.[44]

The approach taken by these courts seems to oversimplify a problem better described in terms of spheres of influence rather than of duties that literally stop at the water's edge. There were several factors in this brace of cases that argued for airport liability. These included the public nature of the facility, its intended function as a receiver of air traffic, and the knowledge–underlined by the physical surroundings–that emergency ditchings were not a unique occurrence.[45] To be sure, factors of comparable weight bolstered the defendants' cases. The cost of training and maintaining rescue personnel is significant and by hypothesis would require trade-offs in other areas of airport operation, which by definition is permeated with safety concerns. Moreover, the private pilot is likely to have more freedom of choice in his selection of risky activity than the typical maritime or industrial claimant. Yet would it not be more satisfactory to say that transportation terminals owe a duty to incoming and outgoing users with respect to known perils, and to make the determination of whether that duty has been breached a question of fact? In one of the ditching cases, it was alleged that the airport previously had secured a fire department helicopter and trained a rescue crew; and it appears that when the accident occurred the airport alerted the fire department, which sent out a rowboat, though it arrived too late to save the crashed airman.[46] That may have been enough to measure up to the requirements of any duty that existed. But with respect to the basic definition of obligation, it would seem that these courts defined too woodenly the issue of whether "duty exists as a matter of common law."[47]

Representations and power. The ability to plan for disaster does cut both ways, because if one may consider at leisure whether to maintain rescue units one may also rationally bow to competing alternative demands for resource use. But the airport case has some special elements. An airport serves figuratively as well as literally as a beacon and, therefore, may be said to hold itself out as able to treat incoming travelers in a way that gives due regard to the hazards of aviation. Although the airman chooses the risks of flying, the airport is involved in that choice, through both promotion and reception. Further, it may be noted that, in one of the Illinois cases just described, the drowned airman received instructions from another airport's control tower that directed him to the airport off which he crashed.[48] This presumably enhanced the representational background of aid and succor that confronted him in his undoubtedly harried state. Most significantly, these facts manifest the nature of the power that various airport functionaries exercise over pilots.[49] It would thus be reasonable to say that the question of whether airports must expend some resources to rescue those imperiled in their immediate vicinity deserves an affirmative answer. How much they must expend is another question. The answer must take into consideration, among other things, an empirical guess as to whether the imposition of a duty on airports will create significant disincentives to careful conduct on the part of pilots. But, even here, humanitarian considerations may dictate some response when the pilot has already made his mistake. At the least, it seems arbitrary and obfuscatory to say simply that pilots are not invitees at the fields to which they are directed and off which they crash. In assigning liability in cases of this kind, one must consider that in such occurrences fortuity is not statistical unpredictability, and one must reckon with the desperation of the human plight involved. One who receives transport vehicles as a business should incur obligations as high as those the law imposes on carriers.

Customers and shades of voluntariness. In more mundane commercial situations, a person's status as a customer may combine with the enterpriser's control of the premises to support a decision that the firm should have taken steps to effect a rescue. Illustratively, in the case of a little boy who caught his finger in a store escalator, the court found a duty to prevent aggravation of his damages—a duty that flowed both from the child's status as "invitee" and from the fact that the escalator was an instrumentality under the defendant's control.[50] But applying the basic calculus of duty is not easy, given the varied factual circumstances of cases dealing with the relation of businesses to their publics. In such cases, problems often arise from the plaintiff's contribution to the riskiness of a situation, which may militate against merchant liability. On the other hand, too rigid a doctrinal perspective may lead to results unjust to customers. For example, in a decision involving a drunken patron, his invitee status and the nature of the tavern business make highly questionable a holding that the tavern operators have fulfilled their obligations by turning him out at closing time and leaving him in front of the establishment adjacent to the highway.[51] In an astonishing imposition of free will analysis, the court in effect says that if the plaintiff had stayed where he was put he would not have been hurt. Noting that the plaintiff was "able to walk without assistance" and in fact "wandered onto the highway," the court found him contributorily negligent.[52] This seems a badly mistaken analysis. Especially given allegations that the defendant's employees had continually coaxed the plaintiff to buy more drinks, this was a situation in which all effective power lay with the tavern owner. The court's rhetorical statement of the issue—whether "the defendant [had] a continuing legal duty to follow and protect plaintiff simply because he had become intoxicated in his place of business"[53]—makes it all the more startling that its answer is negative. The fact that the defendant's employees ordered the plaintiff out, combined with their role in his drunkenness and their control of physical power that could have been used to put the plaintiff in a safe place, should have created a duty.[54]

In the case of inns and taverns, it may present a more sympathetic fact pattern when the proprietor grants admission rather than effecting eviction. In one case a court took the "voluntary intoxication" path to bar recovery to the wife of a man who died in a fire that started in a mattress in the defendant's hotel room, when the management had given orders that the decedent should not be admitted as a guest because of previous incidents of intoxication and cigarette burns in rooms.[55] Although this intoxication rationale may yield a proper result on the facts, depending on the situation surrounding the decedent's registration,[56] it might serve only to paper over the crucial circumstances of other cases. Arguably, the result should be different if, in the context of orders to bar a person's admission, staff members allow him to register when he appears in an obviously drunken condition or weighted down by brown paper bags in the shape of liquor bottles. Surely, it ought to be different if an employee admits someone he knows he ought to keep out and then ignores frantic telephone calls for help.[57] In that case the power conferred by inn ownership would clearly impose obligations to act, which would be enhanced by the original failure to follow orders that were made in recognition of the facts that gave rise to the duty.

Yet the relation of merchant and customer does not create unlimited duties to act. For example, the march of consumer rights has not progressed far enough to oblige a supermarket to provide carryout service, even when it has ordinarily done so. This is the burden of one decision,[58] although the facts are so redolent of the patron's willingness to confront risk and of a practical interruption of whatever causation was supplied by the defendant's failure to act[59] that the reach of the case is narrow. The court excepts "abnormal" conditions of "unusual risk" from its statement that no duty exists. Less satisfactorily, it dismisses arguments based on the market's custom—arguments that have some bite in the context of store images projected to consumers and reliances created. Throughout the case as litigated, the particular plaintiff can never escape the wallow of assumption of risk. But on facts less persuasive that the customer acted foolishly, there would come to the fore the question of how much reliance was created by the usual provision of a carryout service. Customary performance, projecting images of shopping aid into the community,[60] might thus create duties. On the other hand, when policy is traditionally cash and carry and when competitors might steal a march by instituting the service, the customer's suit seeks to enforce chivalry alone. Power is sufficiently in balance—the consumer having sufficient information and the ability to adjust his behavior to the facts—that no obligation should lie.

Landowners and guests. A category that overlaps entrepreneurship is that of the ownership or control of land, and the access to resources for rescue which that brings. The power which landowners possess in that regard should entail substantial obligations to use those resources. There is much to criticize in the infamous decision in *Yania v. Bigan*,[61] in which the operator of a coal mine allegedly taunted a visiting neighbor to jump into a water-filled cut and then stood by as he drowned, an event that drew moral but not legal condemnation from the Pennsylvania Supreme Court. The court held that the defendant had no "legal responsibility" for the plight of the drowning man, emphasizing the voluntary nature of the plunge. Given this determination, the court could find no obligation in law to rescue, neglecting entirely the relation of landowner and invitee. We need not now reach the question of whether the defendant's taunts could legally be held a sufficient imposition on his dare-prone guest to support recovery.[62] They at least supply background coloration for his failure to aid one whose life was endangered on his land.

One must wonder whether the court would have reached the same result in the case of a host who did not aid a social guest who broke a leg falling downstairs, even though there was no showing that the stairway was negligently maintained or marked. To leave helpless a guest in that situation seems clearly actionable, whether it is characterized as a failure to act or something else. The fact that the landowner contributed to the peril of the drowning man—whether or not that contribution was in itself actionable—simply accentuates his obligation to use the physical energy at his disposal to effect a rescue. There is strong analogy in authority creating a duty when one's instrumentality is involved in the creation of peril, even if not tortiously.[63] Another useful analogue appears in the cases that impose obligations on mobile vendors to take special care for child customers.[64] But one also must face the broader issue: as Warren A. Seavey said in an outraged comment on *Yania*, it is whether the law should deny "the existence of any decency in the relation of host and guest."[65] When there is such a relation, the law tends to enforce a standard of decency, and the error of *Yania* lay in the court's failure to follow that tendency. But as relationships become more tenuous, the issue of whether the law should require compensation for refusal to do the decent thing looms more difficult, demanding examination of the sources of power controlled by those who fail to expend available resources to aid endangered fellows.

Trespassers. Some of the harder questions arise when the visitor to land is a trespasser. Clearly, to paste that label on a visitor will not alone absolve landowners from duties to act for his safety. In the case of children, an ameliorating doctrine is fixed with particular firmness in our law.[66] But there are some decisions involving children that go much further than the conventional child trespasser doctrine, and in language not restricted to those of tender years. An important recent pronouncement by the Massachusetts Supreme Court dealt with a failure to turn off power in an elevator when the eleven-year-old plaintiff was known to be trapped in the shaft. The court's response had an oratorical tone: "It should not be, it cannot be, and surely it is not now the law of this Commonwealth that the owner in such a situation is rewarded with immunity from liability as long as he ignores the plight of the trapped trespasser and takes no affirmative action to help him."[67] A similar holding governed a case in which the youthful plaintiff fell from a neighbor's bicycle, which he was riding on the neighbor's premises. The court steadfastly refused to find the bicycle an "attractive nuisance," but it declared that the landowner might be liable nevertheless if he knew or was chargeable with actual knowledge that the youngster was trying inexpertly to ride the bicycle and was in danger of injury. "An owner of property may not stand idly by and watch another, who is guilty of nothing more than trespassing, walk into danger."[68] This principle has quite a broad reach and demands testing, which I shall undertake immediately below as well as later in this book.

A fascinating analogue is enmeshed in a tangle of French and American law surrounding the case of an intoxicated seaman, who wandered up to the gangway of a ship not his own. Officers of the ship were at least solicitous of the drunken man: they attempted to converse with him, set a chair down on the dock for him at least twenty feet from the water, tried to sober him up with coffee, and restrained him from leaving the area because he was in no condition to travel alone. Unfortunately, however, the ship's personnel then left the drunk man alone for a few minutes—the chief engineer going back to the vessel to get his jacket so he could help the man get back to his own ship, and the second engineer simply going back up the gangway to return aboard. The seaman thereupon wandered off the pier, fell in the water, and drowned. The trial court, emphasizing the officers' constructive efforts at lifesaving detention and that it was reasonable to believe the drunk man was safe while the chief engineer went for his jacket, held that the seaman's widow could not recover. It reached this conclusion after analyzing the case under a combination of the French Civil Code's general negligence provision and the noteworthy section of the French Penal Code that makes it a crime to "voluntarily abstain" from giving aid to one in peril.[69] By contrast, the appellate court decided that American law applied and reversed in order to give the parties further opportunity to develop a record on that legal premise. However, it noted American precedents that had held that it was not within the scope of a seaman's employment to help a drunken fellow member of his own crew back to ship.[70] Although this disposition of the problem slants toward the defendant, it is not fully decisive, and the case raises important issues on the borderline of visitor-passerby classifications with respect to the responsibilities of those who control property.

Visitors at the fringe. We brush close here to the purer question of whether there is a duty to act on behalf of the person whom fate throws in one's path. Taking as a point of departure that question, with the law's traditionally negative answer, let us proceed on the assumption that the helpless individual has not crossed the property holder's threshold but lingers near its border. One should note at the outset the problem of incentives that inheres in the rule,

the implications of which are considered below, that one who undertakes to act must do so with care. Focusing now on the facts
in the drunken seaman's case, one finds particular difficulties in
the reality of constantly arising possibilities of competition for
one's energies. In that connection, it is not clear from the reported
opinions in that case why the second engineer chose to return to
the ship just about the time the chief engineer went back to get his
jacket. One may speculate that he felt it necessary to return to
duties to which he had been specifically assigned. A useful comparison appears in the question of whether the ship's master would
be required to delay departure if he knew that to shove off would
necessitate leaving the drunken man on the dock alone. In both
cases, it seems reasonable to say that one need respond to the peril
of others only in accordance with the general requirements of his
own employment obligations. This standard, it is true, will entail
some deterrent to aid, since part of the rationalization for "not
getting involved" in the first place is doubtless an inarticulate,
fearful sense that one knows not the complications that may
arise,[71] intruding on his established responsibilities. The best solution to such cases probably is a rule, either statutory or judge made,
that applies a relaxed standard of care to gratuitous efforts at aid.
While preserving reasonable freedom of action, it would thrust toward removing disincentives to help endangered persons.

Reflection on the case of the drunken seaman draws out further
vexing problems. What if a drunk man's wandering carries him on
up the gangway of a ship not his own? Is he to be treated like any
unwelcome trespasser? Should the law enforce civility to the point
that the unwilling host must expend energies on the unwanted
guest's behalf? Might it reasonably root this duty in the natural
hopes of any sailor that he would be treated the same in that plight,
and in an enforced recognition that anyone who docks in a French
harbor must expect that now and then he will have to aid the stray
sailor who inevitably will wander by in his cups? Beyond that,
might a rule requiring reasonable aid rest on a notion that the
privilege of docking carries certain minimal welfare obligations,
in default of public police or physicians at every pierside? We will
return to these questions.

Injured rescuer. Lurking in an adjoining trench are issues of how
to assign liability when it is the rescuer who is hurt. It may make
a difference whether the rescuer sues a culpable third party whose
tort imperiled him, or the rescued person himself; and in the latter
situation results may vary according to whether the rescued per-

son significantly contributed to his own plight.[72] Moreover, courts have denied recovery to those whose business is rescuing when the injuring hazard was "inherently within the ambit of those dangers which are unique to and generally associated with the particular rescue activity."[73] In general reference to questions involving rescue, it should be noted that, even when there is no duty on the part of bystanders to save individuals in peril, there is explicit political recognition of the worthiness of heroic action. Presidential Medals of Honor give the nation's tribute to those who go beyond the call of duty in civilian as well as military life. Illustratively, a Department of Transportation press release records the award of medals to several railroad employees, including one who crawled twice into a burning train car to save three trapped victims.[74] It may be significant that the release mentions no monetary compensation, implying that virtue is its own reward in such cases, at least when exalted by recognition by the Secretary of Transportation. Yet the law often does impose monetary liabilities on those whose culpable conduct creates a peril from which others undertake rescue and are thereby injured. A patrol guard's "impulsive" action in descending into a ship tank to save both a fallen man and his unsuccessful rescuer merited an award to his survivors under an admiralty doctrine characterized by Judge John R. Brown thus: "[T]he greater the risk, the greater the seafaring man's obligation to respond, and the greater the risk, the greater is the reward where rewards can be made."[75] Although questions of how far a culpable actor's duty stretches to rescuers may occasionally lead to logic-chopping,[76] the maritime law is in the forefront of humanitarian concern with its thrust toward eliminating the "deterrent to voluntary, impulsive response."[77]

To encompass another variation on the problem, the law presumably would go beyond requiring compensation to rescuers from those who endanger third parties and also would place liability on an injured person whose carelessness placed him in a situation in which the plaintiff was injured in the attempt to aid him.[78] But it is a more difficult case when the question is whether the rescued party who is not negligent must pay the rescuer for his injuries. Here the obligation, if there is one, spills over from tort into judicially constructed bargains.[79]

Reduced standard for rescuers. In connection with a suggestion made above, I should refer specifically here to the specific legislative attempts to encourage rescue, or at least to remove disincentives, manifested in the so-called Good Samaritan statutes. A majority of states have passed these laws, which generally exempt from tort liability those who administer emergency care, unless their conduct is more culpable than ordinary negligence.[80] These laws often limit this exemption to doctors and other medical personnel, but several statutes cover all persons.[81] Some commentary has found the limitations to doctors repugnant on grounds of unfairness to the rest of the community,[82] and it is at least arguable whether such statutes will produce significant gains in the emergency altruism of physicians.[83] However, it would seem that such laws strike a practical and desirable balance which avoids the tint of injustice in penalizing the frantic rescuer for inadvertence born of haste and pressure, and incites a marginal number of successful rescue attempts that will presumably outweigh the costs of occasional folly.[84]

These controversies aside, a recent decision seems wise in its practical separation of spheres of public and private responsibility, in the case of a police officer who negligently injured a plaintiff while saving her. In this Alaska litigation, the court denied the policeman and his governmental employer the protection of the Good Samaritan law although the officer literally tore a girl from the jaws of a lion; the suit was for injuries to the child caused when the rescuer's gun accidentally went off as they both fell to the ground after he shot the lion to death.[85] The court, dealing with a law that exempted from liability for ordinary negligence those who rendered aid "without compensation," reasoned that the defendants could not use the statutory shelter because the policeman was under a duty to rescue the plaintiff. This seems a proper recognition of the obligations that attend the exercise of deadly police power, even in the conduct of a rescue operation.

Manufacturers and sellers. In this survey of primarily economic relationships and duties that arise from them, I should also advert briefly to the liability of manufacturers and sellers. I have offered elsewhere a broad representational perspective as the primary analytical framework for these problems generally,[86] but here I should like to place that analysis in a still broader context of power relationships. One who uses modern media to generate demand for his product operates in settings in which the control of power matters in many ways. An omission to provide a given safety device may be negligence but usually would not be classified in terms of a "duty to act," primarily because it involves a long-range planning function and the necessity for choice among a wide variety of design possibilities. Nevertheless, it does involve a failure to use resources for the safety of others, and this often occurs in a context in which the producer controls knowledge unavailable to the consumer. There is judicial commentary that would support a view of this sort of production decision as forcing a hazardous bargain on the consumer.[87] By contrast, others might say that the market offers consumers enough choice to make that a strained description. I would prefer as more exact a characterization of this kind of decision as an unjust imposition made possible by the possession of superior power. In such a case the power derives both from specialized knowledge and from the control of media and is wielded in a situation in which it is practically impossible for the consumer to avoid a peril about which he may not know and for which he is given no feasible option to acquire protection.

Reflective of the tensions and ambiguities in some consumer goods problems is the death-dealing potential of cigarettes. In the late nineteen seventies, one would be loath to say that cigarette manufacturers possess a monopoly of information about the lethal qualities of their products. Power in the sense of exclusive control over information does not, therefore, exist. A common law action might theoretically be mounted on the basis that the cigarette companies deliberately engage in a form of image creation designed to undercut well-established medical belief, with a substantial certainty that many thousands of premature deaths will occur annually as a result. There is indeed psychological literature indicating that smokers are enslaved to the point that they are literally unable to obey their own rational impulses.[88] Because it is not likely that Congress would pass laws prohibiting the sale of cigarettes—that indeed such a statute would probably generate considerable disrespect for the law—one is forced to conclude that there is a reluctant social consensus that enough freedom of choice exists that we must tolerate this commerce. Yet, although we permit sale, this does not prevent us from fashioning rules to reflect social costs generated by prolonged and skillful advertising campaigns. So, in theory, the well-known practices of cigarette advertisers in alluring and entrapping vulnerable individuals, such as college students, might support a remedy in cases in which the hypothesis of free choice were disproved.

Because of the information that already exists in the market, a remedy for cigarette injuries would face difficult hurdles. Rationality is multifaceted, and the politics of cigarettes is inherently contradictory. However, aside from the peculiar characteristics of that product—and the widespread information about its known dangers—it may be said generally that when a safety hazard is discovered while a product line is on the market, producers and sellers must act swiftly to communicate the danger to those who may encounter it. From a time well before the Food and Drug Administration enforced its present recall policy, which has occasionally put a firm out of business in the process, that has been the common law.[89] With the rise of comprehensive federal regulation of products hazards, this kind of issue has become a legal battleground. The question of when a danger is apparent enough for action will depend on circumstances, but the basic duty now is clear and increasingly enjoys legislative sanction.[90]

METHODS OF CREATING RELATIONSHIPS

Representations and undertakings that involve matters other than the sale of goods often serve as a basis for the imposition of tort and tortlike duties. I deal here first with the creation of obligations by representations, including those with a contractual base or a quasi-contractual cast, and then move to cases in which it is argued that the defendant has a duty because he already has acted in some way.

Representations

The field of labor relations provides an important recent benchmark, in a decision that holds that a collective bargaining agreement which gives a union the right to compel compliance with safety codes does not obligate it to do so. The court said that to read the agreement otherwise, allowing an employee to sue the union, would deter the "give and take negotiation" necessary to collective bargaining and would deprive the union of discretion to exercise its power relative to all the circumstances existing in the industry.[91] This seems a reasonable result, particularly in terms of the framework of power which the court discusses. The employee gives up power to the union in exchange for the weight and flexibility of massed power that this gives him. And when the collective bargaining agreement does not make the union's duty specific and mandatory in certain areas, arguably it ought not to be held for a reasonable exercise of its discretion that trades off one aspect of safety to gain other advantages. But one may visualize cases more sympathetic to the union member; illustratively, a court should not dismiss out of hand a complaint that accuses the union of blinking corruptly at safety violations. Particularly where physical security is involved, the employee has a right to expect good faith and indeed the observance of fiduciary standards on the part of his bargaining representative. Thus, although the result in the case summarized seems correct, there should be a remedy when power so entrusted is abused.

Technicalities and insurance coverage. A rather different problem involving tort liability for undertakings with a contractual flavor concerns the lender which informs its borrower of the possibility of securing credit life insurance. Does the lender have a duty to give notification of lack of coverage to a borrower who has expressed in writing a wish to have insurance but has not confirmed that desire with a formal contract? In a case of this kind,[92] the lender's testimony was that the plaintiff had discussed making an appointment to fill out an insurance application because of her husband's inability to be absent from work during business hours, but there was a controversy over whether the lender had mentioned that it was necessary to complete an application. It was clear that the borrower couple had signed a statement with the words "I desire Credit Life & Disability Income Insurance coverage." They also signed a loan settlement statement on which a monthly payment box indicated a charge for "mutual mortgage insurance," at the same figure named in a Truth in Lending statement for credit life and disability insurance. However, the first monthly payment letter sent out by the defendant omitted this figure. The plaintiff's husband died within the next month, apparently with no further communication on the subject. On these facts, the court refused to impose liability on the lender, citing on a tort count the general principle that it is not a tort to fail to notify an insurance applicant of lack of coverage, and saying with respect to a contract claim that completion of an application was a condition precedent.[93] Given that the contract holding is correct, the tort dismissal requires discussion.

Certainly we are compelled to examine the power relationships more closely. The defendant lender arguably had created an expectation of insurance coverage, in an atmosphere in which its apparent financial expertise created an aura of reliability. It seems unresponsive to this reality to say, as does the court, that the "plaintiff was charged at law with the knowledge of the steps necessary to make a contract of insurance."[94] Within the first month of payments in this case, the plaintiffs had encountered at least three pieces of paper that bore on the matter of insurance. The two they signed indicated a desire on their part to get the insurance and at least implied a generation of momentum on the defendant's part to furnish it; let us eschew for the moment a technical definition of contractual "intent." Given these circumstances, it would be reasonable to place the defendant at risk, at least if one believed the plaintiff's denial that association employees had reminded her that it was necessary to complete an application. But it would also not be unreasonable to rule the other way, as the court did, given that the plaintiffs were not helpless to act and (if the defendant's testimony were to be believed) needed only to overcome the inconvenience of filling out a form they knew to be required. Yet the result in the particular case does depend on who is believed. And, at least with respect to the tort branch of the action, courts should not ignore the fact that borrowers move in a sea of relative ignorance, significantly reliant on the perceived expertise of those who manipulate forms across the desk from them.

Somewhat at odds with the savings and loan case is a decision that holds liable an employer who failed to make a timely payment of a medical insurance premium, which was billed for a period during which the plaintiff was still the firm's employee, although the bill was received after the employment was terminated. Accenting the legal problem was the fact that the insurable event was the premature delivery of twins, in the context of a provision in the Blue Cross–Blue Shield policy that required coverage for 270 consecutive days prior to a birth.[95] Since the premium at issue was withheld just after the birth, the court reasoned that the employee had "every reason to believe that coverage was in effect."[96] Proceeding from that premise under a contractual theory of liability, the court awarded damages for mental anguish, saying that hospital insurance is a matter of "mental concern and solicitude" with heads of families. At the core of this case is the employer's possession of information. That information was its knowledge that it had deducted a premium and its knowledge that it had received a bill—a bill that came to it because of its exercise of power over this facet of its employee's life. In these circumstances an efficiency argument for the employee is rather strong, since the medical benefits were clearly an incentive to work for this firm. Moreover, the sociology of power provides a particularly strong basis for requiring compensation from the employer. Beyond the court's necessary exercise in defining "contractual" rights, a meaningful and useful characterization of the decision is that it is one imposing liability on a party which received information because of a relationship involving the dependence of another and failed to act on that information or to communicate it to the dependent person.

In such a situation, the power to control events crucial to another's well-being imposes an obligation that smacks of a trust.[97] While judicial estimates of efficiency may be injected into this judgment, it is suffused with ethical content.

Stringing along and hoping. An interesting and recurrent factual profile appears in the case of a stevedore's employee who claimed injuries from carbon monoxide inhalation, following the failure of a ship's officer to fulfill his pledge to turn on a ventilating system. Reversing a verdict for the shipowner in an indemnity action against the stevedore, the Supreme Court disagreed with a holding of the court of appeals that the plaintiff behaved unreasonably as a matter of law, taking note that the jury had found that the employee "acted reasonably in continuing to work for a brief period in reliance on the officer's promise."[98] The case is rather less difficult than some of those discussed above because of the directness of the representation, though it was not a contractual promise. Here it is the pledge itself, linked to the control of the officer over the energy latent in the ventilating system, that creates the duty to act. The longshoremen had threatened to walk off the job unless the ventilating system was turned on. Their reliance on the officer's promise deprived them of their one bargaining chip in the situation and left them helpless to protect themselves against a known danger. The failure to use available power in this circumstance, even if it was not one in which the defendant was in a position to compel continuation of work, is justly actionable. This kind of profile appears and reappears in many guises throughout personal injury law: the individual who carries on, hoping that his pleas or his reliance will bring action from a person who is in a position to prevent injury to him. A prime example of a category of cases in which one finds this type of situation repeating itself is that of sellers' failure to repair defective products after requests from consumers.[99] In a certain sense, the plaintiff in cases of this kind is in the position to avoid the risk most cheaply up to the fatal moment. Yet the law sometimes provides–and perhaps more often should provide–a check against imposition, recognizing situational restrictions on freedom of action.

Undertakings

At varying points on the borderland of tort and contract, the last three cases discussed share the element of some kind of representation or implication of intent in a setting charged with manifestations of control over power—in one case, physical energy; in others, the power resident in the manipulation of legal rights and communication about matters of personal finance. I turn now to the legal problems that arise when one person claims that another should have continued to give aid because the other embarked on a course of action in that direction. One may begin with the conventional rule that those who undertake rescue operations must act with due care.[100] But the concept of undertaking embraces cases far beyond rescue. Not surprisingly, cases of vulnerable children provide especially compelling instances of continuing duties. Such a sympathetic profile appears in the decisions in which "Good Humor Men" and other rolling vendors are held liable for their failure to protect child customers. In one such case,[101] a four-year-old plaintiff asked a mobile confection salesman to wait for him so he could go home and get a dime. The vendor told the child he would "meet him up the street" and then traveled two hundred feet up the block beyond his house. The eager child, having got the coin and hastening to catch up, was struck by an oncoming car as he ran from behind a parked vehicle toward the defendant's truck. Basing its decision in part on the fact that "the driver undertook to direct plaintiff's activities" and in part on an "invitee" analogy, the court said that the jury could have found "that the driver should have maintained his lookout for the child throughout the seven-minute period which elapsed between the driver's direction to the child and the accident." Thus, the circumstances, including the enticement of the doughnut sought by the plaintiff and the adult status of the vendor contrasted with the child's tender years, define a relationship. And on the basis of that relation, the law dictates that the vendor employ his energies in the preservation of the child's security, even if this requires a diminution of other profitable activity.[102] As has been the case with much tort doctrine and other law relating to children, this judgment is made apart from purely cost considerations.

Insurer inspections. In the area of undertakings, a subtle relationship of power to performance emerges with claims that insurers did not inspect insured premises carefully and thus breached a duty to persons hurt by dangerous conditions there. The hornbook law is that of section 324A of the Second Restatement, which imposes liability on one who undertakes to render services to another "which he should recognize as necessary for the protection of a third person or his things," if physical harm results to the third person, and:

(a) his failure to exercise reasonable care increases the risk of harm,

(b) he has undertaken to perform a duty owed by the other to the third person,

or

(c) the harm is suffered because of the reliance of the other or the third person on the undertaking.

A leading decision imposing insurer liability emphasizes specific conduct that included the defendant's representations that its engineers would take an active part in its insureds' safety programs. Finding that the insurer's engineer made many observations of a hoist that caused the fatal injury, the court concluded that the defendant knew or should have known that the hoist was being used for elevator purposes.[103] The court notes that the engineer was experienced in testing such machines, and that the employees of the insured were not. The holding that a jury could find a lack of due care in inspection thus depends on the superior knowledge possessed by the defendant's engineer; and it is his failure to expend energy that he could have used in the implementation of that knowledge that brings liability upon his insurer employer. That liability stems from a failure to use power in a certain way, in a situation in which power flowed from a common wellspring with dependence. In this case, that dependence was manifest in the fact that only the engineer was in a position to initiate the requisite safety measures.[104] This was the practical reality of the social situation created by his appearance on the job with the imprimatur of the employer, combined with the superiority of his knowledge and ability to inspect as well as the relative inability of the employees to secure the critical information.[105]

It is instructive to compare briefly a trio of other recent decisions in which insurers confront claims based on failure to inspect. Facts persuasive against insurer liability appear in a case in which the insurer did not undertake to inspect an area where an accident happened, in a situation in which it inspected only parts of a plant to which attention was called by management or by accident reports.[106] In such a situation, no basis in power relationships exists on which to fix liability. Slightly closer is a case in which workmen's compensation premium rates were publicly set to include allowances of 2.16 percent for safety and inspection engineering. It seems unsatisfactory to say, as the court did on these facts, that this money could be appropriately allocated to "the holding of safe-

ty conferences or the distribution of safety literature."[107] One may
assent tentatively to the proposition that, when there is no separate contract for safety services, such a vaguely labeled premium
account does not compel "safety inspections on every job site covered by such insurance." Still, one may wonder whether the court
would have reached the same result if the allowances had been 15
percent or 25 percent. If the figure was of that magnitude, the law
quite reasonably could require inspections as a proper corollary to
public regulation of the financial return to one in a position to
supply safety services. Insurer liability in that kind of case would
provide legal recognition of the realities of dependence by covered
workmen on the protective intention manifest in the creation of
the safety account, and of the rate-setting agency's effective con-
ferral on the insurer of power over safety conditions. Thus the result in the case summarized, superficially agreeable on the facts,
seems less pleasing on analysis.

Providing an interesting comparison is another case in which
two federal district judges consecutively achieved diametrically
opposite results in a suit against an insurer of a supermarket,
brought by a fireman's widow on grounds that the defendant had
failed to discover and report fire hazards on the store premises.
The first judge found that the insurer's contract with the market
did not sweep the fireman within its protective orbit, and also held
that there was no duty in tort, although he conceded that there
was an obligation to members of the general public who might be
in the building "in the normal course of its operation."[108] This
concession immediately raised the question of whether a distinction could be justified between firefighting professionals and other
people, a question to which the second judge gave a negative answer.[109] The second judge utilized Restatement section 324A,
quoted above,[110] adding that the plaintiff's presence at the fire was
"reasonably foreseeable" and that the defendant's "duty to exercise reasonable care in inspecting the premises extended to him."
Although the legal language is somewhat cryptic, the result of this
second decision seems more persuasive. Indeed, the fact that the
plaintiff's decedent was acting "in his official capacity," as the first
judge stressed in denying liability, only serves to emphasize the
likelihood that fire hazards would compel his presence and quite
possibly cause injury. That fact surely does not weaken the nexus
that connects the insurer to him, as well as to citizens generally,
in regard to its ability to expend resources in the exercise of power
available to it, and only to it. In the view offered here, the central
questions are ones of what power exists, how it may be used, who

is dependent on its exercise, and what relations create that dependence. If those relations flow from a contract, legally enforceable by the state, a public employee should be able to claim a duty when he responds—as charged by law—to the consequences of careless performance.

Physical control as a determinant. I may highlight some features of this analysis by reference to a denial of liability in an unusual recent suit involving an insurer. The theme of ability to control events pervades the decision of the court in *Great American Ins. Co. v. Bureau Veritas*,[111] an action for indemnification by the owner of a ship and its insurers against a ship's classification society for alleged carelessness in a survey of the vessel. The court rejects arguments that the defendant was negligent in its survey, that it did not measure up to its own rules of surveying and classifying, and that it breached its warranty of workmanlike service. Regarding each point, it refers to the fact that the shipowner had possession of the relevant information about defects. With respect to the claim for violation of the classification society's own standards, the court contrasts the brief contact with a vessel that a classification society has when it makes annual surveys with the constant touch the owner maintains with a ship. Concerning itself with the implications of imposing an absolute form of liability, the court says that to do this would not be commensurate "with the amount of control that a classification society has over a vessel," in addition to being incompatible with the contractual arrangements. Bolstering this analysis is the fact that the owner knew about allegedly crucial defects and elected to take the risk of waiting to make repairs.

The problem of devising liability rules applicable to those who test and certify is not an easy one.[112] However, the case of the classification society gives significant guidance in that effort, relating to the power of the parties not only to acquire information but also to act. The undertaking inherent in a certification may deter the party to whom it is made from making further investigation or taking safety measures. The certification itself confers considerable power on its maker because of the image of technical expertise that it projects. However, when the possessor of a vessel acquires knowledge of its defects, the analogy of breaking the causal chain[113] is an apt one. The locus of physical control is both an artifact and a metaphor of legal responsibility.

11. Relationships More Closely Personal

Student and school. I shall now extend the analysis beyond primarily economic relationships to those in which personal elements of intellect or emotion typically predominate, subordinating or excluding considerations of monetary profit. Several interesting cases have arisen recently in the category of relationships between student and educational institution. This is not surprising, because the aura of parens patriae lingers on despite coed dormitories and in spite of louder wails than ever that institutional discipline has become a thing of the past. Perhaps in all cases involving the effects of student liberation, complaints are perennial and typified, and the only thing that has changed is the center of cultural gravity. Consider a trio of decisions.

The first of these cases involves the application of traditional negligence law to a situation in which the student, a high school football player, was willingly submissive to conventional authority. The court affirmed awards for the youth's death, which occurred when coaches failed to call his parents, or a doctor, after his collapse from the heat during wind sprints in summer training.[114] Essential to the decision was medical testimony which declared that heat damage becomes progressive to a point at which it is irreversible and which emphasized the necessity for speed in the application of remedial measures. The intellectual superiority and personal maturity of the plaintiffs' decedent served only to accentuate the damage to his parents in this case; not even offered was the rationalization that he who goes out for football in the Louisiana sun must live or die with the consequences.

In this case, given the emotional pressures that impinge on high school football practice, the issue of moral control is at a point of high tension. It may not overdramatize the matter to say that the analogy with seamen is almost exact. Indeed, a university professor who viewed the youth lying *in extremis* on the floor of the school cafeteria appears to have had to overcome shyness to force a phone call to the boy's mother.[115] The authority of the coach borders on the despotic in such a situation. And the problem is not that the coaches did not fix their attention on the youth's plight. Discussions proceeded apace, along with various attempts at first aid. But it was little enough that the law required—a timely phone call for expert assistance—and one perceives in the facts no competing demands on the energy required to take that step. The decision is based matter-of-factly on standard negligence principles, but one may find deeper roots. It is true that Louisiana coaches—particularly these coaches—will likely be more careful in the future when confronted with heat stroke. It is not so obvious that a decision the other way would have created any significant disincentive to participation in summer football practice. Given that opposite results would not produce symmetrical effects on primary conduct, it is useful to probe into the nature of the bargain. For the decision seems to indicate that even the student who in all awareness would surrender himself up to the risks that felled this young athlete should deserve the protection of a rule that compels more responsive action, when a danger abstractly understood by both parties materializes. In practical terms, this would mean that there is no way that a waiver of liability clause should stand against a claim for the fatal consequences of a failure to call the assistance that community hindsight would deem necessary. Results of this kind, I suggest, would manifest a recognition that in psychological terms the principal practical power in high school athletics flows from the coach. Channeled broadly from wild community enthusiasm for the gridiron game, the coach's authority arises more immediately from the student's acceptance of command and the associated implicit belief that the giver of the command knows best. Thus, with this isolated tragedy in Orleans Parish as a point of departure, one comes to see the common law serving as a check on the best-intentioned mishandling of power —power derived at one level of theory from the public through its school system, but practically and primarily from consent to organized athletic activity.

Limits of parens patriae. Quite different in their factual bases, and more reflective of evolving controversies concerning student-school relations, are issues presented in two cases dealing with the duties of universities to matriculants. The plaintiff in one of these cases was a black youth from New Jersey who was admitted to the University of Arizona, where he contracted the disease coccidioidomycosis ("Valley Fever"), which occurs twenty or thirty times more commonly in blacks than whites. The court's denial of liability features a parade of classic arguments: "catastrophic" financial burdens on defendants, impracticality of loss-shifting, and implications for the whole state vis-à-vis tourists. Moreover, "there comes a time when an individual must take it upon himself to be responsible for his own education and well-being. No person can be insulated against all the risks of living."[116] Much of the same flavor appears in a court's rejection of a claim that a woman freshman's university permitted her "to become associated with criminals, to be seduced, to become a drug user and further allowed her to be absent from her dormitory and failed to return her to her parents' custody on demand."[117] A university, says the court, is neither nursery school, boarding school, nor prison. Quite importantly, "no one is required to attend." And those who are permitted to enroll "must be presumed to have sufficient maturity to conduct their own personal affairs."

The result in the case of the young woman may well be justified. There appears to have been no failure to disclose information that was not common knowledge in the community. If the complaint is taken at its face, the parents were naïve about the temptations that would face a young woman away from home, possibly for the first time, and about the power exercised by the institution over students. Although one may speculate that the daughter's dependence on her parents and her general home environment sought a place of transference in the university, the pleadings as summarized by the court reflect no basis for a reasonable expectation that this could be effected and reveal no exercise of authority by the university that would correlatively justify the creation of a duty. One probably would want to know more about the representational background of this student's matriculation before being confident that no grounds for liability existed. For example, the catalog might have implied a paternalistic interest on the part of the university, or specifically on the part of dormitory counselors,[118] that the summarized pleading does not reveal. But on the facts as given, the case is not established.

Information and dependence. By comparison, the Valley Fever problem may present a closer case. The university may have possessed specific information, communication of which to the plaintiff might well have changed his decision to enroll there. It is not clear that to print a catalog entry on the incidence of Valley Fever in blacks would have been unduly costly, given the prolixity of self-important heraldry, semipuffery, and dull recitatives that march through catalog pages.[119] Surely, it is rather hollow to speak of a person being "responsible for his own education and well-being" in a situation in which he does not possess material information about risks to his health. Somewhat more persuasive, at first glance, is the homely judicial philosophy about the risks of living. In this regard, the question becomes whether to categorize Valley Fever in the generalized bundle of risks that all must face without specific defenses, or whether its status as an endemic disease classified it with open trenches, slippery sidewalks, and the risks of cancer from cigarettes or side effects from prescription drugs and thus demanded a warning. The distinction with the products liability cases is clear enough. The educational product of the university does not carry the inherent risk of anything but intellectual stimulation—or contamination. But universities exist in specific environments and their offering of that product may be mingled inseparably with the special physical risks of those environments. Perhaps the central question that occurs to intuition is one unanswered in the decision, and that is whether, in a day when heavy recruiting of able black students is common, this New Jersey plaintiff was the object of special efforts to gain his presence at Arizona. If that was the case, then the university falls close to the position of any purveyor of goods who must disclose special incidences of risk to particular classes of consumers. This admittedly speculative comment demands confrontation with a fact of university life that has evolved with the century, and leads me to suggest, in deliberately broad terms, the outlines of a possibly emerging conclusion: modern educational institutions represent great clusters of power, and, even given a laissez faire approach to student life, perhaps the law should recognize a new relation of dependence fostered in students by that power, a relation quite akin to that of industrial workers with their employers.

Lovers' duties. A useful comparison to these decisions, and especially to the problem of the seduced freshman, appears in an old criminal case involving unconsecrated love. Does a weekend assignation create a relationship dictating that one partner must expend energies to save the other from the fatal consequences of an overdose of drugs? The issue is not common in the reports, but in 1907 the Michigan Supreme Court gave a hard-shelled answer in *People v. Beardsley.*[120] In rejecting criminal liability, the court emphasized that the decedent was not married to the defendant, and also that the decedent had continued to "carouse . . . voluntarily," an activity in which she had "ample experience." We may conjecture whether this righteousness would have been attenuated had the decedent been more generally virtuous or had the case been for civil damages rather than a prosecution for manslaughter. The decision is a reversal of a jury verdict, signaling that the rough sense of the community in early twentieth-century Pontiac was that helplessness imposed an obligation, even when it was helplessness stemming from a very adult form of horseplay. Given this belief among ordinary people that dalliance entails duty, we may wonder why a court more sympathetic to the prosecution in such a case could not declare a constructive bargain: if you will spend the weekend with me while my wife is out of town, at least I will see to it that you don't kill yourself in a stupor. By comparison, the reviewing court's emphasis on the voluntary nature of the undertaking has a smack to it of a hard bargain struck and adhered to— implicitly a sense that there was no undertaking to rescue if the tryst soured, leading to desperate acts and culminating in emergency.

Perhaps the lesson is simply that illicit romance is one of the last unregulated markets. Surely we stand here at the boundary of duty's protective embrace. Yet physical proximity and the relative ease of calling a doctor, combined with the joint nature of the temporary enterprise and the presumed advantages it had produced for the defendant, argue for the imposition of a duty. Except for the court's morally laden condemnation of a "debauch," the case presents surprisingly close parallels with very different episodes of pleasure seeking, such as the instance of boyish shenanigans in a public swimming pool.[121] The creation of law in this particular setting goes beyond constructive bargains, and the question of what is legally right depends significantly on the moral sense of the community. At least for the purposes of a civil suit, it would seem more appropriate in a case of this kind to recognize a duty in the first instance, and then to refer the circumstances for judgment by community representatives, rather than to tailor the standard of conduct to a judicially imposed rectitude.[122] Had the case been an action for damages, a jury verdict for the plaintiff would have reasonably defined the responsibilities of power within a deteriorating human relationship.

III. *Protection against Third Parties*

Thus far, the discussion has dealt primarily with the nature of relationships on which obligations are founded. I turn now to an inquiry into problems defined more by external circumstances, often fortuities of the moment that surprise both the injured person and the party against whom a duty is sought to be enforced. Specifically, I shall deal with the problem of the duty of one person to protect another against culpable acts of third parties, an area that recently has spawned some difficult issues.

First, I shall examine a number of questions concerning the duties of those whose business inherently involves caring for the persons of their customers. I begin with an example of a broad concept of obligation, a far-reaching duty which provides an umbrella for decision in a case involving a robbery and threat of rape to a hotel guest. The incident occurred in a 1,200-room hotel where a large ball was in progress.[123] The complaint alleged that "criminals, sex deviates and vagrants" were allowed "to wander indiscriminately about the hotel," and it was proved that at the time of the incident, there were on duty only one security officer, a room clerk, and a bellboy. Moreover, there was strong and specific evidence of the room clerk's failure to respond when it was reported to him that the crime was occurring, including the fact that he did not call police on duty in the ballroom. The court held that the jury could reasonably have found a failure to perform the hotel's "general duty to protect their guests." In these particular circumstances, the room clerk's lackadaisical attitude in the crunch may have swallowed the more general lack of security planning. Yet the decision also stands in terms as imposing a general duty to allocate protective forces in reasonable numbers, a judicial recognition of any hotel guest's dependence on the innkeeper. The room payment is the most obviously identifiable fuel of his duty, but the obligation also arises from psychological bases related to the circumstances of hotel keeping. Strong, if implicit in the background of this decision, is the image of the weary traveler who wants to let down his defenses and who assumes that corridors and rooms are secure. A similar reality underpins the imposition of legal obligations upon those who control residential rental property.[124]

In such cases liability rests not simply on bargain or even on risk-bearing capacity but on a duty of fiduciary dimension. Many threads cross here. The implicit feeling of security engendered by a hotel's image leads the guest to seek refuge there; certainly, it deters him from making independent arrangements for his personal security. Beyond that, considerations of humanity enter. Not only entrustment by the guest of his personal safety but also a bedrock obligation founded on a relationship in which one person effectively has another's security in his care require the power holder both to provide and to maneuver against the terror of potential criminal assault. With this kind of case one is drawn back to the roots of tort law in considerations of public safety. Private suits for personal injury originally were bound quite tightly with the public weal. The hotel case partially closes the circle. The law effectively realizes that hotel keeping has public aspects and confirms that a hotel's interest in the safety of its guests has overtones of community concern.

Boisterous passengers. In suits by persons injured in more generally turbulent situations, courts have taken a variety of approaches. In one case, in which the "churning and agitation" in an overcrowded bus got "out of hand," the Pennsylvania Supreme Court defined a standard that may be extrapolated to cases of unsettled crowd conditions generally. Justice Michael Musmanno, speaking for the court, said that the driver had a duty to stop the vehicle and demand order or to eject troublemakers.[125] His opinion spoke of an "enlightened and humane interpretation of the duties of common carriers" and referred to the "responsibilities" attached to the "stewardship" of the driver. If the law gives the driver the privilege to restrain or eject unruly passengers, this ability to exercise physical control logically entails a duty to do so in boisterous conditions. The passengers' dependence on the driver is virtually complete. Almost as much as the seaman relies on the master, they are at his mercy. It should be noted that in this case there were regulations that limited the number of standees, but a larger principle looms in the background. It is true that in the immediate situation the driver is a victim of circumstance in a world that he, like his passengers, did not make. But circumstance has thrust power upon him, and if he does not respond to the demands of danger and dependence, his employer must pay for injuries caused thereby.

Surging crowds. Somewhat more difficult, in line with the magnitude of the chaos, is the determination of duties in the control of larger crowds. One finds little difficulty in requiring compensation from a storeowner whose saturation advertising scheme lures a crowd to watch Ping Pong balls dropped from an airplane, when a resultant stampede injures an onlooker.[126] More illustrative of competing social demands is a case in which a woman recovered $400,000 against a commuter railroad for injuries sustained when she was pushed into a moving train.[127] The per curiam opinion that affirms the judgment does not deal with the facts. However, a dissenter says that the evidence indicated that the culprit was an impatient passenger and contends that, since in a rush hour crowd it is impossible to identify such individuals in advance, there could be no claim of negligence. This point he joins to an argument from precedent that there should be no recovery in such cases unless there is a breakdown in scheduling that unrelievedly overburdens the platform, or there is a restriction of free movement. This particular drama was played out against a background of municipal emergency, a subway strike that shunted large numbers of passengers onto the defendant railroad. It is in that context that the dissenter declares that one should not call the railroad negligent for failure to control the crowd on the platform, because it already was fighting a battle on another front—to keep people from making hazardous sorties across the tracks.[128]

In situations of this kind, it is hard to locate with confidence the gravitational center of individual power. Given that the life of subway-stuck commuters is nasty and brutish, it might reasonably be argued that they must live with their decision to contend with an overcrowded platform. Although for many there seems little choice at all in the circumstances described, the railroad must itself grapple with the reality that masses of prospective passengers would prefer to take a chance with the arbitrary movements of an uncommanded regiment than enter the overstrained and exorbitant market for taxi seats. The railroad's only alternative is to hire a battalion of police to control ingress to the station itself. The decision appears to put it at risk if it does not do that. It thus makes the railroad the insurer of a mob caused by a strike of its competition. The search for justice within overlapping centers of power and of choice is not an easy one here. Assuming a world of total flexibility in placement of costs, it would seem that if loss is to be shifted the proper risk bearer would be the general public. But certainly the defense that one cannot identify particular aggressive individuals in advance is not dispositive on the question of whether there has been an actionable failure to exercise control, since such an enterprise must deal with probabilities of harm to its visitors from circumstantial packages of risk as well as from notorious bad actors. And given a legal and political quilt in which it is impractical to weave public liability, one might reasonably place responsibility on the carrier, since its own view of the situation is somewhat broader if not calmer and its power to control the situation is greater, both in law and in its actual ability to bring physical force to bear.

Reckless individuals. It is useful to compare with this problem in the public transportation area a case that arose in a private ballroom, whose attractions necessarily entailed "a certain amount of innocent bumping." The unavoidability of such contact helped persuade the court to deny a customer's claim for an especially violent bump by a "fellow [who] kept coming and all of a sudden, bang! We were pushed right over."[129] The court in this case adopted a view much the same as that of the dissent in the commuter train case. Given that some bumping was inevitable, it says that this particular bump was "unusual and not reasonably to be apprehended." Though "the bump may have been deliberate," the defendant was not "bound to anticipate it." It should be noted that the defendant did anticipate some problems in crowd control, for three policemen and two employees were keeping an eye on the floor. But in common sense terms, the decision effectively ratifies a ratio of five security personnel to 1,800 or 1,900 dancers as sufficient and simply recognizes that one can't be several places at once. The court's summary of the record does not indicate that the bumping dancer's ferocity had caused such a stir as to bring it to general attention, although the plaintiff had seen enough that he virtually cowered in the middle of the waltz. The practical explanation for the result may lie principally in the plaintiff's choice of this environment for his recreation, given his general knowledge of the prevailing conditions. One might reconcile with this decision the affirmance of the plaintiff's judgment in the commuter train case, on the basis that the unusual conditions caused by the strike as well as the control exercised by a public transportation company should have required a freer use of resources to preserve personal safety. In the ballroom case, the court in effect tells us both that the defendant appropriately exercised its power in the planning sense and that its tactical position did not possess a superiority of control supporting an obligation to stem this sudden onslaught.

Employees and criminal attacks. The case of deliberately criminal acts, a generalized introductory vehicle above, now provides a useful focus for this discussion of obligations to protect one's fellows against the behavior of third parties. Here again one encounters the employee as suitor, this time claiming that his employer has not sufficiently shielded him against the risk of crime. A very sympathetic case that reached the Supreme Court involved a woman telegraph operator who worked a night shift in an isolated part of a railroad yard. She sued for injuries from a beating by an intruder for whom she routinely opened a door, through which she could not see and to which she had to admit trainmen who came to get messages. The court said that a claim that there was "reason to know the yards were frequented by dangerous characters" was enough to allege a "likelihood" that the plaintiff "would suffer just such an injury as was in fact inflicted on her."[130] A much more recent decision[131] lends significant independent support to this principle, in an engineer's FELA suit. Claiming for injuries suffered on layover in a bunkroom attack, he proved a history of "occasional invasions" of the room by "undesirables." This was enough, the court found, to take the case to the jury.

A somewhat different spirit characterizes a Second Circuit decision in a case in which the plaintiff's decedent, a railroad ticket agent, was fatally shot in the back as he opened his office early in the morning. The court found unpersuasive an offer of proof that there previously had been ten robberies or attempted robberies at stations of the defendant carrier located between four and thirty miles from the decedent's station. The plaintiff had tried to show by correspondence and conversation between the ticket agents' union and the railroad that the latter knew about the risk to employees. The majority opinion somewhat sloughs testimony from a union official that he had requested "that the steel doors be removed from this station [at which the plaintiff worked], as well as other stations and also that a peephole be put in there and a siren alarm to protect the employees, including protection when they open these offices at six and six thirty in the morning."[132] Despite this, the court insists that liability under the FELA would require a showing that the employer knew or should have known of "the special dangers found at a particular location."[133]

Dissenting from a denial of certiorari, Justice William O. Douglas argued that it should be a jury question "whether it was reasonable for respondent to refrain from implementing safety suggestions at the Mineola station until the wave of robberies reached that station."[134] This seems rather a more sensible and sensitive approach than that taken by the Second Circuit majority. It implicitly recognizes the agent's helplessness, as well as the railroad's position of control with respect both to his working hours and to the resources that might be used to protect him. The complaints by the union, making at least a general reference to this station, serve to emphasize that concentration of power in the railroad. They also provide a distinguishing comparison with a suit against a union, mentioned above,[135] for failure to demand enforcement of safety codes. Moreover, the ticket agent's case is clearly distinguishable from a waiting passenger's claim of negligence with respect to an attack by persons loitering at a rail platform, when there was no persuasive showing that the assailants aroused suspicion in either the carrier's employees or the victimized plaintiff.[136] It is implicit in the court's opinion in that case that the railroad's employees would have had no privilege to eject the eventual attackers before the assault. The finding of no negligence is simply a counterpart of that fact, providing confirmation that the case involves no actionable default in the use of power. The injury was truly a fortuity from the standpoint of relations between railway and passenger, and any shifting of loss should be done socially.

Hostage situation. The conflict between interests in life and property, implicit in cases of failure to provide security, becomes explicit when one person refuses to give up his money to another under the threat that the other will kill a third. That was the situation in the dramatic case of *Boyd v. Racine Currency Exchange,* in which a robber carried out a threat to an Exchange employee that he would kill a customer if the employee did not admit him behind a bullet-proof partition. There were allegations that the defendant had not instructed its employees about proper conduct in circumstances of that kind or attempted to furnish them with guidelines. An Illinois appellate court held that the jury might reasonably decide that the Exchange's employees "could have done something but did nothing to protect their customer from physical harm,"[137] emphasizing that the defendants kept large sums of money on their premises at all times, which served as a lure to robberies. The Supreme Court reversed, saying it was "speculative" whether acquiescence to the robber's demands would have spared the decedent and suggesting that to accede might have exposed the defendant's employee to harm herself.[138] The court also opined that to allow recovery would provide further incentives to other criminal acts of that kind. This argument has some power, reinforcing the undoubted rule that one is privileged to defend his property against armed robbery, a privilege which is especially broad when he is actually grappling to save his property.[139]

But the case is a close one and I am inclined to think it was wrongly decided. It is true that, in quite a literal sense, power in this situation came from the barrel of the robber's gun. However, an important element of power also resided in a well-established legal relation, that of customer and merchant, within which the peril to the plaintiff's decedent arose from the very source of the profit of a firm that arguably could have better used its ability to control risk. The result would be rather more satisfactory had the defendant informed its customers that its policy would be to sacrifice their lives to preserve its money.[140] Certainly in the circumstances that in fact existed, the contention that the case is one for the jury seems reasonable with respect to the defendant's combination of planning and maneuvering as it bore on the risk that materialized. The allegations of neglect to instruct employees imply a more general culpability: that is, in the failure to set up an alarm system that would permit temporary submission to robbers' demands and yet also facilitate the recovery of stolen money. At this juncture default in maneuvering ties back into the planning function and becomes enwrapped in it, accenting the origin of a duty that arises from the ability to deliberate and choose. To be sure, the problem of defining the responsibilities of those against whom hostages are held is not an easy one. However, at least in the absence of explicit warnings of a "money before life" policy, the extreme relation of dependence of a customer in this position −rooted as it is in the nature of the business involved−would blend with the defendant's power of control to support the creation of a duty.[141]

I would emphasize here that the kind of dependence that occurs in situations like that of the money exchange−or in employment situations like that of the railroad ticket agent's case described above−is a die-cast sort of helplessness. Speaking in strictly economic terms of a "cheapest cost avoider" in instances of this kind does not capture the reality of the situation adequately. At the moment of the crime, that rubric provides no solvent. And before that moment, the speculative question of whether cost avoidance could be achieved by the potential victim's refusal to continue in the relationship presents an alternative which would commend itself to few judges, not to mention persons engaged in commerce. The possibility of a warning does provide a theoretical solution, subject to Calabresi's caveat about the tendency of people to undervalue risk to themselves.[142] Yet here again the dependence created by reliance on an established commercial enterprise, or by the employment relation, embodies a moral content that properly may influence judicial decision.

THE CASE OF VIOLENCE IN THE TAVERN

Now I shall carry this inquiry about obligations to defend against criminal conduct into the tavern, where, quite as much as with currency exchanges, the very nature of the business tends to bring out a facet of the worst in human nature. It seems clear that in some measure tavern owners have a duty to quell violence. This duty derives generally from the relation of patronage, with a particular, if implicit, basis in the notion that taverns are a place where one goes to relax and let down his guard. The baseline of obligation appears in a case in which there was evidence that an ex-boxer patron was "vicious and sadistic," and that the owner had ordered an employee not to serve him and to keep him out of the place if possible. The court held this sufficient to support a plaintiff's verdict against the tavern for failure to protect him against attack.[143] It follows that, once a "brewing altercation" becomes obvious, the bartender has a duty to mediate or call for aid.[144]

It is little extension to require that tavern employees take steps to head off threats of violence in the immediate future. A court imposed liability on a tavern in a case in which one patron announced that he was going home to get a gun and would come back and shoot another customer with it.[145] In the murderous patron's subsequent attempt to carry out this threat, a shot fatally wounded the plaintiff bystander, who had not heard the gunman's original statements. The court, which rejected an argument that the action should fail because the threat was that of "an intended criminal act," listed alternatively a number of alleged omissions on the part of the defendant's employees, which were described in the plaintiff's complaint. Although some of these items seem only makeweights,[146] the court found in the situation a core of duty to guard against dangers that are cognizable or reasonably foreseeable. The burden of this case seems to be that an obligation exists when an owner has information about the possibilities of violence, intelligence which places his patrons in a dependent relation to him. Given the uncertainty of such situations and the range of defensive alternatives, courts must leave plenty of room for discretion in maneuver, but it should be emphasized that one still may be culpable in the exercise of discretion. In cases of this kind, the power that the tavern owner wields over his premises effectively entails an entrustment of customers' safety to him and provides a foundation for the creation of a duty to act. It may be stressed again that in die-cast situations of this kind it is not fully descriptive of reality to parse the problem in terms of cost avoidance. The tavern owner is, practically, the only cost avoider, and the question of whether he must respond to the danger has a strong moral flavor related to the dependence of his patrons. Even if the net welfare gains to be derived from tavern operation were estimated to outweigh the cost of an occasional injury of this kind, a judge might still properly require compensation on the basis of that dependence.

On a parallel plane, it seems proper that the bystanding tavern patron who intervenes to stop violence should have a claim against the establishment, at least under a Dram Shop statutory provision that imposes liabilities "for injuries . . . caused by an intoxicated person."[147] This liability would derive generally from the broad entrustment rationale just mentioned. It would stem specifically from the owner's duty to intervene, when the bystander in effect fills a breach created by the owner's failure to have enough help around to stop fights. Compensation thus must be paid for inability or refusal to employ physical force in the fulfillment of an obligation of legal power. Overarching this creation of duty is the state's interest in the welfare of crime victims, reflected in compensation legislation for victims as well as the proposal to extend payments to rescuers as well.[148]

Intervenor's carelessness; voluntariness. The case of the intervening patron poses several varied problems. Sometimes an intervenor's foolishness may be reason to bar his recovery. This seems the core of a decision denying an award to a man who responded to tavern owners' appeals for help,[149] with the court's concurrent finding that the owners were not "negligent" appearing rather facile.[150] Sheer recklessness of an intervening patron's conduct aside, a plea by tavern owners for aid against violent conduct arguably creates a duty founded in the desperation of the risk that produced the request. Such a duty might reach beyond conventional negligence law, but the plaintiff's volunteer use of his energy in such a situation may support the imposition of liability against the tavern. This is because of the pecuniary benefit that his act confers on defendants who have a primary obligation to the safety of customers,[151] as well as the welfare bonus it produces for the community. Moreover, in a somewhat different setting, it seems wrong to hold that the knowledge that a club has no bartender should alone prevent compensation to someone injured in the attempt to stop a fight. In one case of that kind, the court bases its denial of recovery on the fact that an intervenor "voluntarily entered the clubroom"[152] and remained there with that knowledge. However, since the court is unable to muster a definitive finding that the plaintiff's insouciance in the circumstances should bar him, the decision arguably evades the realities of power in the situation. These circumstances include the tavern owner's legal control of property where alcoholic beverages are served, his failure to employ physical force adequate to that occasion, and the socially desirable nature of the intervenor's response to a situation created by the owner's default. The case is not free from difficulty, but the balance of desirable incentives would seem to lie with a rule imposing liability on the establishment.

This is not to deny that there may be cases in which the voluntary character of an intervention should itself save a proprietor from liability. A German decision rejected a claim by patrons who remained in a tavern in response to the owner's request for aid against two tough-looking strangers who lingered near closing time. Beaten by the strangers in their attempt to help the owner, the plaintiffs sued him on the ground that he had tacitly agreed to indemnify them; but under technical rules of *negotiorum gestio*, the court could not find an economic outlay that was voluntarily made.[153] If a court were dealing with these facts under a liberally construed Dram Shop Act,[154] this would seem a doubtful result if the attackers became intoxicated on the premises. Otherwise, when defensive action is taken in behalf of the owner himself, the gratuity of the intervention would thrust against at least tort liability. Given that the intervenors had at least brief opportunity to consider the risks, the fact that the owner temporarily lacked adequate ability to defend himself would not constitute an actionable default in the use of power vis-à-vis the eventuality of rescue. Where only his security is jeopardized, his fortuitous temporary dependence creates a situation in which considered intervention is to be accounted only a credit in the ledger of heroism or a basis for restitution.[155]

Parking lots. A further wrinkle on the issue of proprietors' duties to protect against criminal attacks appears when the assault occurs at the physical fringe of the establishment. Rather extreme facts fuel a holding sympathetic to a woman patron's suit against a bowling alley, for crippling injuries inflicted by a man in the parking lot after her refusal of sexual solicitations made by him inside the establishment. There was evidence that police had been needed to handle past violence at the alleys, and in fact the defendant employed a professional football player as a bouncer. But the bouncer's contribution on this occasion was to warn the plaintiff not to go into the parking lot "because that goofball is out there," and then to accompany her to the door and tell her to "please be careful." Quoting a precedent to the effect that a warning is not sufficient if the circumstances make it ineffective, the court reversed a directed verdict for the defendant. It held that a jury could have found that the defendant's assistance in the face of the danger was inadequate to secure the plaintiff's "right to enter the parking lot and obtain her car."[156] The case is an easy one on its facts but deserves mention because of its emphasis that warnings do not invariably dissolve duty. That is especially so when, as here, so high an original obligation was imposed by the actual possession of physical power as well as legal control over premises.

In a more difficult case, in which a patron attempted to defend someone whose presence on the defendant's property was rather casual, the court denied recovery.[157] The incident began when a youth named Yosemite returned from an out-of-town drive to see some girls, a trip undertaken with a friend who had left his car in the parking lot of the defendant drive-in. On their return, an alleged gambling creditor of Yosemite demanded payment from him and they fought, eventuating in Yosemite's flight to the cooking area and his unsuccessful appeal to the defendant's manager to call the police. At this point the plaintiff intervened. He made a somewhat officious although generally inoffensive remark that drew a fist from Yosemite's tormentor. This was a result not entirely unexpected to the plaintiff, since he testified that he knew that interjection into the quarrels of others ran "the danger and risk of being involved in it yourself," but he sued the drive-in for failure to fulfill its duty to him.

The decision approached the question, first, from the standpoint of whether the defendant owed Yosemite a duty, which the court denied because the youth's status was "no better . . . than that of a licensee." Proceeding from the premise that the defendant owed no duty to someone in that position "to prevent assaults by third persons for reasons personal to them," the opinion reasoned that the "plaintiff's attempted rescue . . . did not constitute a justification which affected absence of defendant's duty to plaintiff—a duty nonexistent because the plaintiff "voluntarily exposed himself" to a danger "fully known and appreciated."[158] However, it would seem that if there were a duty to someone in Yosemite's place it might well create a duty to an intervenor despite his appreciation of the risk; and it is surely arguable that there should be a duty, at least, to make a phone call. The boundaries of that duty would depend in part on the nature of the custom of using the defendant's lot as a staging area for romantic junkets. It must be noted that the evidence showed that at one point the manager was preparing to call a wrecker to tow away a car which had been left on the lot. But one still would want to know if general averages reflected a relatively lenient policy toward those who parked without immediate consumption, adopted in hopes of future business. It is true that, even if this were so, in some circumstances it would be impossible to divine a relation of dependence and trust. It would have been chutzpa indeed, for example, for Yosemite's friend to have sued the drive-in for failing to try to stop the theft of his car from the lot. But when a serious danger to personal safety was urgently conveyed to drive-in employees, and the amount of intervention required was only a phone call, a condonation of parking for public relations reasons seems sufficient to support a duty.

Obligations from conduct of business. We may go further yet in our exploration of theory, edging ever closer to the pure bystander case. For example, it could even be contended that if Yosemite had run down the street from two blocks away to ask for help the failure to make a phone call should be actionable, at least assuming this could be done without expectation of revenge from his assailants. For the operation of any such business, carrying along with it the physical ability to save passersby from desperate danger, is a social privilege as well as a legal right. Under the analysis offered here, that compound of right and privilege, and the ability to expend energy that is attendant to it, would presumably support the imposition of a duty.[159]

In theory, this notion of duty entwined with power to respond to fortuitous emergency might reach even further. We may raise for the first time here the question of the duty to act of the private home dweller. In line with the present topic of defense against third party assaults, let us consider the case of the homeowner who opens his door in response to an evening ring on the bell, finds an attempt at entry by one fleeing mayhem, and then pushes the terrified quarry back out at the mercy of his pursuers. The proponent of duty in this instance would have to contend that the lawful possession of even residential property entails certain minimum obligations to one's fellows in the community. He would have to argue that, when circumstances place a property holder in a position to render aid with no more inconvenience than admitting the newcomer and phoning the police, the temporary existence of a desperate dependence in a passerby requires that the call be made. In practice, the possessor's justifiable fear of being physically involved might often be sufficient to dissolve the duty. But if he is physically secure, I would contend that the law may require him to compensate for failure to aid, because of his de facto control over the physical person of his unexpected visitor and his ability to expend minimal energies to secure help.[160] This is arguably the message of the famous Vermont case of *Ploof v. Putnam*,[161] in which the court imposed liability on one whose servant untied from his private dock a boat that had moored there to avoid the perils of stormy weather. In the hypothetical case put above, injecting the premise that the homeowner can act without danger to himself would obviate the problem in *Vincent v. Lake Erie Transp. Co.*,[162] in which the court awarded compensation to one whose dock was damaged by a mariner who kept tying on during a violent storm. If the fleeing person were to force his way through a door held ajar by the curious homeowner, and the pursuing mob injured the possessor or damaged the premises, then the rule of *Vincent* would clearly apply, requiring the one who sought haven to pay compensation.

PRIVATE DUTIES AND PUBLIC CONTROL

Wrapped up with the problems discussed above is the question of how to draw the uncertain line between public and private duties to protect citizens from criminal conduct. This question arises under garish light in *Sunset Amusement Co. v. Board of Police Commissioners*,[163] in which the California Supreme Court ratified the denial of a license renewal because of the petitioner's "failure to control its patrons and prevent public disturbances." The traffic situation around the establishment compelled the pell-mell discharge at closing hour of hundreds of customers, many of them inebriated. There was evidence that from time to time the defendants threw out customers for causing trouble, only to have them redirect their aggression onto the surrounding community. The court found, in part, that the Board could have concluded that some disturbances outside the defendant's property "were attributable to petitioners' failure to control or restrain those patrons who, when ejected from the rink for disorderly conduct, were likely to cause further mischief outside the premises."[164] Justice Stanley Mosk concurred separately on the refusal to renew the license, on grounds of inadequate parking facilities, but disagreed with the imposition of "significant responsibility on licensees to control the conduct of departing patrons after they have reached public streets and sidewalks."[165] This, he said, would encourage the placement of essentially public policy functions in the hands of relatively untrained private security forces, possibly exacerbating disruptions and resulting in violations of constitutional rights. The point is a weighty one and joins the issue on a difficult problem.

Yet, if we examine the question from the standpoint of the control of power, the refusal to renew seems justifiable on the ground that the firm did not appropriately exercise its ability to control the egress of its patrons or their collective level of intoxication. Creating dangers to many customers as well as to the neighborhood, the situation evokes the analogies of nuisance and even of responsibility for the release of ultrahazardous substances from one's land. The probability of injuries resulting from traffic congestion or from violence exploding out of unruly knots of persons makes it an accurate metaphor to visualize the defendant's establishment as a temperamental machine, emitting outbursts of physical energy against which battered neighbors or patrons are essentially helpless. It may be that this decision signals that as a practical matter one may not run certain kinds of amusement places, thus providing a regulatory analogue of absolute liability at common law. But although this seems Draconian given the helplessness of the business to control its customers, the more passive helplessness of injured patrons and neighbors deserves legal priority. In one sense it is simply a case of having undertaken but not having followed through. In another view the most apt characterization of the case is that it is an instance of failure to protect dependent persons against criminal conduct. In any event, the decision provides an important benchmark at an intersection of spheres of public concern and private obligation to control power.

Criminal law parallels and sources. It is appropriate, at this juncture of our discussion of private liability for failure to prevent third party crimes, to refer briefly to certain aspects of criminal law and some implications they carry for the imposition of civil obligations. There are several parallels in the criminal law for duties to act that have been imposed in tort cases. Applying to offenses that include the most serious crimes,[166] these penal duties range from categories arising from relationships to those based on statute.[167] They include, notably, duties based on undertakings, although the case literature does not appear to be abundant.[168] Some courts even have imposed criminal duties on a strict liability basis, although not without considerable dissent.

Of course, beyond the direct imposition of sanctions, legislation may express community sentiment in a definitive way and thus provide scaffolding for a duty. The fact-gathering abilities of legislatures combine with their status as elected representatives to provide a predicate for the use of criminal laws to support private claims, although the fact that a penal statute does not embody a specific tort remedy may indicate a desire to constrain judicial activity in that respect.[169] Professor Allen Linden has properly noted that the factors that play about cases in which statutes are involved are usually multifarious, and that the rationales offered by many decisions are makeweights. It may be, as he suggests, that one can say no more than that a statute is simply one element that must be weighed along with the full range of policy considerations that affect any case.[170] I would stress at this point only that courts should be particularly sensitive to legislative efforts to rectify imbalances in various forms of power that crop out in relations between individuals. Under the present analysis, it would seem that the California court acted wisely in the amusement park case, giving effective approval to two layers of public safety regulation by affirmance of a private party's obligation, imposed through a licensing authority, to control the antisocial acts of third persons. This is an appropriate judicial recognition of the political judgment reflected in the licensing board's decision, a judgment that defines the duties of power in a community setting; and it reflects as well the social welfare interest in ameliorating the lot of victims of violent crime.[171]

THE PROFESSIONAL BYSTANDER

I conclude this examination of duties to aid crime victims with a speculative discussion of the special problems posed by the case of the professional bystander. Illustrative of these problems is the issue of whether a journalist has obligations to aid those enmeshed in the troubles that make the news which is the staple of his existence. The question is presently hypothetical in terms of reported precedent, but the importance of the competing interests makes it an excellent vehicle for examination of the problems of policy and philosophy in this inquiry. Consider the documented case of the reporter who accompanies muggers on an expedition, watches them execute a robbery (in broad daylight), and then interviews them about "the possible consequences of getting caught."[172] Let us assume that the model whose victimization was recounted in a magazine article based on this crime had recognized the writer's description of the assault, as she well might have done if his literary ego or a meticulous editor had required that all details, including place, must be correct. Should she not be able to claim that the writer owed her a duty of warning? He would defend by arguing that the muggers simply gave him a privilege to accompany them for an event that surely would have occurred anyway, that in his position he could give no warning without fear of substantial danger to himself, and, finally, that the social value of his description would outweigh the victim's injury in the final accounting. Perhaps so.

But now suppose the victim is badly hurt and slumps to the sidewalk. Disregarding the question of whether he should identify the assailants to the police, would not the journalist owe a duty to help? At the least, his proximity, his possession of the physical strength to render aid, and his willing witness of a crime should impose that obligation. Moreover, the fact that an affirmative answer seems compelled to this question strengthens the case for a duty of prior warning, putting aside the problem of danger to the onlooker, because of the substantial coincidence in both cases of the elements of power that exist in his relation to the victim. The intuition of countervailing social benefits attending the opposite result is strong and, combined with the dangers that exist in fact, may save the day for neutral reportage, but the case is not an easy one.

Social nexus. A rending pair of news photos from a Bowery street import further complexity. The pictures show a young woman walking her dog in the predawn hours who "stops briefly, then turns helplessly away from a stranger who moments before had pleaded for her help as his life ebbed." The shoeless unfortunate, apparently the victim of a beating, "died before help arrived."[173] Deferring the problem of the casual passerby's duty, do not the literal focus of the photographer's attentions on the victim's plight and his direct use of the situation for the acquisition of information support the imposition of an obligation? Moreover, do not the public's construction, maintenance, and policing of the street on which he plies his own trade provide the basis for a duty, given no risk to himself and only the necessity for a phone call? It might be noted that, ironically, there is a certain implicit reliance by the photographer on the general level of police protection while he snaps his picture, though admittedly that protection had failed the dying man. The case stretches rather beyond that of the reporter who plans the chronicle of a mugging, but these factors of commonwealth involvement tend to create a social nexus between the professional bystander and the crime victim, at least in the case where the stakes are high and the risk low.[174]

Journalists and hostage situations. The outbreak of kidnappings and takings of hostages in the last few years highlights the journalist problem with terrible intensity. Indicative of the policy tensions is a newspaper story that relates the smuggling of an elevator key into a cellblock in a District of Columbia courthouse, undertaken to rescue hostages from convicts. The report is headlined "Prisoners Prove Adept at Manipulating City's Media."[175] With reference to the question of the journalist's obligation to hostages, consider the following characterization by a reporter who covered the story: "In the 68 hours . . . the media and the convicts had treated each other alternatively as quasi-friends, pacifiers, negotiators and messengers." Certainly, any questions of duty in such a case are pretty theoretical; to prove the element of substandard conduct necessary in a negligence action would be virtually impossible in practice, because of the hornbook rule that in emergency conditions the standard is only what is reasonable in the circumstances. Yet it is worth emphasis that in theory the control of media power, which gives the journalist his access to the prisoners and thus his story, should impose especially high obligation with respect to the persons whose very plight lends the report its high drama. Certainly there may be a duty to refrain from action. A simple example of how the obligation might become concrete inheres in the chief federal judge's request to journalists not to report that a technician had entered the courthouse, recruited in what proved an unsuccessful effort to cut television cables leading to the cellblock.[176] Would not a radio or television report of this fact, in the tense minutes as the key was being smuggled in, provide grounds for a tort action by the survivors of hostages slain if the prisoners had heard the broadcast? And although this obligation to refrain from doing something may not be dispositive that there are correlative duties to act, may it not be indicative of judicial bias in that direction? For example, it arguably would be reasonable to impose liability for a reporter's refusal to carry a message while he was shuttling between the tense lines of prisoners and jail officials.[177]

The obligation would become subtler and less capable of judicial imposition as the facts move more into the area where the reporter perforce becomes a psychotherapist and a negotiator.[178] But this does not negate the theoretical case that a duty exists, its roots nourished by the power that the situation gives the journalist, and on which he feeds. His position makes the hostages his dependents, and the law should enforce the trust that this dependency creates. Although the functional role of the professional bystander is unique, the principles governing his control of lifesaving power are the ones generally applicable to the creation of duties to act. A broad definition of an analogous range of duty for professional power holders appears in a very recent California decision, in which the court imposed liability on psychotherapists for failure to warn of a patient's threats to kill the plaintiff's decedent.[179] The court approvingly cited precedents which it characterized as holding that "the single relationship of a doctor to his patient is sufficient to support the duty to exercise reasonable care to protect others against dangers emanating from the patient's illness."[180] In this case, the power locked in information created an obligation, even though the relation between therapist and third party existed only through the medium of the patient's threats, and although the physical danger was not so immediate as in the typical hostage case. And this obligation arises not simply because the physician is in the best position to avoid the costs of violence—his opportunity in that regard is obvious and in the circumstances solitary—but in large measure because of a social judgment that he should do so. In the view offered here, respect for the value of an imperiled life requires action when one with little expenditure can save another to whose plight events intimately connect him.

iv. *Plaintiff's Own Conduct a Hazard*

Destructive child. Parallel to questions of obligation with respect to the acts of third parties is the case in which the person who seeks judicial creation of a duty has by his own conduct created physical danger to others or acted in a significantly disruptive way. Exemplary of this kind of problem is a recent case which arose from an apartment manager's order to a five- or six-year-old boy to leave a playground for throwing dirt.[181] The child's mother had told an older son to take the little boy to the playground, a fenced area located near the manager's apartment-office in the complex in which they lived, and told the little boy not to leave until someone came for him. The manager, who testified that he saw the child throwing dirt at his daughter, ordered him off the playground. The little boy departed, but he said that he was fearful of his mother's anger if he returned home without an escort. He thus went with a friend to play with a toy car in a parking lot, where an automobile struck him.

The court, declaring that the boy's mother had observed a high standard of care in having him escorted to a fenced playground, found that the manager had "breached his duty by ordering Chris from the fenced playground without escorting him the short distance to his home or notifying his mother that he was no longer in the playground." The court found extra weight to support a plaintiff's judgment in the fact that the manager was the father of a small child himself, saying that he should have known about the behavior of children and opining at another point that the boy behaved "in the normal fashion of a heedless child."[182] On facts that included the child's residence in the complex, the decision seems right. It would be on especially solid ground if it rests on an unarticulated background of a custom of escort or notification in such circumstances. Even without them, the case provides a welcome counterweight to another decision in the same jurisdiction, which refuses to impose a duty on a tavern operator to see that its drunk patrons are not left in harm's way.[183]

Let us ask, however, whether it changes the issue significantly if the child is an interloper from down the block. In that case, an apartment manager may be caught in a multifactored bind. Among various duties, he presumably would have a certain obligation to keep an eye on the playground. Indeed, although it is not manifest in the case discussed, the duty of a person in that role might include enough supervision to prevent childish intentional torts. If that were so, must he then learn the address of a troublemaking child and escort him to a home out of the complex, forsaking more direct alternative demands on his energies? It would seem that a rowdy trespasser, impinging on other duties of the manager, would forfeit the claim of duty, even if the playground could be expected to attract a certain number of gate crashers.

Handling disturbed employees. Somewhat less problematical, but not free from difficulty, is the question of what constitutes reasonable care in the management of a raving employee. The facts of an illustrative case, which spells out the employer's liability side of a fine line described earlier,[184] are summarized in the court's holding that "a seaman who, because of inordinate intoxication, becomes uncooperative and boisterous, should not immediately be shackled to a bunk with two sets of irons, and then left unattended."[185] As I briefly suggested above, the despotic authority of the master, which gives him the privilege to place a violently dangerous seaman in irons, cuts both ways. Power brings obligations; and in situations like this an authoritative text on nautical medicine defines these to include the application of as little force as possible and indeed prescribes the use of "kindness and consideration," as well as "constant supervision."[186] The court's uncritical use of these standards betokens its recognition of the power conferred by captaincy and accentuated by the helplessness of intoxication, however "voluntary" at the outset, as well as by the geographical isolation of shipboard. Here the judiciary exerts post hoc regulation of the simple use of physical force in a situation in which all rational control of that force rests with one party to the transaction. And the imposition of an obligation to act with "kindness and consideration," an application of practical medical standards by the law, reflects a judgment that seems to go considerably beyond considerations of efficiency, including even short-term morale. It shows that at least on some occasions the law will demand decency from those who hold superior positions over their fellows.

Defendant's nonnegligent cause of hazard. Reasoning from principles of duty developed here with reference to occasions on which the plaintiff's arguably culpable behavior endangers others, it would seem to follow that liability should fall on a defendant who fails to take remedial steps when his accidental conduct creates a dangerous situation. In one case the court required compensation from a motorist who accidentally hit a trolley pole and knocked it into the street but did nothing to remove it from the road or to warn approaching drivers.[187] The reasoning of the decision is not entirely persuasive, for it uses as a principal analogy the case of a private contractor who does the "lawful act" of opening up a street and thereby incurs a duty to warn of the excavation; by contrast, this motorist did not intend to do anything that would cause an obstruction. However, his participation in its creation, and his acquisition thereby of information unavailable to those who would be imperiled, properly serves as a basis to require use of his energies to prevent injury. Surely there will be situations in which the possession of strength or information comes so fortuitously, or the social fundaments of a relation are so thin, that it is wrong to penalize a failure to use power. But when one's own accident plays a crucial part in the creation of the danger, it is appropriate that he be required to pay.

v. A Thesis on the "Unrelated" Bystander: The Law as a Manifestation That "It Tolls for Thee"

I turn now to the most difficult case, that of the "pure" bystander, who stands in no conventional pre-existing relation to the party needing aid. It is useful here to distinguish the problem of the person whose life or security is seriously threatened within a rather short time but not immediately from that of the victim who requires help in a matter of seconds or minutes.

Duty when peril emergent. I shall concentrate on the case in which the peril is quite emergent and the plaintiff is a casual bystander. Exemplary would be a *Yania v. Bigan*[188] situation in which an unrelated third person walked by and noted the drowning man's plight but moved on without trying to help. In previous rehearsals of the general question, the contentions that the imposition of a duty to act is akin to slavery and will generate officious intermeddling have clashed with the arguments that the state lawfully imposes more onerous interferences with personal freedom and that moral revulsion itself provides an important basis for the creation of a duty.[189] At its point of greatest breadth, the analysis offered here suggests that the law properly may require bystanders to respond in emergencies in which there can be shown a de facto though quite fortuitous relation of dependence. This obligation would be imposed only when the person with the power to help can render aid without significant possibility of physical harm to himself, either actual or reasonably perceived, and without substantial personal inconvenience.[190] Part of the rationale for this duty would stem from the saving of overall welfare costs in the preservation of a life imminently threatened.[191] Quite important, especially in opposition to the "slavery" argument, is the boost to social morale that arguably would flow from the creation by the law of extra incentive to help others in peril. By codifying the deep moral sense of the community on this point,[192] a clear requirement of duty actually would remove a tension between law and social belief and well might contribute to a suffusion of greater feelings of responsibility and trust across community strata and beyond the closer personal relationships. I should note in this connection that the press seldom reflects as good a community feeling as that manifested on occasions when someone is rescued from an emergency predicament, or when hostages are released. And yet, as appears below, one must confront difficult situations in which the imperiled party's needs are argued to impinge on the power holder's interests and rights in controlling his own energies.

Stranger on the doorstep. We return at this juncture to the point on the borderline of duty where the private residence lies. Beyond an important old salient of case law,[193] the question arises of whether a homeowner must shelter a freezing stranger who appears fortuitously on the doorstep. By parity with my argument concerning the stranger fleeing attackers,[194] my answer is that at least there is a duty to call the appropriate public agency. I must note that it is an important facet of the hypothetical that the stranger appears fortuitously. To divert a long parade of horribles, I should emphasize that it would go far beyond the thesis advanced here to allow an action by one who deliberately selects a particular householder as a target for welfare demands and then sues when they are not met. Indeed, one generally must distinguish cases in which the plaintiff has the initial ability to control the situation— indeed to create it. Moreover, on the facts hypothesized, it is well to consider a behavioral point that relates to the perception of the person who controls the power to rescue: in an age in which *The Sting* evokes admiration for swindles by nice bad guys, one must make considerable allowance for the householder's skeptical belief that he is being set up for a con game—or a mugging.

Societal contribution. But the thrust of duty outruns these necessary caveats. In particular, a powerful justification for the imposition of obligations on many bystanders derives from the fact that the power they control, including physical energy, is owed significantly to social organization. Here one must deal directly with what I have termed the social fundaments of relationships. The present political consensus has approved a commonwealth that makes substantial inputs to education and other elements of individual welfare, in large measure because citizens perceive in it a system that maximizes utility. And because of the contributions society makes to individuals, it is appropriate for it to require that in fortuitously created relations its citizens respond to pleas to preserve life and limb which would be answered if its official agents were on the spot and acted in accordance with the social consensus on welfare. In emergencies where aid is refused despite a practical absence of risk to the power holder, the imposition of tort liability would provide an effective mediate remedy between a totally laissez faire approach and criminal punishment. On one hand, it seems superior to an unvarying policy of nonintervention, given the difficulties that approach creates with respect to public perceptions of justice. And although it would impinge on liberty, it would not do so nearly to the extent of the imprisonment that might follow criminal conviction.[195]

Behavior studies. With the advancement of this thesis, it is well to consider at least preliminarily the question of what effect human behavior as measured should have on the law. The studies of Bibb Latané and John M. Darley, among others, have revealed that one's inclination to take rescue action varies inversely as other persons are present.[196] Moreover, when others are present, their relation to the subject whose reactions are being tested will significantly influence his behavior: the presence of a friend will inhibit rescue behavior markedly less than that of a noncommunicative stranger. Among other explanations for these phenomena, Latané and Darley suggest that the apparent perceptions of others will contribute to a perception in the subject that the situation is less serious than he would think if he were alone Also, the presence of others tends to diffuse responsibility. These results, as the investigators note, subsume many characteristics and inner psychological tensions: lack of experience in dealing with crises, a cultural commitment to *machismo*, and a conflict between the attempt to avoid feelings of guilt and shame and the desire to keep from looking silly in front of strange companions.

What are the implications of these data for legal rule-making? The high proportion of those who respond in emergencies when they perceive themselves as alone with the victim suggests that the imposition of duties in these circumstances would not impinge on general patterns of behavior, and would in fact tend to confirm them. By comparison, it might be contended that the diminished frequency of intervention when there are several bystanders indicates that legal requirements of action should be less stringent in those situations. Certainly as a practical matter, in terms of possible litigation, the diffusion of responsibility would often produce overwhelming problems of proof of causation. Yet problems of proof aside, it properly may be countered that the rule should be the same for those in multiple bystander situations as for those who are alone. Supporting this position is the proposition that, beyond perceived sanctions, the existence of a known rule of obligation would lead to an increase in intervention and probably a reinforcement of cooperative motivations among those fortuitously thrown together in emergency situations. It would be useful to conduct a study that examined knowledge of the law in a population newly exposed to the idea that there is a legal duty to help persons in peril, as is now the case in Vermont,[197] and sometime later tested their reactions in group situations. If the argument advanced here is correct, then a change in the law, reflecting what most people privately consider to be proper behavior, would have positive effects on conduct.[198] In turn this would produce welfare benefits in the prevention of injury and death.

It may be suggested that the award of money damages is an inappropriate remedy in cases involving failures to help those in peril. The tort depends, after all, on notions of humanity and decency. The requirement of judicial judgment as to whether liability should be imposed at all should assure that compensation awards would not cheapen the concept of duty. At the threshold, the court would determine whether a power holder can justly be ordered to compensate for his failure to use energy or information for the benefit of another. The court would be constrained in this decision by its reading of mores generally and its sense of the practical political limitations on civil obligation.[199] A judicially imposed standard would always be significantly influenced by the existence of an emergency, and, in practice, courts would likely be chary in their award of compensation for failure to render aid. However, it would seem important that the rule be stated rather broadly for hortatory purposes, with the aim of producing the salutary consequences outlined above, and also because this would encourage a broad construction of duties in cases in which power is abused.

Cowardice aggravated or courage bolstered? The view that to impose a duty to help those in peril will increase respect for the legal system does not win universal acceptance. A contrary argument suggests that, if the duty embraces the spectrum of relative cowardice common throughout the population, it will have "a high potential for unnerving the citizenry rather than cultivating public respect."[200] Moreover, it is conjectured that legal penalties for failure to aid may well reduce the incidence of rescue, for example, by discouraging bystanders from fixing their perceptions on endangered persons and therefore even from reporting their plight to others.[201] But there is no showing that the imposition of duties to act has undermined natural altruism in the many cases in which an obligation exists by virtue of a relation. Moreover, any reasonable requirement of rescue would make substantial allowance for pleas of feared harm to oneself as an excuse for refusal and would relax armchair standards of performance for those who did plunge in. Therefore it would seem unlikely that to impose duties would discourage perception of emergencies or response to them. Further in the teeth of arguments against obligation, there remains insistently the thought that the existence of legal duties might provide a bolster to the better angels of human nature. Finally, the contention that a duty that applies to rather callous conduct must be practically broad enough to sweep in normal timidity seems exaggerated, if the law makes reasonable allowance for the potential rescuer to avoid substantial risk to himself.

Slow death and social default. Generally beyond the writ of the common law, and penal sanctions as well, is the situation in which the plaintiff's peril is one of slow death, and in which the defendant's failure to expend energies to save him is no more than part of a generally lackadaisical attitude on the part of society. Here, as a matter of tort theory as well as philosophy, the determination of causation would become impractical. In the case of one dying of starvation, the difficulty lies only partly in the problem of trying to fix responsibility at a given point in time. It inheres more profoundly in the fact that the failure of one passerby to give him money or food is inseparable not only from the inaction of scores of others but also from that of society itself.[202] Though the tragedy is not lessened, diffusion makes it virtually impossible to fix responsibility except politically.[203]

Summary

I shall now undertake a summary of the factors and principles that bear most heavily on the question of whether the law should impose a duty to act on private persons for purposes of civil liability. Besides reviewing my general examination of private duties, this will provide bases for further study of specific private relations, and for analysis of the tort liability of governments and officials for abuses as well as defaults in the use of their power.

I have evolved as a working principle that one has a duty to aid others in situations in which hazardous conditions necessitate assistance for the preservation of life and of physical integrity, and in which one possesses the power to expend energy in that task without serious inconvenience or possibility of harm to himself. I have suggested that this duty, vindicable by tort judgments, also should apply on occasion to the protection of other vital personal interests in relations of transactional superiority and helpless dependence. Many of the relationships on which this kind of obligation will depend will exist well before the situation that gives rise to the injury and will involve an established reliance interest in the plaintiff. The case of patient and physician is exemplary. However, as these cases move gradually away from cleanly defined relations with contractual overtones, the duty continues to exist, as in the case of doctors whose principal bargain relation is with a third party, such as an employer. And it will persist even when the relation is one created by emergent circumstances. For example, it will apply in many cases in which a power holder is able at minimal expense to save a potential victim from the threat of immediate injury by a third party. Usually, in cases of that sort, the defendant already has acted in some way that effectively has placed the plaintiff's security in his hands. But beyond that, I have suggested that there are some situations in which the fortuity of an emergency in the vicinity of a power holder may impose on him a duty to act.

In the view I have put forth here, power becomes the ultimate generator of many duties in tort. This perception, I believe, will clarify analysis of the development of the law for all those concerned with its policy bases. Once that analysis is made and judgment is required, the views of those called upon to judge may differ reasonably, according to perspectives of public policy refined by as dispassionate a view of the issues as is possible. My own view places some emphasis on the social sources of many kinds of power, ranging from the ability and opportunity to practice a profession to the rights of untroubled possession of land or leasehold, and even to the personal energy so dependent on a secure social basis for distribution of the means of physical sustenance. Besides providing legal recognition of this reality, the imposition of broadly defined duties would manifest the law's recognition of the breakdown in sources of personal support once provided by tightly structured communities and extended families, and of the attendant loss of social adhesive. What seems most important, whatever choices are made, is that courts pose and confront questions related to power and dependence, and particularly the influence of humanitarian considerations.

The considerations relevant to the question of whether an obligation exists are indeed numerous. Courts must take into account not only whether there is a conventionally recognized legal relation between the parties but also whether others are in a position to render aid. Other considerations would include the alternative possibilities of energy use that immediately exist for the party sought to be charged, and the pressure of competing obligations which draw on his energies. As the situation becomes less emergent, less demanding of instant action, calculated balancings of cost factors become more important to decision. Whatever the factual circumstances, judgment invariably will require definition of the nature of the power possessed by the person who would be able to give aid; and it will be necessary to identify the source of that power, whether in a relationship with the imperiled person or in socially cultivated abilities or characteristics. When a relationship is the principal font of the power and generates dependence, the case is usually strong for the victim. It is typically much stronger from the power holder's point of view when the primary source of his power is a personal resource that owes its existence and development only generally to social organization. However, in some situations that in itself may be enough to support a duty. Indeed, in that connection, questions sometimes useful as rough testing standards are whether a government official who knew about the plaintiff's plight would reasonably believe that it is his obligation under the law to render aid,[204] or whether officials confronted with the problem ordinarily would exercise their discretion to do so.[205]

I have offered this analysis as an alternative—sometimes as a complement—to recent scholarship relating to tort liability. I have suggested explicitly, and it has often been implicit, that an exclusive focus on cost avoidance will not yield satisfactory answers in a branch of the law that has been reflective of a variety of social judgments that reach beyond efficiency concerns.[206] But it has also been both implicit and explicit that for reasons of morality and fairness, related both to the social basis of civilized existence and to basic ethical requirements of respect for life, I would not require a strict reciprocity in the sense of defining the risks to which both parties are subject.[207] Nor would I accept as definitive a theoretical framework which is founded principally on causation with legal duties seen as rooted primarily in volition in the sense of action. While Professor Epstein has argued ably for a strict liability formulation so founded,[208] I have indicated my belief that courts are equipped to deal with many cases conventionally classified as non-action, and I have suggested that the blurred boundaries between action and inaction[209] require an alternative analysis to deal with problems in which the issue is primarily one of control and dependence and not of cost avoidance on one hand or causation on the other. I also have suggested that the uncertainty of the line between strict liability and negligence seems to demand more investigation of the categories of tort culpability.

Although I have deliberately confined this work to a limited wedge of cases, the analysis has radiations that extend through personal injury law, bidding judges to give more explicit recognition to the social protein of duty between private parties as well as between individuals and the commonwealth. An advantage of the perspective offered here is that it would require fuller attention to the moral bases of decisions about whether to shift wealth between power holders and those injured on occasions when well-directed uses of power would have saved them from harm. Broader vistas of application for this analysis will require further examination. Here, it is well to conclude with a particular case that evokes powerful arguments for imposing a duty, in a situation in which the traditional view of the common law has been that no obligation exists. Assume that a janitor breaks a leg working late Friday night on an upper staircase of a high-rise office building and lies helpless on the landing. An executive who works on the adjoining floor walks by, laden with a full briefcase. He perceives the janitor but ignores his pleas for help. No one works in the building on weekends because there is no heat then, an economy measure that is due to rising energy costs; thus, no one else comes on the scene for three nights and two days. The janitor suffers serious injury from spending the weekend in an unheated building without food or water.

Should the executive have to compensate for this added injury? It is true that it is at least questionable whether his refusal to aid was inefficient in a conventional exchange sense. He entered into no bargain relationship with the janitor. Moreover, given his impersonal status as no more than the employee of a tenant, his relationship to the janitor is such that his decision to pass by may not have a substantial effect on morale in the custodial crew. Yet a court properly might take into consideration the impact that legal condonation of such conduct would have on social morale generally, and even the consequent marginal effects on productivity. Less speculatively, to apply a line of argument already begun, the welfare problem created by the prolonged exposure of the janitor impinges on a public treasury that makes significant contributions to the building of skyscrapers. Police protection, tax advantages, locational privileges, quite possibly grants supporting the activities of various tenants—these only exemplify the role of government in giving the overworked executive the opportunity to pursue his business in the lofty quarters of his modern keep. A commonwealth related so symbiotically with productive activity may require from it a correlative concern for welfare and may impose liabilities when failures to use readily available energies cause injury in even informal and fortuitous relations.

The need for a broad view of duty appears more clearly in the light of the impersonalization of society in times of recurrent political stress and international crisis, when a sense of national unity and interpersonal concern appears even more necessary to social preservation. The dislocations of modern life lend special force to the large general notion that power confers obligations, and buttress the principle advanced here: that transactional superiority imposes duties on those who control power over the security and interests of other persons who stand in known relationships to them, however temporary. These duties support rights in favor of dependent individuals in many situations and against a variety of power holders, including other private citizens, firms, and governments. Room for moral decision still remains. One must be wary of the conviction that the law can make us better. Yet it is appropriate to emphasize that decisions either way have implications for social norms and to argue that law-making agencies should take care that their judgments do not make us worse. As always the law involves hard choice and uneasy compromises, in the great area of swirl between social benefit and individual choice. But, as it is, our law has well established the principle of due care as applicable to even tenuous and transitory relationships, and even between actors and others unknown to them. In such a legal world, it is appropriate that the law encourage the judicious use of power in situations of perceived peril, the more so as it aids known and identifiable persons. In this sense, private as well as public law may generate incentives for caring as well as obligations of care.

PART TWO

Public Duties to Act:
Vindicating Personal Interests
against Invasion and Neglect
by Commonwealth Power

Introduction

Citizens who suffer personal injury often may claim that the government caused or could have prevented harm to them. The clearest case is that of injury caused by an emission of physical energy from a government instrumentality or by the use of physical force by an official of the commonwealth. Somewhat more subtly, actions of government agencies in the control of various abilities and forms of knowledge may damage one who is consigned to a position of submission and acceptance unless an agency of the law proclaims that he has a legal right in the matter. Lying further toward the frontier of governmental duty is the claim that the commonwealth should have preserved a citizen from injury by another private person. This problem merges, at its most extreme boundary, with the issue of whether government owes a private citizen succor against fortuities of his life that he cannot trace meaningfully to the actions or omissions of either government or other persons. I shall deal with this problem only at its margins here, but it provides a constant background for the issues which I primarily consider.

My principal purpose in this part is to explore the question of when governments have a duty to give protection to citizens threatened by harm to personal interests. As in the last part, I will focus primarily on the framework of power relationships that I believe provide the key to much of modern tort law and related areas. Thus, I shall parallel questions of governmental responsibility with problems of private duty discussed earlier. The terms in which power is defined will be the same broad ones used in the preceding part, comprehending the possession or use of energy, ability, and information. In a remedial sense, the issue most often posed here will be whether governmental default should invoke judicial response, typically by the award of damages, but I shall also examine some analogues in which the problem spills over into one of legislative policy. The inquiry will deal with a number of factual settings, ranging from rather routine problems of traffic control to the profound and far-reaching questions that arise when citizens attempt to enforce claims for police protection or seek commonwealth response to various welfare needs. I must emphasize that I shall be dealing with numerous complicated areas of governmental function, several of which each might well support a full-dress, discrete study. But although I shall not always plumb the richness of the factual background in these areas, I believe this approach will prove fruitful in the effort to develop a general theory of governmental obligation with respect to personal injuries. In that endeavor I shall often use as guideposts established tort doctrines, as well as undertaking to suggest other principles that govern tort law and the surrounding territory, including some aspects of "constitutional tort" theory.[1]

vi. Highway Safety as a
Paradigm of Liability for
Planning and Maneuvering

The area of highway safety is a natural starting place for this study. With the passage of legislation that manifests deep congressional concern with death and injury on the roads,[2] it has acquired legal significance that reaches far beyond such petty doctrinal issues as whether painting lines on the street involves a "corporate" or "governmental" function.[3] I shall begin with the superficially simple question of government liability for failure to erect or maintain traffic control signs or devices. In the least complex legal strata of this territory, one finds laconic authority imposing on a municipality the duty properly to maintain a "Stop" sign which a statute requires it to erect.[4] Yet even at this level of the subject controversy may arise. It may be reasonable to draw the line against requiring notification of motorists that they are about to cross a boulevard designated by ordinance as a through street, but it seems quite artificial to say that to rule otherwise "would require all law-enacting agencies of government to maintain constant signals notifying its inhabitants and the public at large of all enacted laws."[5] And one may at least question the broad use of this authority, in turn, to support a decision against a motorist who claimed there was a duty to maintain a stop sign where one had been before, although it had been removed at least several months before the accident.[6] In supporting that result, the court meets head-on a claim of "moral obligation," replying to an argument in a sister state's precedent that emphasizes the notion of a right of reliance in motorists. It queries, sensibly, whether a motorist can reasonably rely on a sign that has been nonexistent for many months. Rather less persuasively—and less sensitively—it asks with some incredulity whether a city "fairly [could] be required to post notices on one street that STOP signs *had been removed* from crossing streets?"[7] Although it concedes a "possible moral obligation," it cannot find a "legal duty," concluding with the traditional argument that street signs are a facet of police protection for the "public generally."

On the facts of that case, the plaintiff's argument that an existing sign should have been preserved is not compelling, given the lapse of time between the removal of the sign and the accident. The decision gives one pause, however, in light of the court's statement that "the very existence of an intersection is open notice of potential traffic hazards." One wonders what the appearance of the signless intersection in fact signalled to approaching motorists, and whether there was a known history of accidents there. The situation may present no more than a case of contributory fault, and in that case the law is simple enough and the decision proper. But surely there may be instances in which a government should be liable for its failure to notify the public of a change in a traffic control system, if this creates a hazard where none has existed before. The government's role in the building and maintenance of streets creates a certain dependence on its management of traffic flow, and arguably this dependence should generate legal duties as well as "moral" ones when the government defaults on the trust implicit in that relation.

I already have cited one court's adoption of the view that the duty sought to be enforced is one owed to the public generally rather than to a particular individual. This argument, one of the most successful defenses that governments mount against suits for failure to use their power to avoid injury, also finds favor in a Florida appellate decision,[8] which involved the collapse of a stop sign following a police officer's attempt to prop it up after a collision had knocked it down. The court, confronted with a precedent in a suit for the death of a prisoner[9] that has served as a bellwether for a nationwide liberalization of liability for police torts, sought to limit the effect of that case with an argument quaintly aromatic of products liability "privity." Noting that all the recent Florida decisions which granted recovery against municipalities dealt with situations of *"direct contact or liaison"*[10] between the plaintiff and the defendant's employees, the court distinguished these patterns of "privity" or *"direct transaction or confrontation"*[11] from its instant problem of the fallen sign, which it characterized as involving only a "public duty." But "privity" has no more solving power concerning governmental reality than regarding the facts of the consumer world, if one speaks in terms of the expectability of injury. And an appeal to privity is persuasive only so far as it dovetails with a calculation of comparative costs and benefits of accidents and prevention, and with the nature of the relationships that exist between government and citizen and the compulsions and entrustments that are intertwined with them. The fact that those likely to be harmed do not have direct personal contact with governmental officers does not effectively distinguish the risk of failure to make sure that a fallen stop sign is re-established from that of failure to take proper care of a prisoner.[12] Indeed, a recent decision has rejected defenses based on both "public duty" and "discretionary" rubrics to impose liability for failure to maintain a sign which had disappeared.[13] Analogy further supportive of liability appears in the sphere of private duty, where we have noted that one who nonnegligently knocks a pole into the road must remove it or give warning to oncoming motorists.[14]

The properly applicable principle would appear to be that an officer's knowledge of a dangerous condition, plus a relationship temporarily created by the circumstances of a fortuitous event, imposes an obligation at least to share that knowledge with those likely to be endangered. Here the wavy and blurry boundary between "action" and "duty to act" becomes entirely obliterated, and private and public duties coincide, as one views the case in terms of both acts and roles and of the nexus that has arisen between the person with the information and those citizens whose safety depends on it. It is the knocking down of the pole that creates the nexus in the case against the motorist. It is the role of the policeman that creates it in the case of the stop sign. Given these parallels, it would seem curious that the possession of information about hazards and the ability to communicate it or to remedy dangerous conditions should impose liability on a private person but not on a government. In both cases the basic obligation is one to an unidentified group, but the "public" aspect of that duty should not render it less enforceable against a government than a person. The key to duty in both cases resides in the dependence of the unknown plaintiff—in the one situation involuntarily created by an unintentional but violent act, in the other fostered by a role entangled in a web of assumptions about what government usually does for motorists. Accenting that dependence is the fact that the plaintiff has no opportunity for self-help in this kind of case. And, highlighting the breakdown of the barriers between action and nonaction, the policeman's default has created quite as much a peril as the motorist who drives away from the fallen pole.[15]

Nuisance theory; reasonableness standard. Two decisions dealing with traffic signals present a different slant, tilted by the extra reliance that an existing signal engenders. In one case, particularly compelling on the facts because the city had nine hours' notice that a light was not working, the court disdains distinctions between governmental and proprietary functions to hold that a nonfunctioning signal "may be determined to be a nuisance by a jury under proper instructions."[16] It finds overtechnical an attempt to distinguish traffic signals from chuck holes with reference to the nuisance characterization. An even more expansive view appears in a brief opinion of the New Jersey Supreme Court, in a case in which a township police officer failed to take over traffic control when an overhead signal maintained by the state highway department broke loose. Although the principal duty was the state's, the court declared that "the municipality must act reasonably . . . until the appropriate authority, here the State's own agencies, can take over."[17] Specifically, it held that there is a duty "if a police officer learns of an emergent road condition which is likely not to be observed by a motorist and which holds an unusual risk of injury."[18] Delimiting the standard, the court allowed that the city might prove that its failure to act was due to "competing demands upon the police force," and said that the jury could impose municipal liability only if the deployment judgment was "palpably unreasonable."[19]

Despite this qualification, the court's basic rule is one that slices through rolled-up problems of discretion and negligence, embodying a recognition that governments have a duty to act quite analogous to that of private parties. Of course, judicial decision in cases of this kind necessarily must take into account governmental problems in the reconciliation of competing demands. It should be noted, however, that the court's articulation of the culpability standard on this point may introduce an unnecessary inequality into legal doctrine, unless one is prepared also to apply the standard of palpable unreasonableness to private parties faced with competing demands. That would seem unwise, for the conventional use of the concept of unreasonable conduct provides a tool that is serviceable yet will not bog down courts in discussions of whether "palpably unreasonable" is to be analogized to "gross negligence" or even to "wanton, wilful and reckless conduct." In any event, whichever standard of reasonableness is selected, it should be applied to government and citizens alike, with courts simply factoring in the extra burdens that government may face because of multifarious demands on their police resources. It should be added that when the issue involves an ability to exercise power that is crucial for personal safety the basic level of obligation of governments should tend to be heightened, providing an appropriate counterpart to the relaxation of their duties in particular cases to account for their peculiar burdens.

Governments not insurers. The analysis proposed here does not require that governments become insurers for all injuries causally connected with their maintenance of streets; it would impose liability only for harms caused by their mismanagement of the power conferred on them by citizens. In this connection it is useful to refer to another New Jersey decision, rejecting the claim of a mailman who was hit by a car as he tried to clamber over a snow pile created by a plow. The court in this case declares that it is not a municipal duty to "broom sweep" all streets of snow removed by plows.[20] The common sense of the decision probably lies in the obviousness of the danger, but it is also basic that the case simply involves no misdirection or default in the use of power. It does seem too broad to suggest, as the court appears to do, that there may be no recovery when public benefit "far outweighs any slight, private detriment." If this were so, might not one conclude that there is no duty to warn of a signal light gone awry because the use of the device itself saves so much in traffic costs? To follow this approach would enmesh us unprofitably in old distinctions, entailing frustrating efforts to define the conceptual boundaries of activities.[21] A sufficient explanation for the result in the snow plow case is that there was no negligence.[22] But this means not only that the benefits of governmental management of the broad problem were greater than its toll but also that municipal activity did not impose unfairly on one who was in a position to preserve himself from perceived risk.[23] I should emphasize that there are many instances in which government is held for default in services that it has undertaken to perform although the activity confers social benefits that far outweigh an occasional victim's injury, when the default seriously breaches an obligation of practical trust that the circumstances impose. A classic example is the case of air traffic control, in which the pilot is completely dependent on the tower for his basic weather information.[24]

Superior information and duty to warn. Impenetrable fog on a thruway lies over the factors of governmental allocation and citizen choice as they hang in delicate balance in an interesting recent decision, which affirms an award against the state of New York. An auto passenger sued for injuries caused when her husband had a collision as he drove through the fog, which was caused by the uncontrolled burning of muckland over a period of several days. The court of appeals[25] affirmed a decision of the court of claims, which had found that the state police should have either closed the thruway portion completely or stopped traffic at both ends of the affected area and convoyed vehicles through the smog.[26] A dissent reveals conflict on the facts as well as on the wisdom of the decision. It in effect accuses the majority of insufficient attention to the comparative risks of shunting traffic off the thruway onto other roads similarly afflicted by smog, or of the use of convoys.[27] On the facts, these may be reasonable arguments. However, I wish to address here a basic principle that arches beyond factual controversy: when government commands the power to give both warning and aid necessary to avoid a particular danger, it has an obligation to provide them when the magnitude of that danger is much better known to it than to those whose security is threatened.[28] Of course, a proper reason to deny recovery would be foolish persistence in the face of nonvisibility. But, as a practical matter, one must consider the case from the standpoint of the motorist who hopefully waits for the end of the fog at the next bend in the road, vaguely reasoning through growing uneasiness that otherwise ·some more stringent control would be in effect. Again, our view of the justice of this case may be as murky as the facts,[29] but the inquiry should focus on the possession of information and ability to avoid accidents, in circumstances that effectively create an entrustment of safety because of the perception they reasonably produce in the citizen about governmental role.

HIGHWAY DESIGN: CHOICE, KNOWLEDGE, AND FAIRNESS

I turn now to the generally more complex area of highway design liability. Many thousands of traffic accidents each year are at least partly attributable to various characteristics of roads themselves. A recent independent survey of the Capitol Beltway, which rings Washington, D.C., revealed "built-in boobytraps virtually every mile." These included four-inch I-beams set in concrete, used as mounts for route markers, as well as exposed abutments preceded by guardrails that tend to guide whatever hits them into the abutments. Also evident were "short sections of blunt-ended guard rails, too short to shield the objects behind them, and capable of spearing a vehicle and its passengers."[30] At the national level, some evidence concerning highway design is positively melancholy. For example, a survey of more than 560,000 highway bridges found that about 88,900 were "critically deficient," including 24,000 on federal aid highway systems.[31] Figures of this kind eventually pose the ultimate allocational issue of what value society places on lives in its choice of road designs. This involves a complex calculus, but models are available and specialists can adduce figures on "acceptable outlay[s]" to avoid accidents.[32] Beyond easily quantifiable economic deprivations, loss statistics may include both "affective injury to the family," primarily sorrow, and "affective injury of the nation"—a derivation of an "imperative rule" that commands communities to preserve the lives of their members, "irrespective of the advantage to be derived, and whether or not the persons concerned are families."[33]

Policy choice blurs into tactical maneuver. The cases on highway design incorporate several judicial positions summarized above with respect to duties of routine maintenance and of warning when dangerous conditions arise. One decision that deals with the absence of shoulders on a highway, though it mentions testimony of two engineering experts that there should have been standard hard shoulders, stresses that neither expert denied that the highway met minimum standards for its traffic volume. The court notes also that federal aid programs did not require standard shoulders. Pointing out that such shoulders would presumably have cost substantially more money, the court says that the decision about whether to have them "was a duly considered one, reposing in the discretionary judgment of the governing authority and free—in the specific factual context of this particular case—from collateral attack by tort suit."[34]

The court's examination of precedent emphasizes the policy or political nature of the decision, while conceding by quotation from a previous case that government could be liable for acting "in a manner short of ordinary prudence."[35] One may reconcile a defense of "policy making" with standard negligence doctrine when one views the court's quotation from that precedent of the statement that, "*if a road were constructed of a design imperiling the user, the issue of fault would present no novel problems*,"[36] with an eye to the prior case's selection of examples of questions involving "discretion . . . committed to the judgment of the legislative and executive branches." These examples include matters as diverse as whether there should be dividers or traffic lights or a certain number of lanes in a road, or what the speed limit should be.[37] The question of how many lanes a road should have depends on factors that are sufficiently complex and embodies enough of raw politics that arguably a court should not get involved; and this reasoning may be contended to extend to the question of whether there should be hard shoulders on roads on which travel is relatively infrequent. But it may not embrace all cases that can linguistically be housed under a broad definition of "discretion." I simply wish to emphasize here that as the situation shades off toward discrete, known dangers the planning and preparation decision of how to build a highway will merge functionally with the maneuvering decision of how to respond to perils that arise on that road, with the latter category including both failure and collapse of safety devices or equipment and the emergence of environmental hazards. In this perspective, and relating this discussion to the preceding one, we see that often one may not slice design cleanly away from traffic control.

Close parallel with private manufacturers. The problem of abutting structures illustrates how the exercise of state power in design may justify the imposition of government liability. A per curiam opinion of the Second Circuit finds no obstacle to recovery in a case in which a car hit an abutment that was "improperly obscured by growth, was not properly marked, and was too close to the highway for safety," in a setting in which the roadway lacked proper markings, curve signs, and guardrails.[38] The court viewed the problem simply as one of design choices that were "not in accord with standard and acceptable highway practices in the area." More complex and difficult is a New York case involving failure to erect a median barrier on an express highway, in which the differences between the appellate division and the court of appeals reflect what doubtless will be a continuing area of clash. The appellate division mustered a number of factors that contraindicated negligence: it said there were no hazardous conditions or confusing signs and noted specifically that there was adequate warning of a curve by means of curve and arrow signs. The court of appeals agreed that there was no showing of negligence that brought about the accident. However, where the appellate division had said that the failure to construct a median could in no way "be considered the proximate cause of the accident,"[39] the court of appeals declared that although this did not cause the car to leave the highway it "might have been a substantial factor in aggravation of the injuries."[40] The court of appeals finally affirmed for the defendant; but it emphasized that it would have decided otherwise if there had been proof of causation as well as negligence. Particularly interesting in this regard is its "cf." quotation of a products liability case,[41] in which it had imposed liability for design defects in motor vehicles that aggravate injuries rather than cause them. This analogy and this approach are convincing. They equate the liability of governments with that of private producers. Certainly, definition of the government's obligation must take account of competing drafts on its resources, but this fluctuation of duty with comparative scarcities should follow exactly that which occurs with private entrepreneurs. Again the theme of dependence deserves emphasis: highway design typically involves situations of almost total motorist dependence, in which the government possesses superior information about hazards as well as the physical power necessary to produce safer conditions.

Undertakings and knowledge. The viewpoint developed here casts doubt on the result in a recent suit charging failure to provide an opportunity to make safe turns.[42] The plaintiff sought damages for the death of one child and injury of another, caused when a car violently rammed her vehicle in the rear as she slowed to make a left-hand turn. She alleged that the defendant Department of Highways had neglected to warn motorists "of the great number of accidents at that hazardous section" of roadway and had failed "to take proper action to alleviate this very dangerous situation." She also specifically alleged negligence in failure to construct a left-turn lane after repeated notification of a great number of accidents; but, although the court concentrates on its rejection of this claim, presumably there might have been intermediate alternatives of modifying the intersection or emphasizing warnings of danger. The court contents itself with a statement that it knows "of no statute or reported decision which places an affirmative duty to construct left-turn lanes at a highway cross-over even though the accident rate at such cross-overs may be indicative that traffic has created a hazardous situation."[43]

The court concludes by saying that the law places a duty on the motorist to ascertain whether he can turn safely. This may hide an unarticulated but sufficient determination of the case on grounds of contributory fault. But the decision falters seriously in its insistence that the Department of Highways "does not owe a duty to a motorist to protect him from negligence of another."[44]

It is well established that government must sometimes pay for failure to protect its citizens against the torts of third parties, not only for negligence but even in the case of intentional torts.[45] At least on the pleadings, it would seem that this case fits that matrix of liability. On an intersecting conceptual track, the facts summon the analogy of the *Indian Towing* case,[46] in which the Supreme Court imposed liability for substandard operation of a lighthouse. In the left-turn case, the government has undertaken to construct a highway. At a point of particular danger—known statistically to it—it folds its arms and opts out. Arguably a duty should devolve on government in circumstances of this kind if there is no showing of carelessness on the part of the imperiled individual (as concededly may have been the case on these facts), but evidence only of a desperate struggle to make the best of a highly dangerous situation. In the terms I have been using, it is a planning duty to avoid an expectable disaster in maneuver. I should emphasize that the court need not settle whether the best (or second-best) solution is to establish a left-turn lane, to cut off entirely the possibility of left turns, or to give fearsomely explicit warning of the gruesome toll taken by that intersection. These are proper choices for officialdom.

Expectations and perceptions of justice. Yet it must be emphasized that official choice remains subject to judicial scrutiny, tested by the standard of obligation of power holders. It thus would seem wrong to refer to "policy" and "discretion" as rationales that permit government to ignore dangerous conditions on its own creature of commerce. This is so partly for reasons of expectation, derived from a representational background. Maintenance of such a road may be likened to governmental construction of a maze, which appears as an ordinary if complex footpath, in which the citizen strides inexorably to a dead end where an electric shock awaits him. A dangerous section of highway without the most specific warnings implicitly signals that it is safe for travel at generally accepted standards of motoring behavior. This implication derives in large measure from the level of civilization. Move that level fifty years back, drop living standards generally, and you change expectations; with them change perceptions of justice. Indeed, common expectations are the stuff of duty. And in the present social milieu, the commonwealth's construction of a road, or other public project, communicates a concern for the individual welfare of prospective users that entails the further obligation not to tolerate traps in it, and to rectify conditions that experience proves dangerous.

Here we enter the uncertain realm of the attempt to define fairness. Obviously, one may not expect government to even out all the safety factors across various forms of transportation, or even in one area of transportation. But it seems reasonable that the citizen expect a level of government responsibility for his safety that accords with the standard for comparable activities in which private enterprise undertakes the management of hazardous clusters of energy. Under this analysis, government incurs an obligation if it has knowledge of a pattern of occurrences in which danger proves likely to arise instantaneously and with shattering impact, and in which there is no opportunity for endangered persons to extricate themselves. Specifically in the case of highway building, it will not wash to argue that tolerance of a dangerous condition is insufficient to support the claims of a citizen injured thereby, on grounds that the road represents an increase in total social utility that redounds generally to the benefit of all. The power that inheres in the commonwealth's control over the highway, and in its possession of information, creates a duty.

From one standpoint, this appears clearly as an affirmative obligation. It is not simply a matter of preventing neglect in design, such as the location of unyielding abutments at a place where cars often arrive at high speeds. It follows from the approach advanced here that government has a continuing obligation to monitor data that bear on physical security in its bailiwick, and to act on their implications.[47] To be sure, the reach of such a principle is broad, and it will require definition founded in economy as well as expectations. But one does not need to stretch its application in the case of highway design, given the analogies that course through the area of products frustration. And now one sees the formulation of "affirmative duty" as bound up and intermingled with the enforcement of duties, usually characterized in defensive terms, to avoid damaging miscalculations prior to the moment of emergency. In this sense, the left-turn problem lines up closely with the case of witless placement of abutments. Again the lines break down between original misfeasances and arising duties. Once more the binding theme is one of obligation that power confers on those upon whom others depend.

The comparisons drawn above with private industry do summon a paradox. In extreme cases, the imposition of liability on governments may present graver questions than would requiring compensation from private business. The problem may sometimes involve finding the right pocket and at other times a question of whether there is a pocket at all. On the other hand, in the areas involved here, the role of government as a protector of physical security, and citizen dependence on that role, is such that, if anything, the responsibility of government should be judged more expansively than that of private parties. But in all but the most speculative cases, the analogy presents few difficulties. In fact, in most of the cases addressed in this part, the specter of financial ruin for government does not arise. Indeed, the literature is silent with respect to instances in which the expansion of tort liability has put intolerable strain on the fisc of a struggling government. This is not, however, to minimize the problems of loss allocation and the desirability of matching tort obligations with the appropriate governmental accounts. In the case of highway design and traffic control, for example, tort judgments should be financed at least in part from taxes on motoring as an activity, although the positive externalities of motoring are such that part of these obligations also should be paid from the general revenues.[48]

When the activity involved is even more broadly fundamental to social order, as in the case of police protection, a practical working principle would require compensation to be completely financed from the general revenues—a point occasionally rationalized explicitly in existing case law.[49] In most cases in which an expansion of governmental obligation is suggested here as an analogue to traditional liabilities of private parties, there should be no serious question about the feasibility and administrability of this combination of financing from general revenues and use-related taxation. In others I shall explicitly note that the decision is clearly a political one requiring direct legislative judgment and appropriation. In a very few cases, such as hypothesized tort actions for inadequate education, I shall emphasize the speculative nature of the discussion—and this speculation obviously will embrace the difficulties in selection of the appropriate taxing unit and, ultimately, the political judgment about the levels of governmental services.

VII. Security

I shall now consider various aspects of the provision and delivery of protective and welfare services, respectively, focusing on tactical responses to particular situations but examining also a wide range of implications with respect to rather basic allocational decisions.

FIREFIGHTING

The duty to provide fire protection provides a point at which emotional as well as legal tension runs high, involving as it does the special horrors that fire holds for people generally; it also presents an interesting comparison to the extended discussion below of police protection. I shall first trace the boundaries of obligation. A broad view appears in a federal court's construction of the New York Court of Claims Act, emphasizing that when a fire department official subjects someone to the "compulsion of law" the official's use of "discretion and expertise" to reduce fire hazards will not necessarily bar a negligence action.[50] In this case there was a collision that damaged a ship carrying naphtha, which the Coast Guard had ordered to be transported to a federal explosives anchorage. Believing that the Coast Guard had not done enough to prevent the possibility of explosion, the city fire commissioner ordered the introduction of carbon dioxide into the vessel's cargo compartments to reduce the concentration of naphtha fumes. Suing for damages from the consequent explosion, the plaintiff shipowner claimed that this was a negligent order, arguing that the commissioner should have known that the use of carbon dioxide was "extremely dangerous" because of the possible occurrence of static electricity. Reversing a dismissal, the court found that the shipowner's complaint had sufficiently alleged that the order was without "reasonable basis," in the words of a state precedent.

This decision fits comfortably within traditional formulations of duties to act because it views the commissioner as already having undertaken to act, creating thereby an obligation to exercise due care. Thus harmonizing with conventional doctrine, the case is noteworthy not only because it refuses to allow a blanket defense for "discretion," but also because of its emphasis on the compulsory aspect of the commissioner's actions. In this situation the power of government is at a zenith. It has deprived the shipowner of the opportunity for self-protection and placed him in a position of complete dependence. These elements join to make a strcng case for governmental liability, a case sealed because the official's action increased the level of risk. A poignant contrast, delineating a cutoff line for duty, appears in a press report that members of a volunteer fire department passively viewed a blaze as it consumed an $18,000 house, because the owners had not purchased the department's $7 tag.[51] The volunteers had frequently advertised a policy of "no tag, no service." This publicity, plus the ready availability of fire insurance, combines with the volunteer character of the department to justify the refusal to help as a matter of law as well as morality, although the legal situation might blur if there were persons trapped in the house.[52]

Public benefit argument. Within these broad perimeters of duty, there is room for much controversy. It is appropriate to begin a brief survey of the intellectual history of the problem with the *Moch* case.[53] In that decision, Judge Cardozo refused to impose liability against a waterworks for its failure to supply enough water, in fulfillment of its contract with a city, to put out a fire in the plaintiff's warehouse. Fretting about the problem of indefinite enlargements of duty—a matter of continuing concern to him— Cardozo found that the defendant had at worst denied a benefit, rather than committed a wrong. New York courts applied this much cited reasoning recently in a case in which it was a city that contracted to give assistance to a fire district. The appellate division,[54] affirmed without opinion by the court of appeals,[55] rejected a claim based on the city's failure to have personnel present to handle the plaintiffs' call and to establish safety regulations for use of a relay system. Again the arguments appear that there was no "especial duty nor benefit running to plaintiffs individually," and that the contract "at best was for the benefit of the general public." Although the result may be supportable, this now-tired litany, though more freshly minted in 1928, does not seem persuasive in itself. It is playing with words to separate the fate of individual citizen and general public in this case, when it is clear that the agreement was made only for the benefit of the members of the contracting district. The complexities of contract law raise thorny obstacles to recovery; this problem occupied Cardozo in another branch of the *Moch* case. Yet, while it is disputable whether this particular relationship is enough to justify government liability, the very fact that it is a city that is the obligor must be reckoned with. Under the analysis offered here, the entry of a municipality into the picture may expand rather than restrict obligation because of the very nature of government. The energies and expertise the city commands arguably support a duty to persons outside its boundaries for whose benefit it has contracted to supply services usually thought of as public.

Terror and trust. However, given that to impose municipal liability in that case might extend the chain too far, it certainly is reasonable to say that the power of government should render it accountable for defaults in the use of that power with respect to its own citizens. Thus, one properly may criticize *Steitz v. City of Beacon*,[56] in which the court cited *Moch* to sanctify its refusal of a claim against a municipality for negligent failure to maintain fire equipment already installed. Relevant statutes in *Steitz* said that the city "may contract and operate a system of waterworks" and provided that it "shall maintain" a fire department. In denying recovery, the *Steitz* court argued that municipal liability had been rejected in *Moch* on a contract that was even more specific, one made by a public service corporation and expressly requiring the supply of water on demand by the city for the extinguishment of fires. But this only provokes the thought that Cardozo's court could and should have been bolder in its recognition of the quasi-public nature of the *Moch* defendant, and of the implications of that factor in terms of power relationships.

Moreover, with respect to the facts of *Steitz*, it must be emphasized that a direct governmental commitment to supply fire protection creates powerful filaments of relationship—particularly of trust—between commonwealth and people. Cases of this kind probe the very nature of citizenship itself. The situation stands in contrast to the case of the volunteer firemen who gaze passively at the burning house. The city fire department occupies the field; it discourages, and usually even forbids, competition. The citizen's dependence is at least as complete as it is on any private sellers of services, who surely would be liable for negligent default in the use of their expertise; and it is accented by the factor of government monopoly. It is paradoxical that a rule of liability should thrust in a direction so contrary to the reality of power and dependence. One does not confront comprehensive problems of resource allocation here. Conflagration increased by failure to keep hydrants in repair plays out on a scale less grand. The case evokes homely analogues throughout the law of private liability, which requires compensation responsively to both diseconomies and injustices in individual and corporate choice. It seems wrong to argue, as does a decision akin to *Steitz*, that the only remedy is legislative.[57] In the case of fire protection, with the flaring mixture of terrors and expectations that illumines the citizen's view of governmental obligation, this is very much a situation in which courts should match public duties to private ones.

A few other observations are in order, responsive to potential criticisms of this approach.[58] First, in answer to the argument that such judicially imposed duties would fall too broadly over the population, it should be noted that taxing mechanisms can feasibly be refined to assess the costs of liability upon those who create particular risks or derive benefits with which the risks may justly be associated. Moreover, as is attested by numerous cases in which I oppose or find dubious the extension of liability, I would not make civil obligation a function of only potential governmental control of energy and information; rather, I advocate the imposition of duty only where government power, transactional superiority, and dependence are existing realities which control the circumstances of life for individual citizens. On this basis, the analysis advanced here occupies an intuitively appealing middle ground between the harshness of complete denial of duty and the unwonted breadth of a total socialization of losses, with attendant sacrifice of any efforts at pinning duty to risk creation.

It should be emphasized that, in cases of this kind, the fact that a formal accounting of costs and benefits shows that inaction is "efficient" should not necessarily bar the dependent citizen's claim. The question is not whether the citizen, with full information beforehand, could have opted out; practically, this is not a live option in the cases under consideration. It is primarily a matter of whether government has defaulted on an entrustment associated with its monopoly on a certain kind of power, and what I contend for here is judicial adherence to standards of fundamental fairness[59] with respect to the failure to provide governmental services.

It should also be added that this criticism of the notion that public benefit negates privately enforceable duty necessarily cuts against a summary division of cases in which governmental "takings" require constitutional "just compensation" from those in which the characterization of conduct as an exercise of police power will prove fatal to citizen suits.[60] The independent development of conventional negligence law will often provide an effective counter to immunization on "police power" grounds. At the same time the courts have barred compensation on that rationale, they have awarded damages in many situations in which choices by government officials create risks that endanger persons who have no practical opportunity for choice or for self-defense.

INSPECTION

Closely related to the fire protection cases are problems that arise from attempts to impose duties of supervision and inspection. An important recent English case emphasizes policy considerations in holding that an urban district council breached a duty of careful inspection to the owner of a tract house.[61] The council's inspector had inspected the foundations of the house several times and erroneously pronounced them strong enough to bear its weight. Lord Denning's opinion for the court of appeal emphasized the control that the council exercised over each stage of construction, conducting inspections with the power to compel compliance with bylaw requirements.[62] The decision achieves a salutary result, persuasively reasoned, and invites yet further examination of the basis for imposing duties of this kind. When government enters the field of inspection, a number of elements merge to impose obligations—the legislative expression of concern, the agency's occupation of the field, and both the reliance and the dependence of the citizen. I distinguish here between reliance and dependence, because it is possible for a person to be generally dependent without being specifically reliant. Although there could be specific reliance if there were a publicly filed certificate, fragile house construction also may present a case of general dependence. It is a situation in which the government's possession of both expertise and information combines with its monopoly and the attendant force of compulsion to confer a power to save people from danger and expense. It is also an occasion on which it knows that if it defaults in the use of that power the peril against which inspection is conducted is likely to materialize. These factual elements are at once the basis of dependence and substantially the measure of obligation.

The case of the house foundations is relatively an easy one, since there clearly was an undertaking. It may be argued more broadly that governmental power to compel response to developing situations of danger carries with it an obligation to impose safety requirements within legislatively designated spheres of competence. I do not mean to imply an infinite expandability in the judicial conception of the relevant sphere,[63] but I do suggest that government ought to compensate for negligent conduct of inspections when it reserves a right to conduct them.[64] And, certainly, when government undertakes an inspection, it should be liable for failure to follow up on discovered hazards when a prudent private person in possession of that knowledge and endowed with comparable expertise would seek corrective action. The view I expound here is at odds with a much cited New York decision that denied governmental liability for failure to pursue repair or replacement of a defective heater.[65] That result seems to ignore totally the government's complete transactional superiority and the corresponding dependence of the citizen.[66]

By comparison, important support for a broad view of governmental investigational responsibility appeared very recently in quite a different area of activity, that of vaccine testing, in a decision imposing liability on the United States for failure to live up to its own regulatory standards.[67] The same sort of philosophy informs a decision against the government for a failure of the FAA to follow its own regulations, which caused the plane crash that took the life of baseball star Roberto Clemente and others, ironically in their voluntary efforts to bring emergency aid to Nicaraguan earthquake victims.[68] Going even further, a rather extraordinary recent decision imposes liability on a state government because the real estate division of a state department of licenses did not warn owners and occupants in a mountainside development of predicted danger from avalanches. Rejecting arguments that to give such notice was beyond the statutory duties of the agency, Justice Robert Utter wrote for the Washington Supreme Court that "[n]o special permission is necessary, either for public officials or private individuals, to warn others of some peril to them when a legal duty has been assumed to do so. The law does not require statutory authorization to inform a person that he or she is in mortal danger."[69]

RESCUE

Although the cases examined thus far have dealt principally with rather deliberate planning choices or relatively considered maneuvering decisions, the approach I have taken also would encompass situations in which danger is quite emergent. In this connection, I shall comment briefly here on public duties to rescue, of which an important cognate receives separate treatment below in my discussion of trauma.[70]

Astronautical analogue. It is appropriate to begin with a hypermodern analogue. This is the "Agreement on the Rescue of Astronauts, the Return of Astronauts and the Return of Objects Launched into Outer Space."[71] Article 1 of the agreement, approved unanimously by the General Assembly of the United Nations, provides for immediate communication to launching countries of intelligence of spacecraft accidents or astronaut distress.[72] In the event that astronauts land in a country's territory, Article 2 requires that it "immediately take all possible steps to rescue them and render them all necessary assistance."[73] Moreover, although the agreement requires that launching countries reimburse other nations for expenses incurred in the return of space debris, there is no such provision for expenses in the recovery and return of astronauts, a point on which American commentators declare that "it was generally understood that humanitarian considerations should principally govern assistance . . . not the expectation of compensation, consistent with well-accepted principles governing rescue on the high seas."[74] The approval of this agreement reflects a universal belief that there is a substantial affective public interest in the fate of brave nationals in distress, extending far beyond the substantial investments committed to their specialized training; and the gloss on the omission of expenses for astronaut recovery indicates that significant elements of this concern stretch across national barriers. I do not contend that subscription to this unique document by the United States as well as more than one hundred non-space-flying countries has direct application to the instant problem. But I do think that it provides us instruction about the general views of twentieth-century persons concerning the humanitarian obligation of governments.

Duties at sea. In a more literally down-to-earth way, it is now useful to examine a decision that focuses on the standard of care but relates it rather closely to the elements of duty. In this case, in the stormy setting of the high seas, the United States was required to pay for several acts of negligence in a Coast Guard attempt to rescue a crippled vessel, with a court of appeals sardonically refusing to "be party to adding to the honored motto 'Semper

Paratus,' the words, 'Interdum Prudens.'"[75] The trial court had bottomed the government's liability both on reliance by endangered parties on the Coast Guard's rescue service and on the reliance of other potential rescuers who otherwise would go to the aid of vessels in peril.[76] The court of appeals, specifically rejecting the argument that a "good samaritan" salvor is not held to ordinary standards of care, declared that "if the Coast Guard accepts a mission it should conduct its share of the proceeding with acceptable seamanship."[77] Moreover, it held that the government must accept the burden of establishing its claim that the imperiled vessel would have been lost in any event.[78] In terms of the power relationships involved—including both the control of physical power by the Coast Guard and the metaphorical radiations thus thrown off in that area of the sea—this combination of results and rationales is desirable. And the court of appeals shades the case even more subtly, and correctly, in its handling of the government's claim of contributory negligence. Although the court ultimately rejects the defense on the facts, it refuses to accept the claimants' argument that the Coast Guard "was in full control because it had the 'superior authority of a military branch of the government.'" It comments: "While it is of course true that ultimately, there had to be a 'dominant mind,' the claimants, at the least, had an obligation comparable to that placed upon passengers in an automobile to watch out for their own safety in those jurisdictions which impose such an affirmative duty."[79] This language captures rather fully the complex reality of the power relationship without overemphasizing the dependence of this claimant in the circumstances.

POLICE FUNCTIONS

This brief discussion of the question of when governments have a duty to rescue serves in turn to introduce the case of the plea for police service, the most typical of governmental activities. Around this narrow issue swirl many of the great controversies in modern political life. Here considerations of politics and economics both blend and compete, as do theories of judicial and legislative competence.

Direct Threats and General Menaces

An ideal case to open an examination of the police protection problem, ventilating many of these elements in a setting that offers useful comparisons with rescue decisions, deals with a cry for help that would have required public expenditures over a period of time. This is *Riss v. City of New York*,[80] charged with passion, desperate drama, and particular judicial irony. Linda Riss had forsaken her suitor Burton Pugach for another, to whom she planned marriage. She reported to the police threats from Pugach that "if I can't have you, no one else will have you," but encountered only indifference. A "last chance" phone threat at Ms. Riss's engagement party triggered more pleas from her for help. However, the police also rejected these, and the next day a thug hired by Pugach threw lye in her face, scarring and substantially blinding her. After the attack, the police gave Ms. Riss more than three years of around-the-clock protection, a fact that would seem to undercut defenses based on discretion in resource allocation. Yet it was a line of argument thus founded that persuaded so sophisticated an observer as Judge Charles Breitel, who wrote a decision affirming a dismissal of Ms. Riss's complaint against the city for failure to provide protection before the event.

This opinion, though compressed in exposition, reflects what I view as a recurrent error that has infected much decision making in this area. First, Judge Breitel distinguished cases involving governmental activities that have "displaced or supplemented traditionally private enterprises," naming rapid transit and hospitals as examples. He also distinguished governmental provision of services and facilities for "direct use by members of the public," citing highways and public buildings. Compared with these, he found a dispositive difference in the protection of "the public generally from external hazards," an activity whose supply was "limited by the resources of the community and by a considered legislative-executive decision as to how those resources may be deployed."[81] He feared that the imposition of tort liability in cases like this would effectuate judicial allocation of limited police resources "and without predictable limits," contrasting the "predictable allocation of resources and liabilities when public hospitals, rapid transit systems, or even highways are provided."[82]

Public expectations; judicial competence. With all respect, these arguments are less than convincing. A distinction based on "directness" of service is rather mushy, given the contact that many citizens have with police every day—illustrated, indeed, by the various contacts that Ms. Riss had with them. And the effort to distinguish traditionally private activities may prove too much. As Judge Kenneth Keating pointed out in dissent, a most galling aspect of the result in *Riss* was that the Sullivan law prohibited the plaintiff from carrying self-defense weapons. Taken seriously in a world of well-disseminated information, the message in *Riss* in that context would be to encourage the formation of private police forces and the cooperative hiring of bodyguards, whose services could be divided by times of perceived maximum danger to the employers. Moreover, the argument concerning unpredictability of allocation would have thrust only if one accepted the same point of view with respect to the failure to remedy or warn of a slick floor in a public building or to fix a rut or repair a guardrail on a highway. A key question in all these cases is basically one of whether government has used its power appropriately, but that question is posed most definitively and sharply in an area in which the state historically has monopolized the use of effective physical force, and where generations of cultural backup have conditioned people to expect that police will aid them when bad men threaten their physical security. Besides an implicit reliance on the part of the citizen, there is also a significant dependence heightened by the very possession of physical power by the police department. This power, in the sense of immediate control over usable force possessed as a practical monopoly, is a source of duty. To deny governmental obligation here while imposing it in cases of failure to undertake structural repairs is paradoxically contrary to that reality.

Besides creating theoretical incentives to provide competing police forces, the consequences of a *Riss*-type decision with respect to community perceptions of justice are likely to be negative. What effects on attitudes might one expect in an already fearful public, continuously bathed by news of murder and mayhem, when it finds that police refusal of a specific appeal for help was ratified by the courts? It is worth emphasizing that Ms. Riss's claim was not one for general failure to patrol the city but one concerned with a deliberate choice not to respond to an identified risk; it contrasts in that sense with the case of a citizen who alleges an actionable default because there was no policeman on a given corner at the time that he was assaulted by a stranger. In cases involving general shortages of resources, serious questions of how to finance compensation will arise and will require considered legislative decisions as to further taxation or the shifting of resources. But in circumstances like those in *Riss*, focusing specific risks of known danger, the court is in a peculiarly good position to say that the "considered legislative-executive decision" to which Breitel refers has resulted in a simple default in the fulfillment of what public responsibility has become. Undoubtedly, the imposition of liability would increase governmental burdens marginally, but in this connection it is relevant to cite Judge Keating's acerbic notation that the slice of the city budget that then went to pay tort claims—including "all those sidewalk defect and snow and ice cases about which the courts fret so often"—was less than two-tenths of 1 percent, and his argument that this was "of no importance as compared to the injustice of permitting unredressed wrongs to continue to go unrepaired."[83] The special irony is that the judge's judge, Breitel, rests on the argument that the duty, if any, is legislative; but former politician Keating, in lone dissent, insists that judicial imposition of a duty is only a realization of the proper role of judges.

Crime waves. With this discussion of *Riss* as a background, I shall examine several important cases of the last decade in an effort to define legal standards for the problem of failure to supply police protection. A baseline principle is that it is within the legislative province to bar liability "for failure to establish a police department or otherwise provide police protection service,"[84] in the words of an Illinois statute; moreover, it is reasonable to apply statutory language of this kind to the withdrawal of a previously established police system.[85] However, when the legislature does not make such an explicit choice for immunity, one must resort to analysis of policy factors. Reference to these considerations often will support decisions rejecting the injured citizen's suit, as the discussion immediately below indicates, but I shall also argue that sometimes the realities of power relationships demand judicial imposition of governmental liability.

A persuasive decision denying compensation dismisses a charge that city police failed to halt a wave of criminal activity, with the consequence that a retail grocery was forced out of business.[86] Although it may be somewhat exaggerated to describe this suit as one for municipal guarantee of losses from criminal acts—to use the court's characterization—the result seems correct, largely because of the generalized nature of the problem. The victimization of a business in a community seriously afflicted by a crime wave is the kind of broad-scale fortuity that requires reliance on legislative forms of compensation or public relocation subsidies, or, in extremis, remits the injured citizen to the solace of philosophy. It might be noted that the affective social concern in a case of this kind is in a sense weaker than in the situation in which a single individual is injured after police failure to respond to pleas related to a specific, direct threat.

Pleading requirements; a civil rights perspective. Somewhat similar elements of generality present themselves in both state and federal litigations that arose from the death of Jerome Huey, a black youth who was fatally bludgeoned with baseball bats by four whites of Cicero, Illinois. In the state case, the plaintiff administrator charged that the Cicero police department had failed to use ordinary care to warn the decedent of the unusual perils that existed for blacks on the town's streets. The Illinois Supreme Court, affirming a dismissal, brushed aside consideration of both the statutory immunity for police protection quoted above[87] and the plaintiff's constitutional challenge to that statute. The court focused on the "general rule . . . that a municipality . . . is not liable for failure to supply general police or fire protection." It noted decisions holding cities liable for "affirmative negligent or wilful acts by their employees" but viewed these as exceptions to that rule. It emphasized that the plaintiff administrator had not demonstrated a "special duty"–there were no allegations that the defendants knew of the decedent's presence in the town, or that he had requested police protection, or that he was in "some peculiar danger."[88] The generality of the default charged in the complaint does limit its force significantly, although the claim seems stronger than the one in the grocery case mentioned above, in which the plaintiff described an ordinary crime wave.

A somewhat better rationale for denying recovery persuaded a federal trial court that dealt with a complaint by the same administrator under the Ku Klux Klan Act. This decision posited that an affirmative obligation lay upon the defendant police officers and city officials, growing from their roles "as conservators of the peace," which required them "to take reasonable measures as dictated by circumstances to prevent the consummation of unlawful acts against negroes."[89] The court's announcement of this proposition, relating to the conspiracy section of the Act, joined a declaration with reference to section 1983 that "city officials and police officers are under an affirmative duty to preserve law and order, and to protect the personal safety of persons in the community," a statement which concluded that the failure to perform reasonably in that regard "would constitute both a negligent omission and a denial of equal protection of the laws."[90] However, under both sections the court found itself constrained to dismiss the complaint because the plaintiff alleged no specific acts or omissions causally connected to the decedent's death.[91]

The Huey cases taken together provide an encapsulation of conventional judicial views concerning police obligations together with a reasonable technical position on pleadings. Beyond that, despite its rejection of the plaintiff's claims, the federal court's abstract statement of principle provides an important window on intergovernmental relationships related to this analysis. It helps to define a special role of the federal government under the Ku Klux Klan Act, as the ultimate guarantor of civil rights violated by defaults in the use of the power that resides in local government; and in this process it evinces recognition of the dependence that governmental power creates in citizens whose lives fall within its realm.

Individual choice; allocational alternatives. As is manifest in the cases discussed, police have no obligation to be everywhere at once, shielding all possibly imperiled persons from danger. However, it is also clear that to take on the job of police protection is to incur a duty of reasonable staffing. Thus, it seems wrong to defend the assignment of a single policeman to a sixteen-acre housing project of ten buildings on the ground that the housing authority had "no special duty" to a little girl who was seized, raped, and thrown off a fourteen-story structure. Yet that is the gist of the Appellate Division's position in *Bass v. City of New York*,[92] in which that court finds that legislation setting up the housing authority and vesting it with the power to establish a police force did not impose on it "any greater burden or responsibility with respect to its police force than that which through an unbroken chain of decisional law has been imposed upon a municipality's police force."[93] The court cites precedents that include the *Riss* decision as well as other cases previously discussed, in which the New York Court of Appeals had denied claims for negligent maintenance of fire equipment[94] and for failure to follow up on correction of defects in a home heating unit.[95]

This denial of governmental liability flies in the face of a stipulated history of vicious acts preceding this savage murder, including an attack on another young girl a half hour before the fatal assault. The paucity of assigned officers as well as of police equipment—there were telephone call boxes on the roofs of three buildings but none on the one in which the decedent lived—strongly supports a dissenter's view that "the proof of negligence was overwhelming."[96] The facts also suggest the basic validity of a somewhat emotional opinion in which the trial judge refers to the "helpless, underprivileged" residents of the project, who he says "were entitled to know that they could not rely on their landlord for any form of protection."[97] Indeed, the trial judge's rather sentimental language clothes an approach that emphasizes choice: had they not been "lulled into a false sense of security" by the "occasional glimpse" of housing authority police uniforms, the decedent's family could have made sure that she was accompanied by adults whenever she left the apartment; perhaps they even could have decided to stay "in whatever ghetto from which they had originally come."[98]

But given the limited nature of the choice that presents itself in such a situation, and the dependence that did in fact exist, analysis should allow nothing to blur a basic focus on the planning obligations of those who undertake to supply police services. Even if one concedes that it was "not the legislative intent to have the housing police department assume the *total* police function," but only to supplement the city police, the fact remains that the housing authority's possession of information, media, and perhaps manpower gave it superior ability to control the situation. It could have considered various combinations of more policemen and more protective machinery; if necessary it could have publicized warnings to residents, thus reimporting into the picture the possibility of self-help. It is true that, compared with *Riss* on the facts, the relief sought in *Bass* would require a broader commitment of resources. Yet the problem remains concrete and identifiable, not simply a generalized complaint about "crime in the streets." And a judgment for the child's parents does not imply liability without limit for crimes committed after further allocation of police and technology to the project. What judges can do in such a case is what they have historically done when standards are markedly poor, and that is to set minima. If these should prove ruinous, which seems unlikely, the legislature may take a comprehensive view of the subject and make readjustments. On the concrete facts, the decision remains interstitial enough that it does not impinge on the delicate balance between deciding the law and making the law. Although the case is not free of difficulty, at least in instances of default so egregious, it is proper for courts to require a provider of police services to compensate victims of its lassitude.

This is not a wholesale condemnation of judicial concessions to discretion in the assignment of police power, even of some such judgments that deny protection to large-scale social units, but it is only to say that it is inadequate to paper over rejections of liability with "special duty" talk. Illustrative of a possibly proper rejection of governmental liability is the case of a teacher who was killed at school by a student, litigated on the general allegations that the city had assigned no police to control a "dangerous condition then existing at the school" about which it "knew or should have known."[99] The decision, which was on a motion to dismiss, may be rationalized as a practical determination that in the circumstances there was no breach of duty, given the competing demands for resources. However, the court's argument that there was no "special duty," pitched on the basis that to rule otherwise would impossibly burden the city, is not independently persuasive. Indeed, it seems wrong to deny that there is a basic duty owed to those who teach in violent environments, arising from their very status as public employees who are expected to be at work every day, from their helplessness in the face of murderous attacks, and from their resultant dependence on public protection. It bears emphasis that this is a situation of de facto entrustment of personal safety to the government by those who choose to work in public schools; when that trust is failed, the costs should be charged to society's police ledger.

Responses to known danger. I shall deal now with cases in which police have rather precise knowledge of a particular hazard but in which their response to that danger is flawed by some kind of default in their use of the power that they possess. Two recent decisions in this category involve alleged failures to detain intoxicated drivers, with the result that they subsequently killed other motorists. In one case,[100] the drunk driver had caused an earlier collision with another automobile, and the plaintiff alleged negligence in the failure to arrest on that occasion. Squarely facing the duty issue, the court declared that there was "no special duty" owed to the plaintiffs and emphasized that the defendant village "did not take any *affirmative* action which resulted in injury to a member of the public."[101]

In another case in which governmental liability was denied, a sheriff's deputy pursued a recklessly driven auto but made no effort to apprehend the driver, although the deputy's patrol car was equipped with an overhead flashing red light. In this case, in which the ensuing collision killed five persons and injured another, the

Supreme Court of Arizona reasoned that the duty of the defendant county was "patently one owed to the general public, not the individual plaintiffs."[102] The decision, overturning a judgment by a lower appeals court, seems particularly vulnerable given a prior case which the supreme court attempted to distinguish. In this precedent, reversing the dismissal of an action for failure to install and maintain a fire hydrant, the court had said that, "when a city assumes the responsibility of furnishing fire protection, then it has the duty of giving each person or property owner such reasonable protection as others within a similar area within the municipality are accorded under like circumstances."[103] In the reckless driving case, the intermediate appellate court struck at the heart of the matter in its argument in support of a cause of action on the deputy's lax response. That court properly rejected distinctions between "misfeasance" and "nonfeasance," noting that "any lawyer clever enough to draw a mandatory injunction in terms of restraint can, where public duties are involved, usually transform a nonfeasance into a misfeasance."[104]

Power monopoly and dependence. The correct solution in both drunk driver cases would seem to derive from a notion of public duty rooted in power and dependence. This concept of duty is framed with special sharpness in the pursuit case by the particular circumstance–emphasized by the appellate court–that there was "a clear opportunity for the defendant deputy to arrest prior to the occurrence of this accident."[105] In that case it seems an artifice no more respectable because of its perennial use to distinguish duties owed generally from duties to individuals, especially when the provision of fire protection has effectively been held to be a duty to "each person." There is some murkiness in the facts in the other case described above, involving failure to make an arrest after an accident, but the court appears to misconceive the realities of power with its ritualistic insistence that there was no special duty and that the claim did not involve "affirmative action."

A central point in both cases is that by pleaded hypothesis the policeman could have used the power of his office as well as the physical energy available to him to prevent injuries to members of the community, who because of lack of knowledge of the hazard were completely dependent on the imposition of restraints by one with public authority. In these situations the officer is the only one who could have effectively prevented harm that was probable to even a casual observer. The very fact that it is police power that is involved would seem to accentuate the duty to individuals rather than to detract from it. It is inherent in the idea of a police force that it is to take measures of defense that private citizens ordinarily are not able to effect themselves. Even given a liberal law on citizens' arrests, as a practical matter most people lack cultural encouragement—and usually the physical power of restraint and pursuit—to undertake this kind of task. In defining the sphere of obligation, the legal system should take full account of this effective monopoly on power.[106]

Practical limits on duty. Yet, certainly, obligation must be tailored to reality. By way of illustration of the leeway officials must have, the bare fact that the paroled inmate of a state training school is a truant would not require the parole officer to guess that he will shoot a pedestrian. This is the burden of a decision under the New York Court of Claims Act,[107] and it seems a reasonable one. But there are facts that give one pause: The truant won parole only with the understanding that he would enroll in a different public school to prevent reassociation with street gangs. This datum takes on special significance given that when he fired the disabling shot he was in the company of two other youngsters, and that they all fitted descriptions of the perpetrators of previous assaults and robberies.[108] The case may boil down to a question of whether the parole officer reacted quickly enough in issuing a warrant within three days of receiving the information of truancy—as it turned out on the day of the shooting. There is some latent conflict between the reported opinions on previous violent proclivities of the paroled youth;[109] but the controlling opinion, in denying governmental liability, seems to accept that a duty would exist if he had exhibited dangerous tendencies.[110] Whatever room for argument may exist on the facts, the thrust of the analysis offered here is that in cases of this kind the courts should approach the question of governmental obligation liberally. In the particular case, this would require attention not only to the nature of the information possessed by the parole officers, but also to the inability of members of the public to defend against attacks and their resultant, de facto dependence on the caution of the authorities. Again the practical inquiry in such cases would often go to whether duty had been fulfilled, involving consideration of the severity of the hazard, the appropriate general level of performance of such officials, and the exigencies of competing demands.

All manner of beast? A recent decision in which it is animals that pose the danger provides a useful comparison with the cases of police failure to protect citizens against vicious or reckless third persons. In this case, which provides a firm baseline for governmental obligation, the plaintiff was savagely attacked by two dogs, whose roaming and viciousness were well known to city authorities. Indeed, in response to a report of an attack by the animals on a pedestrian earlier that day, two officers were making a field investigation which they had interrupted for lunch at the time of the attack on the plaintiff. Reversing a summary judgment for the city in a suit for failure to round up the dogs, the court refers specifically to the elements of knowledge and ability of physical control that I have emphasized in this analysis. It does limit its decision explicitly to "an inherently dangerous condition to human beings created by nonhuman animals, not by other human beings."[111] But it seems questionable that the court would employ this distinction to deny recovery to a claimant injured by a human being so vicious that he posed an immediate danger to anyone strolling outdoors. Why should we hesitate to apply the general rules governing obligation to use power to any case in which a government knows of a specific hazard and defaults in its response, if the hazard is not one taken for granted in community life? It is incidentally worthy of note that the court pauses only briefly, even matter-of-factly, to reject the argument that the action is barred under the discretionary function exception of the state tort claims legislation.

In broad perspective, this is a case in which many elements of duty come together. An obligation to control dogs was manifested in an ordinance, and there was a common law duty to maintain streets and sidewalks. The hazard was one against which the plaintiff was practically defenseless, and the ordinance embodied a societal decision that free-roaming vicious dogs were not properly regarded as part of the urban landscape. In this context the court chose to rest its decision not on the ordinance but on the common law duty to maintain sidewalks, thus explicitly avoiding the morass of "general duty" versus "special duty."[112] I would simply add, re-emphasizing a previous argument, that that distinction itself seems quite vulnerable when officials possess knowledge of a particular danger and there is a specific legal definition of the government's control role.

The politics of public security. It should be noted that a broad field of potential liability opens out in certain cases in which knowledge of looming hazards spurs public authorities to action, though courts ordinarily would not originally impose either common law or statutory liabilities on governmental power holders. An exemplary case appears in the Department of Transportation's adoption of wide-ranging and expensive measures to prevent airline hijackings. This is an instance in which it may be impossible to project with any accuracy the net benefits from protective measures, given the way offenses snowballed as well-publicized early attempts incited new perpetrators. It is indeterminable how many lives or aircraft were saved by the purchase of more than two thousand metal detectors and the employment of fifteen hundred security officers for larger airports, as well as many local officers for smaller ones.[113] But however expansively one estimates the uncertain social benefits of these precautions, it would seem that the government would be liable under the Tort Claims Act for defaults in the use of power by any federal officers involved in this activity, as well as for any of the abuses most commonly associated with the exercise of law enforcement power.[114] Illustratively with respect to defaults, in the event that security guards carelessly allowed an armed individual to escape detection, passengers might claim for injuries that occurred in his piracy of the plane.[115] Here the elements of dependence on expertise and access to information recur in a setting in which the passenger has effectively turned over concern for his physical safety to the security force, and in which there is no meaningful physical power available to him or indeed allowed to him.

Important in such cases is the concept of protective role, analogous from the case of skyjack prevention to the problem of rounding up vicious dogs. There is general agreement that government exists in significant part to secure the physical safety of persons. Within that area of duty, both statutes and common law spell out relatively specific obligations and assign them to particular authorities. When citizens are hurt despite the existence of social protective measures, the principal question under any doctrinal casting of the liability issue is whether the designated officers have defaulted on the use of a power that their roles confer. This is not to comment on the desirability, or possibility, of devising a comprehensive calculus for the equalization of protection across the multifarious categories of risk; or, on the other hand, to imply that certain affective qualities of particular kinds of hazards may not justify specially heavy investment. It is simply to say that in a polity where protective roles are created ad hoc this very fact emphasizes the strength of governmental obligations with respect to roles that are already established and thus incorporated in a political consensus that the commonwealth has a duty to respond to the hazards thus targeted.

Keeping classrooms safe. Typically less dramatic than the area of police power just reviewed, but quite significant with respect to the number of vulnerable lives it touches, is the problem of supervision of school students. I shall refer to a variety of cases, some of which provide only pallid factual comparisons with the *Sturm und Drang* of *Riss, Bass,* and vicious dogs on the loose, but others that arise in classrooms where happy horseplay has long crossed the line into youthful savagery.

A basic doctrinal text is woven in a Vermont decision that concerns the relatively uncontroversial area of protection from dangerous physical conditions in the schoolyard. In this case,[116] which involved injuries sustained by a fourth grader on a merry-go-round in which there was a missing piece of board, the court considered and rejected the argument that liability required "misfeasance" and a "negligent act." It declared, drawing on a sister precedent, that the teacher's duty was not to be negligent whether by "misfeasance or nonfeasance."[117] Moreover, distinguishing the teacher-student relation from the relationships that obtain between most government employees and members of the general public, the court adopted an *in loco parentis* characterization. In this vein, expressly articulating a variation on the theme sounded here, it placed emphasis on the teacher's possession of that "portion of the powers of the parent over the pupil as is necessary to carry out his employment."[118] Thus, the decision matches obligation to its recognition of a power resident in social arrangements but rooted by common conception in natural relationships.[119]

Deployment strategy and allocational alternatives. From this elementary point of departure, one may inquire how an analysis based on power would apply in more difficult situations of resource allocation, when the claim is that the school failed to protect students from the assaults of their fellows. Courts have divided in their responses to this problem. In one interesting case, someone threw a sharp piece of metal at a seventh grader as he entered a shop class, causing the loss of an eye. The majority of a divided court, protesting collaterally that it was not exonerating the school on grounds of "discretionary" immunity, held that there was no showing of negligence in the facts that the shop teacher was not in his room at the time of the attack and that he arrived several minutes late. Crucial to this judgment was the existence of a reasonable plan for deployment of teachers for crowd control during the change of classes. The court noted that the teacher had printed and distributed to each class member a set of rules for behavior when he was not in the room, including an injunction against the throwing of type—apparently the metal object that had struck the plaintiff.[120] The majority appears to slough some evidentiary problems mentioned by a dissenter as to the teacher's assignment for that day, but beyond that the dissent is persuasive in contending that the school should show why the teacher arrived ten or twelve minutes late at the classroom, even if he was acting in accord with a reasonable schoolwide deployment. Moreover, the majority fails to meet the argument that alternative measures could have been devised to prevent this kind of injury, for example, the locking up of type or the appointment of an upperclassman as supervisor in the teacher's absence.

A contrasting decision affirms a plaintiff's judgment in a case involving iceball throwing in a schoolyard, with a brief majority opinion stressing teachers' knowledge of snowball throwing and of icy conditions, as well as the fact that there was no teacher to supervise a "fairly large group of children."[121] A dissenter sounds the theme that there was no notice of the danger, written over a submotif that hymns praise to snowballing as a healthy outlet for children. But this appears ineffectual as an attempt to drive a wedge between manifest knowledge of ice on the ground[122] and intelligence of much prior snowballing. It also seems a weak response to the jury's verdict for the plaintiff, although it is unclear precisely what instructions the jurors received.

Compulsion, submission, and blackboard jungles. With respect to both of these instances of alleged failure in public school discipline, perhaps the most telling point lies in an argument by the dissenter in the type-throwing case that, putting the immunity question aside, the evidence would have gone to the jury had the defendant been a private school. It would seem that in the case of a public school the conjoining of governmental power with the convention that children in all schools must submit to discipline should enhance the institutional duty rather than reduce it. In the type-throwing case the majority's approval of a "plan" seems unequal to the task of containing the slippery eel of discretion. Public controllers of educational resources should meet at least the same standards of responsibility as private ones. Public school students necessarily depend for their physical security on the government that runs their institution, and this dependence argues strongly for the creation of a duty.[123] Indeed, this combination of power and submission parallels the case closely with many decisions involving private employers that I have discussed elsewhere[124]–perhaps even with decisions bulwarking the assiduously protected position of the seaman.[125]

There does reappear here the question of how the government's provision of resources as well as its execution of plans compare with the general level of social performance in the particular activity at issue. Concededly, not only can one conceive a society in which people must send their children to school with a prayer that they will return alive and whole; there are such schools today. But this would seem an area in which courts properly can enforce traditional standards of what is due to those whose presence signifies obedience to a social command, and for whose safety the counsels of prudence dictate the supply of protective services at adequate minimums. The specter of waves of lawsuits from violence-ridden schools should not cloud the vital relation of these minima to the duty, the judicially imposed obligations of which ideally should be financed from the same sources of the affected population as would any tort judgment involving a failure of police protection. When governmental compulsion places young people in a situation of known substantial danger, judicial creativity need extend no further than the application of the most conventional common law of torts.

Riots

RAMPARTS OF THE COMMON LAW. I shall now examine a particularly turbulent frontier of possibility for this analysis–the problem of when there should be governmental responsibility for damage from large-scale civil disturbances. Here "deployment" finds a more literally military connotation, the political factor is quite intrusive, and legislative action is most likely to foreclose judicial determination. Illustrative of the possible breadth of legislative immunization is a case against several California state and local authorities for damage caused by the Watts riot. This suit was based in part on the theory that the negligent arrest of a person for drunk driving provoked an angry crowd and touched off the conflagration, and on alleged negligence in failure to bring the ensuing disturbances under control. The court refused to allow the action,[126] recurrently citing the provision in the California tort claims legislation that exempts public entities and employees from liability "for failure to establish a police department or otherwise provide police protection service or, if police protection service is provided, for failure to provide sufficient police protection service."[127] Leaving no room for judicial maneuver, this draftmanship articulates a public policy that is respectable; but the view developed here suggests that the balance of justice may weigh against it.

Overlap of discretion and "no negligence." Considerations of justice confront the court more directly, without the intervention of legislated immunity, in *Wong v. City of Miami*,[128] which is especially provocative of inquiry into the bases of decisions against governmental obligation. The plaintiffs in that case were merchants whose stores were plundered by persons who "lost restraint" in the wake of a civil rights rally, held in Miami at the same time the Republican National Convention of 1968 was progressing at Miami Beach. They argued that the defendant city had been careless in withdrawing police officers already stationed in the vicinity of their businesses. The Florida Supreme Court's decision rejecting the claim demonstrates most clearly the overlap between the defense of discretion and that of no negligence. The supreme court affirmed a dismissal granted by the trial court and upheld by the lower appeals court.[129] The intermediate court's opinion was rather cryptic and primarily cast in terms of a negation that Florida's recent expansion of municipal tort liability extended to riot damage. In affirming, the supreme court was at pains to combat what it inferred as concessions by the intermediate court that the removal of the policemen was negligence "and that respondents are shielded from liability merely because sovereign immunity has not been relaxed sufficiently by prior decisions."[130] Socratically, it asked whether if the police had stayed, there might also have been allegations of negligence because their presence created extra tension. In the same paragraph that it posed that question, the court declared that "inherent in the right to exercise police powers is the right to determine strategy and tactics for the deployment of those powers." And it concluded, in the light of findings by the Riot Commission about the contribution of police to the heightening of tensions, that "the sovereign authorities ought to be left free to exercise their discretion and choose the tactics deemed appropriate without worry over possible allegations of negligence."

This is a case of great difficulty, and one cannot deny the persuasive quality of the supreme court's argument. But the court does not really counter the force of a simple application of tort law offered by an appellate court dissenter, who characterized the complaint as describing a situation in which the defendant had supplied services and then withdrew them after creating a reliance, and in which the plaintiffs could not cover for themselves.[131] It may well have been that the plaintiffs' proof would have fallen short on this theory, but under the analysis offered here, arguably they should have been able to present it. The burden of the supreme court's decision seems to be that the court could see no way to prove negligence on the facts pleaded in the complaint, but the opinion entangles this rational intuition with a common law discretion defense. That seems unfortunate. As a matter of both clarity and policy, it would be helpful to keep the concepts separate. Beyond that it might reasonably be contended that, given the virtually absolute nature of the political and physical power exercised in a decision to withdraw squadrons of police, and the de facto dependence of merchants on the city's control of this kind of situation, the obligations to avoid miscalculation should, if anything, increase.

Judicial competence and social accounting. There remains available the independent defense that there is no negligence, on which it may be reasonable to rely in many situations of this kind. Still, it is necessary to beware facile repetition of the view that judges should not review basic policy decisions, when one confronts specific situations involving choices that may affect who will live and who will die.[132] The best rationalization for the result in *Wong* may reside in the incentive it provides for increased reliance on insurance. And the appropriate ultimate remedy may be legislative socialization of loss. In my view, however, the allegations of Wong and his unfortunate fellow merchants generate at least a colorable case that the proper account to be charged is that of the police function. To be sure, reasonable official choices among conflicting behavioral hypotheses may provide a valid defense, just as may reasonable allocations of scarce energies to competing demands. But "deployment" does not sweep all before it. Although the concept has proper uses as a shorthand—for example, in municipal defense of suits for losses sustained when there simply is not enough manpower to go around[133]—it should not be a total immunizer. Courts must still decide when power holders have defaulted on their social obligations in particular circumstances.

One dare not minimize the difficulties of the issues of whether and when courts should require the community to spread losses caused when the exercise of civil liberties boils over into mayhem that was predictable if not certain. As the Florida Supreme Court suggested, in a case like *Wong* the matter is one of weighing police choices post hoc in situations that may well have hazardous fallout either way the decision is made. In the end, the question of whether compensation may be judicially awarded will depend on the definition of social accounts. I would simply suggest that judicial caution in the setting up of those accounts should not melt into abstention. The practical question may finally become whether the damage is so general, of such broad community concern, that it is effectively everybody's problem. When civil disturbance goes beyond reasonable hope of containment, it may properly be argued that losses either should be distributed in an explicitly collective way or charged up to personal bad luck in generally grim social circumstances. The minimum *ad damnum* in *Wong* of $100,000 would seem to suggest that this was not the case in that situation. Surely it appears oversimple to say, as another court declared contemporaneously, that "either everyone who suffered damage by riot should recover or none should be permitted to do so."[134] Given control, reliance, dependence, and alleged causation in situations like *Wong*, the case would seem made against a motion to dismiss. As all these elements save causation drop out of pleadings and proof, and as disorder becomes universal, the picture changes enough to say that not only is it a tough world but also it is the kind of bad break that judges cannot repair. When that is the case, the remedy must be legislative or the citizen must hedge for himself with more insurance—next time.

Knowledge of hazard, "duty," and "tort." The analysis offered here provides a reply to a recent decision of the Iowa Supreme Court,[135] which denies recovery to a young auto passenger injured by missiles thrown from a Des Moines crowd of which police were allegedly aware. The plaintiff claimed that the police either did not control the street adequately or did not exercise reasonable care to warn him. The court's thoughtful opinion attempts to dig into the doctrinal roots of the problem. Given recent legislative elimination of municipal tort immunity, it begins with the question of whether there has been a tort. This depends in turn on whether there was a duty, and again the thesis appears, well supported by case law, that the municipality owes no individual duty to particular citizens. Although the court's examination of precedent and critical scholarship is careful, and its conclusion is well reasoned in accord with conventional premises, the decision seems wrong. More persuasive is a dissent, which notes that the city's motion to dismiss admitted knowledge of the dangerous condition and which argues that the case is essentially no different than that of a hazard caused by heavy objects piled in the street.[136]

It is useful to probe briefly some competing notions of obligation and equity that emerge from these rather simple facts. As I have suggested in other contexts, the argument that there is no duty to individuals seems only a makeweight, especially given the frequency with which courts impose duties with respect to routine nonpolice functions. In my view, courts should not be reluctant to recognize obligations stemming from control and dependence, elements at least preliminarily satisfied by a complaint that emphasizes the city's knowledge and implies the plaintiff's ignorance. For purposes of comparison, let us visualize a tireless municipal administrator with a file-cabinet mind, superior intelligence, and a computerized grip on dangerous activity in city streets, sitting at a great control board at which he adjusts risks twenty-four hours a day. Any rational ordering of Des Moines society by him would have to permit numerous risks to exist, and surely no court would account most of these choices as defaults or abuses of his power over streets and travelers in the sense that I have used those words. In most cases of injury related to such allocations, compensation must be sought in legislative socialization and private insurance.[137] But it seems inadequate for the court to suggest, as it does with self-assurance in the case summarized, that the definition of "tort" implicitly accepted by the legislature in its abrogation of municipal immunity cannot include riot damage. Competing basic rules of tort law that I have mentioned, as well as the arguments offered here for a power-based analysis, indicate that judges may properly make other choices. Those choices would be based on an explicit recognition of obligations that attach to those who possess information, strength, or ability, conferring transactional superiority; and they would further be founded on the premise that these duties should be matched analogically between private power holders and governmental ones.

Again it must be emphasized that with cases involving governmental liability the ultimate judgment is a political one, and rather more so than with the liability of private parties.[138] In this regard, questions of some difficulty present themselves about the appropriate limitation on judicial role in imposing new obligations on government. A parade of judicial actions and legislative reactions has recently taken place in this area, with courts overthrowing governmental immunity root and branch, events sometimes but not always followed by legislative responses in the enactment of state tort claims acts.[139] Politically aware judges in these cases must be sensible of the probability of such reaction. Yet judges acting in this way show fidelity to their role of administering justice at the same time they undertake the task of prodding legislatures. Similarly, judges may responsibly opt for new impositions of liability which are suggested in this paper, making ad hoc determinations of injustice in the knowledge that distributional refinements may await legislative carpentry.

MOB VIOLENCE STATUTES. I have suggested that the realities of power as well as the dictates of compassion argue for a more liberal governmental response to the wreckage of civil disturbance than some lawmaking and interpretation allow. And in fact there is substantial precedent for the provision of legislative balm. In many jurisdictions, statutes require local governments to pay for damages caused by mob violence. A Supreme Court decision in 1911[140] rejected a constitutional challenge to such a statute, offered by a city claiming that the law was invalid because it imposed liability without fault. The court held the statute to rest constitutionally "upon the duty of the State to protect its citizens in the enjoyment and possession of their acquisitions," declaring it "but a recognition of the obligation of the State to preserve social order and the property of the citizen against the violence of a riot or a mob."[141] It viewed the law as having "entrusted" to local governments this "duty and obligation." This positing of duty, and of entrustment to local jurisdictions, found a policy basis in a "tendency to deter the lawless," since the tax burden would fall in part on "evil doers as members of the community." One's intuitive reaction that this deterrence is likely to be thin is matched by doubt that such a statute would create significant incentives "to stimulate the exertions of the indifferent and the law abiding,"[142] given not only the present limitations on municipal resources but also the fragmentation of local governments,[143] as well as the volatile social chemistry of modern urban riots.[144] However, despite dubiety about some of its rationale, the basic force of this decision has carried through across half a century, charged with duty and the notion of public trust.[145]

Resource allocation, equity, and dependence. Modern justifications for mob liability statutes present a web of diverse rationales, with the notion that the whole population of a city should be responsible for riot losses because of social judgments about resource allocations[146] weaving across threads of equity.[147] In turn, the equity justification, emphasizing disproportionate impact on the poor, blurs at the edges into collective choices of welfare measures. I would add that significant justification of the concept of community responsibility embodied in these statutes appears in the increasing dependence that residents of modern cities have on governments long recognized to have positive obligations to them.

The nature of this dependence would argue for broad interpretations of mob violence statutes, which sympathetic fact situations have occasionally evoked. Exemplary of a particularly generous judicial response, in a set of terrifying circumstances, is a decision that applies the statutory word "mob" to a group of five young men with reference to the following events: they abducted a young woman from a hospital parking lot, transported her to the next city, and ejected someone from a dwelling where they gang raped their victim; they then left because of their fears of being observed and went to another house where they raped the woman several more times, attacks followed by forcing her to commit sodomy in a car. Although the original abduction was "apparently accomplished in a quiet and surreptitious manner," clearly involving no public disturbance, the court found that the subsequent events did create one. It noted such factors as the necessity of ejecting the person from the first dwelling and the gang members' apparent recognition "that some disturbance was being created," causing them to leave.[148] One can hear the court asking itself angrily, even as laymen, "Where were the police?" and, perhaps, "Why didn't the neighbors respond?" Yet, although the court earns much credit for compassion, arguably this interpretation stretches the legislation beyond common parlance, expanding the statutory language to house a general compensation for victims of crime.

Dependence and control. On the other hand, some decisions have taken too narrow a view of such laws. In one case the court limits the definition of "mob" not only to those who offer violence to one supposed to be guilty of a violation of the law—this tracks the language of the statute—but also to the exercise of correctional or regulative powers "in respect to those matters concerning which the public has assumed jurisdiction to make laws, rules, and regulations," a gloss on statutory language that mentions only "exercising correctional or regulative powers."[149] In the case of an overt group attack on an individual, several factors militate against such restrictive interpretation: the utter helplessness of the victim, the commonwealth's relative ability to suppress civil violence, and the resultant positive obligation of government described by the Supreme Court.[150] This is especially so because of the very fact that the mob has usurped the government's historic function of control of the public peace, abusing the power that attaches to that role.

Emphasis on the elements just mentioned would aid in rationalizing other cases involving compensation claims for mob violence. Exemplary of decisions in which this analysis provides general support for a judicial focus on physical control is a brace of Kansas cases dealing with injuries inflicted by groups of prisoners in jail. In the later of these two cases, the court refuses to impose liability on the city because the prisoners were held in custody by the sheriff,[151] whereas in a case distinguished in that decision the prisoners constituting a mob "were peculiarly within the control of the city officers."[152] The court elaborated the control point in the earlier case, saying that "the city is vested with the power and charged with the duty of preventing mob violence and preserving the peace everywhere within its corporate limits, and it should be easier to discharge that duty where those who are engaged in the riot are in custody and could be controlled by the officers without much difficulty."[153] Beyond this, and congenial to the broader approach offered in this study, is authority indicating that actual physical control is unnecessary to sustain liability under mob violence statutes. The victim's dependence on the local government's preservation of law and order may be rather general. Under a state constitutional provision for compensation to victims of lynchings by "the County where such lynching takes place," the court has no hesitancy about imposing liability on the county where a victim was taken after being dragged from a jail in the next county.[154] Implicit in this constitutional provision and a similar statute is a notion of de facto entrustment of physical security to the commonwealth by all citizens. The focus on prisoners in these provisions is simply a particular manifestation of that wider concern.

It is true that the imposition of public liability for riot damage or mob violence can create a dilemma for police departments. The problem becomes manifest in a concise exposition concerning a parallel issue: "If police are not given broad discretion when the decision is made *not to arrest*, the net effect is to encourage the officer to be less careful in invoking the criminal process."[155] In the terms used in this analysis, to impose penalties for defaults in the use of power may cause its abuse. But the vexing nature of the dilemma does not lessen the rationality of a legislative choice to compensate. This is so whether one reasons that society has fostered conditions that spawn riots or subscribes to a rationale emphasizing compassion for those whose dependence in moments of fortuitous social turbulence is simply more than the police structure can bear.[156] Statutes of this kind properly impose social obligations in situations in which the allotted physical power of government is outstripped by events but citizen dependence remains, an ultimate combination of humanitarian considerations with the state's superior financial power to create a duty of salvage.

Duties of Incarcerators

It is logical to carry the discussion from state obligations to compensate for the consequences of large-scale social violence to the duties of governments in their control of those incarcerated as dangers to society or themselves. I will deal with two facets of this problem which recently have aroused controversy. The first category raises questions of government responsibility to individuals both inside and outside institutions for injuries inflicted by inmates. The second problem, rather distinct but containing elements of the first, concerns liabilities to inmates for defaults as well as abuses of power attendant on their incarceration.

HAZARD FROM THE INMATE. In many suits for injury caused by violent conduct of prisoners or patients, the government's defense rests reasonably on the impossibility of predicting the danger or on a need to balance risk with social and individual advantage. To illustrate the unpredictability defense, carelessness in allowing a prisoner to escape should not be regarded as a default of power entailing liability for his assaultive behavior outside the walls when his record gives no hint of tendencies of that kind.[157] Moreover, even in situations of known psychiatric danger, judicial analysis of negligence claims tends to give substantial leeway to custodians. This has been so with reference both to claims for suicide[158] and to a suit for an assault on a retardate who had been placed in an open ward.[159] In the latter decision the apparition of discretion sweeps across one arc of the case,[160] but it may be sufficient to say in many situations of this kind that there simply was no negligence.[161] Courts have not been quick to find that decisions allowing inmate freedom of movement constitute abuse of power, or even actionable default.[162] And given the delicacy of the balancing that must be done, arguably one should not impose absolute liability for injuries committed by those discretionarily at liberty inside or outside prisons or mental institutions.

Yet I would argue that liability for default in the use of institutional power should be relatively expansive in situations in which the exercise of control over dangerous energies has in fact made substantial contribution to an injury.[163] In the case of citizens assaulted outside institutions, this is because events find these victims so completely at the mercy of the aggressions that may occur in the wake of the calculated decision of release. By comparison, in cases of assaulted patients in open wards, it may be reasonable in some instances to deny compensation, because the plaintiff's own benefit from treatment is bound up so intimately with the risk on which he comes to grief. Even so, because the dependency of inmates is so complete on controlling officials and physicians, judicial decisions should aim to ensure minimums of decency in the quantitative obligations of institutions to provide care for those over whom they have control.[164] It should be added that it is useful to examine the problem without reference to the normative overtones that may accompany holdings of fault in this setting. Beyond that, besides suggesting a broad approach to liability with reference to the conduct of institutional defendants, I would urge that courts severely limit the application of defenses based on "discretion" in cases where compensation otherwise seems desirable.

Levels of "discretion." Johnson v. California[165] contains a powerful statement of affirmative obligations governing officials who possess legal and physical power over the lives of persons with dangerous proclivities. The plaintiff in that case undertook to provide a foster home for a parolee with alleged homicidal tendencies which the paroling authority did not disclose, and was injured when the youth assaulted her. The court defines the outlines of duty in an opinion in which it also rejects an attempt to bar liability on grounds of a state "discretionary function" exception. The setting of standards for parole may be discretionary, says Justice Mathew Tobriner, and even the decision to parole "comprises the resolution of policy considerations." But once that choice is made, the decision whether to warn foster parents of a child's violent tendencies is "ministerial," unprotected by the statutory exclusion. The rationale for imposing governmental liability is a socialized one: "Since the entire populace of California benefits from the activity of the Youth Authority, it should also share equally the burden of injuries negligently inflicted on individual citizens; suits against the state provide a fair and efficient means to distribute these losses."[166]

As the problem radiates outward into the community, however, even the definition in *Johnson* of the boundaries of discretion and of liability may not be broad enough. Warning serves well enough for the case of injuries to the foster parents, to whom it gives a choice. But what about the case of an innocent pedestrian, attacked by the same parolee on the street? Here it seems unresponsive to deny compensation on the basis that the decision to grant parole is "discretionary." That choice hardly ranks on the scale of political generality with "governing";[167] although it may partake of "policy," to call it "basic" would exaggerate. A judicial framework featuring liability for failures to warn on a "ministerial" characterization is inadequate to cope with the problem of decisions to release. That such decisions involve judgment is clear enough; but the level of judgment, in the context of the loss distribution rationale announced by the court, militates against immunizing them on grounds of discretion.[168]

Physical power: analogies. Moreover, if legislative history in a particular jurisdiction should indicate an intent to embrace cases of this kind within a "discretionary" exception, I would argue that this is unwise. By hypothesis one may be negligent in the exercise of discretion; to combine terminology developed here with that often used by the courts, this means that there may be serious defaults in the exercise of a legally conferred power to make choices that concern risks of personal injury. In the event of provable default in the parole decision itself, persons who may be hurt because of the dangerous tendencies of the parolee are effectively in thrall to the control exercised by the authorities. There is no alternative protection for them; the official has a monopoly on the power that allows parole, and his control over the eccentric energies of the parolee is analogous to that of one who is responsible for the demolition of explosives adjacent to populated areas. Through the political system, his fellow citizens have created an entrustment of this power to him. In the case of the victim of a criminal who commits a crippling or murderous act before his dangerous tendencies are known, usually compensation must await the passage of specific legislation. But in release cases, under claims statutes that take their shape from basic tort law, the affective claims on the commonwealth are strong. "Did you hear about poor Ms. Jones? They paroled some crazy kid from the State Home, and he went after her with a knife on the street." It is here that this analysis, elementarily focused at the outset on matters related to the control of simple forms of physical energy, broadens out and bends around problems that characterize dealings with troubled human beings. The thread of principle that joins cases across this spectrum is that the control of power and the superiority it confers should impose duties on officials.

It is true that an exaggerated application of this point of view could have land-mine consequences for parole and sentencing systems. My argument, however, is for an approach that simply nurtures a plant already germinated by the common law. In those situations in which information about dangerous tendencies is unavailable to officials as well as to innocent citizens, common law liability would be unmerited, although a substantial case may still be made for legislative compensation for crime victims. But when the critical information is available, and particularly when the identity of one or a few potential victims is known in advance, as in the California Youth Authority case, a basic case for creation of a duty is made out, with the question of its breach for the jury. It may be noted in this connection that California has now judicially developed a complete matching of private and public duty, with its imposition of an obligation on a psychiatrist to warn a known, potential victim of a patient's murderous tendencies.[169] I would simply emphasize that even when the possible objects of personal violence are more randomized the probability of injury done to members of the public should be analyzed in terms of their dependence on officials for an exercise of discretion that fully considers their rights. This emphasis entails the further point, as was stressed in the first part, that there should be leeway for judicial judgment concerning the fairness of compensation for this kind of injury, even in cases in which a net social monetary gain is hypothesized from the continuation of the practice in question. Although decisions will vary with factual variations, the control of power by officials as well as the helplessness and lack of awareness of danger of the random victim argue strongly for a spreading of such losses.

THE INMATE ABUSED. I now turn inward upon the institution itself this inquiry into the control exercised by imprisoning and committing authorities. It is clear that under the common law of many states jailers are liable for negligence in failing to provide adequate protection for prisoners from injuries inflicted by other convicts,[170] as well as for direct brutalities of prison employees. But state remedies have not always proved efficacious for prisoners claiming injuries caused by persons or conditions in the institution. My focus here is on issues that have thus arisen as a matter of federal civil rights law, issues concerning which it is helpful to examine the nature of the power that is being exercised.

First, viewing legal rights at a very basic level, it is clear that it is an abuse of power of constitutional dimensions to impose certain forms of physical restraint on prisoners. This is surely so in such egregious circumstances as an occasion on which two mentally retarded youths were bound and spread-eagled for seventy-seven and a half hours in a public area of a state hospital, as punishment for alleged consensual homosexual acts.[171] A court finds that proof of these brutalities would support a judgment of cruel and unusual punishment under the Eighth Amendment, citing a precedent that refers to "evolving standards of decency" in what the court calls a "humane society." The same constitutional provision has been used to justify a requirement that death row prisoners in solitary confinement be given reasonable opportunity for exercise.[172] Moreover, a court has awarded money damages to prisoners for deprivation of due process by the use of solitary confinement as punishment for recourse to the legal system.[173] And punitive measures for the "mere expression" of beliefs also have been enjoined, at least when there is no likelihood of circulation that would upset prison discipline.[174] The grounds for relief vary in such cases, from cruel and unusual punishment to due process to freedom of expression. But a theme that implicitly ties these decisions together resides in the malignant exercise of the control given by law to jailers, a natural result of which is an intolerably high level of prisoner fear and frustration. In one case, awarding judgment for $15,000 against an individual prison defendant, the court cited a $9,000 figure as "illustrative" of the cost of psychiatric care for emotional harm of the kind caused to the plaintiff prisoners.[175] It should be added that the spectre of personal liability unleashed by this decision produced immediate effect on primary conduct, in the state's expeditious purchase of liability insurance against similar claims.[176]

As one moves into the related territory in which incarcerating authorities take deliberate intrusive action in the name of habilitation, a focus on realities of power provides a basic rationalization for recent judicial opposition to mind-altering surgical procedures.[177] Coercion, or the overawed prisoner's or patient's lack of ability to give a meaningful affirmation of willingness to undergo the procedure, will vitiate consent in many such cases.[178] In those circumstances, an operation of this kind would technically become a battery under traditional tort analysis, and under related constitutional principles it would be enjoinable.

The direct application of physical force to prisoners, for a variety of motives, presents the clearest case for judicial employment of remedies for abuse of power. Cases like spread-eagling for three days provide the most brutal manifestations of prison abuse, but official conduct may remain insidiously vicious as it shades away into offenses less obvious. Beyond outright battery, the continuum is one that begins with the deliberate creation of conditions that seriously menace the dignity as well as the physical security of prisoners. It runs through the rather passive allowance of physical arrangements that permit violations of personal security and, finally, extends to the case in which an inmate claims that insufficient steps have been taken to give him medical aid or, more generally, to rehabilitate him.

Use of dangerous practices. Illustrative of the intentional creation of conditions that pose grave threats to personal dignity are the facts in a notable case in which federal courts found it necessary to undertake supervision of some Arkansas prisons. One of several practices cited by the trial court in that case was the use of trusties as guards, conferring authority that effectively included the ability to "sell favors, easy jobs, and coveted positions" and to "extort money from inmates on any and all pretexts."[179] The court cited universal condemnation by penologists of the use of trusty guards, as a breeder of fear and hatred between the guards and the guarded and as tending toward brutality and the endangering of the lives of inmates. To impose money damages or institute corrective orders in a case of this kind only carries out the logic of requiring compensation for the unlawful exercise of physical force by prison authorities. We may expect greater controversy with the arrival of salients that push culpability further, illustrated in the hint by a federal district court that the maintenance of grossly unsafe conditions in a penitentiary shop might be cruel and unusual punishment.[180]

Blinking at brutality. Slightly subtler in terms of control of power, but no less terrifying for the prison population, is the problem of permissiveness to brutality practiced by inmates upon each other. The Arkansas case again is instructive. The district court adduced evidence of inmate stabbings and homosexual attacks so frequent, and instilling such fear, that it was not unusual for men to come to the front of the barracks and cling to the bars all night—a practice known as "coming to the bars."[181] The trial judge was quite prescriptive on this point. He posited that barracks were compatible with "a well run penal institution," but only if they were confined to small groups "properly classified and selected and subject to adequate control," and he held that the barracks in one prison did "not satisfy those conditions."[182] Affirming his judgment, the reviewing court did not find it necessary to examine these findings in any detail,[183] thus apparently confirming that governmental default even in what might be characterized as an architectural planning function may be a constitutional deprivation.

Chief Justice Warren Burger's statement that when a person is put in prison "we have tolled the bell for him . . . we have made him our collective responsibility"[184] provides a partial basis for decisions that grant relief in the categories of prisoner injuries described above. Beyond that, it implies a standard for the obligation of government to provide rehabilitation and supply therapeutic services to those subject to imprisonment and other forms of confinement.

Rehabilitation. With respect to the provision of rehabilitative care, the remarkable trial court decisions in the cases titled *Wyatt v. Stickney*[185] provide a detailed judicial prescription. Dealing with claims of inadequate treatment brought by patients in a state mental hospital and an institution for mentally retarded persons, Judge Frank M. Johnson had found patients subject to a "dehumanizing" lack of privacy and serious physical deprivations related to crowded housing, inferior food, and poor sanitation.[186] After conflicting testimony from psychiatric experts about the appropriate ratios of professionals to patients,[187] he undertook to construct orders that set out "minimum constitutional standards for adequate treatment of the mentally ill"[188] and "adequate habilitation of the mentally retarded."[189] These orders included precise details concerning minimum floor space in resident units, as well as number of toilets and privacy requirements; an articulation of specific guidelines for nutrition; and injunctions and other rules concerning the use of patients for hospital labor. Judge Johnson also mandated an "individualized treatment plan" for each patient, which would enumerate the patient's specific problems, describe treatment goals, and give a description of proposed staff involvement with specifications of responsibility.[190]

Reviewing this comprehensive edict, the appellate court resolved to "pretermit decision as to the remedy decreed by the district court,"[191] proportionally to its order of a remand to facilitate "the parties, amici and court moving together to meet the constitutional requisites."[192] However, in principle it effectively upheld the district court's approach, one which carries broad implications responsive to the analysis presented here. Implicit in the district court's orders is a profound concern with personal dignity, the protection of which is at the root of all tort and constitutional doctrine that enjoins or compensates for miscarriages of power, ranging from outright abuse to default. A distinctive feature of these orders is that they impose obligations on government with respect to persons whose incarceration is due to congenital conditions, or medical fortuities occurring later in life, and not to the commission of a crime. The *Wyatt* decisions thus represent a judicial articulation of a state concern that extends not only to the consequences of control exercised to protect public interests from emergent peril, but also to the effects of a control imposed because of the dependence of the helpless. They involve the judge in the fashioning of minimum levels of personal dignity for persons in that position, and on a constitutional scale. Read broadly, the message would appear to be that whenever the state confines persons, and for whatever reasons, the federal judiciary may set such minima;[193] and it seems clear that it should not differentiate between the dignity due a retarded person and a prisoner.[194]

Desperation and social morale. The trial court decisions in *Wyatt* raise serious issues from standpoints of both judicial competence and judicial resources. Cognizant of these problems, the court of appeals offered a cooperative, negotiating approach, but one that stood quite firm with reference to the basic obligation of the state. Without blinking the difficulties involved in granting this kind of relief, I think it important to emphasize that Judge Johnson's opinions reflect the unity of negative injunction and prescriptive compulsion in such cases. To order inhumane treatment stopped is by itself insufficient to the task; the judge who does this risks disrespect for his order unless he undertakes at least to sketch guidelines about what will be required. The decision does carry legal remedies a long way from the simpler tort applications of the duty to act. Some may say it is too far, but my study of the diverse doctrines I have analyzed here has gradually impressed me how straight and direct is the road that runs from tort law protections of personal interests to constitutional vindications of civil rights. Again, this is not to underrate the problems presented by the district court's broad mandates, which will require much exploration and debate.[195] These orders are troubling because our constitutional arrangement does not envision regular judicial undertakings to realize for us as well as to articulate for us our better selves. But the depth of deprivation—and the desperation of the pathetic claimants—provides important rationalizing bases for this kind of remedy, when piled upon the factors of control and dependence inherent in conditions of confinement. Moreover, there is a strong affective element in this type of case, one connected with the permeation of publicity about conditions in such institutions. In this regard, a decision like *Wyatt* may render a proper balance of a subconscious social morale account, with the judge serving as an appropriate surrogate for the community. A telling analogue appears in the modifications of attitude toward imprisonment that reportedly take place in judges who spend even a night in prison.[196]

Abusive deprivation of therapy. I shall now consider a class of case that is typically more emergently compelling than the *Wyatt* problem because of its particularity and immediacy, but which also sometimes presents peculiar subtleties. This is the case of the individual prisoner who sues for deprivation of specific medical care. At a relatively simple level of analysis, there is a clear example of abuse of power in a case in which guards forced a surgery patient, a victim of polio, to walk out of a prison hospital in violation of instructions given for his care and without a surgical discharge. Sustaining an action against the warden, the court finds that these allegations show, "at best, a deliberate indifference to appellant's condition and the surgeons' orders."[197] Moreover, it holds a claim stated against the prison doctor for discharging the plaintiff from the hospital, as well as for requiring him to stand and failing to provide him with adequate medication; it says in this connection that although courts "cannot go around second-guessing doctors . . . neither can they ignore gross misconduct by a doctor."[198] In terms of the analysis offered here, a persuasive explanation for the result as to the warden lies in a concept of abuse of power, perpetrated by one who owes his superior position to the force of legal compulsion that gives him physical control over the plaintiff. With reference to the doctor, it might be argued that we should assess his conduct on the basis of the standards usually used to judge medical care—including their often implicit reference to the power that is fused with the use of medical skill—rather than focusing on the use of governmental power. But the court's use of "gross misconduct" phraseology, in the context of its application of "deliberate indifference" language to the warden, suggests that the characterization of abuse of power may properly apply to the doctor as well.

This view seems implicitly confirmed in an earlier decision[199] which upholds a complaint alleging that a wounded man, taken into custody, received no medical attention for a developing infection. The root of the offense again lies in the use of the power of incarceration, in this case depriving the plaintiff of the opportunity to seek medical aid that a rational free person would have sought. Given the emergent problem of a wound, it is that exercise of governmental power, rather than a failure of medical judgment, that seems best to rationalize this noteworthy application of the Ku Klux Klan Act to a raw pleading; the decision came four years before the authoritative and liberalizing construction of the legislation in *Monroe v. Pape*.[200] On the other hand, as I will suggest below, the application of a medical rather than governmental perspective generally seems more appropriate in situations where the case lacks such a compelling aspect as the failure to attend a wound.

Decisions that deny recovery for deprivation of medical care in prison encompass a broad spectrum of reasoning. In one case, in which the court's recitation of the facts supports its statement that there was "no indifference or intentional mistreatment," it does set forth a baseline allocational standard: the state must "furnish at least a minimal amount of medical care for whatever conditions plague the prisoner."[201] The stated reason for this require-

ment, quite compatible with the present analysis, is that imprisonment substantially deprives a prisoner of the "ability to seek and
find medical treatment."[202] But the court's denial of compensation
on the facts suggests a practical guideline to decisional results.
This is that once treatment is undertaken judges are reluctant to
find constitutional deprivations in suits dealing with medical judgment. That is the case with respect to an instance of refusal to call
in a specialist,[203] as well as a decision not to prescribe medication
for a condition that usually causes no pain, especially given the
necessary sensitivity of prison physicians to problems of addiction
to medicine.[204]

A recent effort by the Supreme Court to provide guidelines on
the subject[205] deals with a case near the borderline but, according
to the principles developed here, decides it correctly. The plaintiff
prisoner was injured when a bale of cotton fell on him, and claimed
cruel and unusual punishment in the failure to provide him adequate medical care. Although the court of appeals upheld his complaint, the Supreme Court reversed this decision with particular
reference to the alleged deprivations caused by the prison physicians.[206]

The difference between the lenses applied to the case by Justice
Thurgood Marshall, writing for the majority, and the lone dissenter, Justice John Paul Stevens, is interesting. Justice Stevens first
emphasized certain particular occurrences, including the placement of the plaintiff in solitary confinement because he would not
work when he could not do so, refusal by prison guards to let him
sleep in the lower bunk which a doctor had assigned, and the fact
that he was forced to wait twelve hours to see a physician because
a clearance had to be secured from the warden. Then, stacking
together a number of events of this kind, Justice Stevens characterized the complaint as being one that "the system as a whole
is inadequate."[207]

By contrast, Justice Marshall emphasized the positive aspects of
the prisoner's treatment, especially the fact that "medical personnel" had seen him seventeen times over a three-month period and
had treated a variety of problems. Synthesizing a range of precedents including prisoner cases and many other decisions involving the "cruel and unusual punishment" language of the Eighth
Amendment, Justice Marshall proposed a standard of "deliberate
indifference to serious medical needs of prisoners."[208] This requirement, he said, was unfulfilled by the particular complaint because
of the numerous instances of medical contacts which the prisoner

had had. Specifically, and in line with the analysis proposed here, he rejected arguments that "more should have been done by way of diagnosis and treatment," and that several options not pursued should have been taken up. At most, he said, these would be malpractice, suable under state law.[209]

Medical judgment and the shadow of malingering. Given the position of a prisoner practically cut off at the moment of his travail from immediate legal determination of his claim, and possessed of a belief that his medical needs are being ignored, one is wary of cutting off federal remedies. But there are practical psychological reasons in the background as well as a desire to remit to the states what are, after all, simple negligence cases. In particular, doctors who take care of prisoners face recurrent problems in sorting out sufferers from malingerers. A vivid recent account pictures an examination in a county jail of a middle-aged alcoholic, who says that he has "a bad G.I. bleed," and that he thinks he's "gonna die," presumptively indicative only of a previous bleeding ulcer and a mastery of lingo. Yet, despite suspiciously inconsistent answers to other diagnostic questions, the doctor finds the man's "abdomen's really rigid . . . stiff as a board," and decides to send him to the hospital.[210] A refusal to do so that caused harm would arguably have been an actionable default in the use of power, but in such a case the locus of power would seem medical rather than governmental. Surely, courts have properly drawn the line against liability in many such cases. However, this distinction between kinds of power highlights the reality that a dismissal of an action for inadequate care is basically a denial of a negligence claim, often on the merits although in some federal cases it at once reflects judicial perception of the appropriate boundaries of federal jurisdiction concerning common law tort claims that lack constitutional foundation. In any event, it seems to blur the issue to say that "Federal courts do not ordinarily interfere in matters of internal prison discipline and management."[211]

It should be emphasized that as medical judgment shades into administrative fiat the case for prisoner relief becomes stronger. Scrutiny of some decisions, occasionally involving a look between the lines, suggests that an explicit liberalization of liability rules might be justifiable and just. Illustratively, behind the brief denial of a convict's claim that he "merely . . . should have been admitted as an emergency patient on two occasions"[212] may lurk complexities that defy facile dismissal. This is hardly an argument for absolute liability, but rather a call for careful balancing of important interests in conflict. Yet, while pursuing this balance, one must remember that actions that are socially reasonable in the circumstances may inspire great frustration and even dreadful fear. Giving a pleader his allegations, a prisoner who really believes he has cancerous warts on his penis[213] must be terrified when a prison physician is recalcitrant about calling a specialist. And, important in terms of this analysis, the effective control that the doctor exercises over the prisoner's freedom, directly derived from governmental compulsion, prevents him from getting the opinion he could seek if free. Certainly, the stronger the prisoner's subjective belief in the immediacy of peril, the more an unsympathetic rejection of pleas for treatment is likely to stimulate the most profound anxieties. Here not only the prisoner's frustration and his fear but also his own perception of the justice of the situation would argue weightily for his claim.

However, the most apt inquiry in most situations of this kind would seem to remain one of whether the doctor acted reasonably as a matter of craft, and courts that deny recovery frequently join an affirmative answer to this question to a judgment that it is inappropriate to focus on the use of governmental power in such cases. Sometimes, tragically, the diagnosis will be wrong. In one close case, in which the trial judge found no grounds for relief but the appellate court thought that a liberal construction of the plaintiff's complaint required a full evidentiary hearing, the prisoner's fear of cancer ultimately proved justified although the doctor insisted that his complaint was only hemorrhoids and refused tests and x-rays.[214] Buried in such cases, one suspects, are latent hostilities in physician as well as patient, mental calluses built up by platoons of malingerers on the examining table. But when the most serious accusation is one of careless judgment, considerations of both power relationships and economy thrust toward the simple conclusion that there has been no misuse of governmental power and thus no violation of a civil right; and often, though not always, those considerations will also militate against a finding that the physician has miscarried in his use of medical power.[215]

Concepts of governmental and medical power. The framework of analysis that emerges is this: All cases dealing with requests for medical aid by prisoners and inmates will involve a situation of total physical control by the institution and a relationship of virtually complete dependence,[216] made especially poignant by the fact that with his freedom the prisoner could and likely would seek therapeutic care in the case in which his suffering is in fact a warning. In such situations, it is an abuse of governmental power to keep a prisoner from competent medical care—and knowingly to provide incompetent aid may itself justify a claim.[217] Indeed, a committee of the American Bar Association has argued that there is a substantial risk-enhancing factor in the very exercise of power by government through its prison system, and has recommended a legislative compensation system for injuries thereby incurred by prisoners.[218] This broad solution would dispose of the necessity to distinguish cases within the category of prisoner injuries, and some vexing problems attendant to that task. I therefore might be inclined to vote for such a scheme as a legislator. However, from the standpoint of judicial decision, my view is that once competent medical personnel is provided, generally no claim exists for abuse of governmental power. The violation of personal rights by deprivation of care for illness or injury is then properly viewed as not principally governmental but medical,[219] and this distinction has special significance regarding federal constitutional litigation as well as secondary implications for the theory of liability and thus the size of compensation awards.[220] Among other specific consequences, this means that there would be no civil rights claim against a doctor for malpractice in the rendering of care, unless he could be shown part of a conspiracy with prison officials.

This analysis does not derogate the serious nature of the obligations that entrustment of anyone's body to a doctor entails, obligations that arise from the power inherent in the physician's professional status. But the fact that there is no choice in physician selection by prisoners does not make a doctor's default in the use of medical power a misuse of governmental power. To repeat, this is not to deny the validity of the terror of the rebuffed patient who is sick and knows it, but only to say that his plight is not sufficiently related to the government's control over him that the commonwealth must compensate him on the basis of that control. It should be reiterated that in some cases of this kind there simply is no miscarriage of any sort. In this regard, given that often the line between doctoring and administration will be hard to draw, I would simply stress that it would be a better legal world if the courts announced their conclusions more directly without resort to the mask of "internal discipline." At once, I would note that when medical services are carelessly rendered to a state prisoner, there is always theoretically a remedy at state law; and I would suggest without present elaboration that, in theory, a showing that state courts deliberately ignore valid claims for relief in such cases would be another way to approach the highway marked civil rights.[221]

To conclude this discussion of governmental obligations to prisoners, there seems an especially strong analogy in the seamen's cases, discussed at the beginning of this study in the area of private duties to act.[222] In the case of prisoners, there prevail with even more force the conditions of physical isolation, of dependence for the most basic sustenance, and of required obedience to discipline. The exercise of governmental power in cases of incarceration thus provides even firmer support for a broad view of duty.

VIII. *Welfare*

Victims of Trauma

A compelling case of public duty to act under this analysis, with a primarily legislative focus, is the problem of trauma. Trauma is ubiquitous and epidemic and has been called "the nation's most important environmental health problem."[223] The year's toll in 1971 was 114,000 fatalities, 50 million injuries with half a million permanent impairments, and an estimated total social cost of $21 billion.[224] It has been estimated that proper ambulance equipment and training of personnel would save 60,000 lives a year.[225] Recently, interest has begun to grow toward developing systematic solutions of the problem. The formation of the American College of Emergency Physicians illustrates the concern of medical practitioners, and an educational committee of that organization has issued guidelines for the establishment of review training programs for residency in emergency care.[226] In a parallel development, the Commission on Emergency Medical Services of the AMA has undertaken to classify hospital emergency facilities with reference to their ability to handle various kinds of situations.[227]

At best, the job of trauma care is a difficult one, and the difficulties begin with transportation of the seriously injured person. A recent report records the financial problems of a private ambulance service, which refers most emergency calls to public rescuers on grounds of superior speed in response, and whose owners complain about the "distasteful" nature of the nonemergency calls that are their precarious bread and butter.[228] By contrast, public rescue work, while much more exciting, involves such strain that it is considered "the hardest job in the fire department."[229] The obstacles to life saving may be surmounted, however, and when proper resources are devoted to rescue services, the results can be rather dramatic. The development of a city-owned service in Utah, with an "elite 138-man corps of emergency medical technicians" and twenty-two new ambulances, has significantly reduced average call times and saved many lives.[230] The designation of forty downtown Illinois hospitals as trauma centers has cut the death rate for injured persons after first aid arrives from 8 percent to 2 percent, which is approximately the same as that on Vietnam battlefields.[231]

Spotty performance. The results of recent investigation have indicated that these advances in allocation and technique are not uniform. A study of ambulance service in Utah reports that "the scope of first aid . . . varies drastically"[232] and that many attendants giving first aid could not even qualify for a standard American Red Cross first aid card.[233] There is a statutory predicate for a leap forward in societal response to trauma in recent legislation which requires states to have highway safety programs approved by the Secretary of Transportation.[234] However, there is a large gap between the promise and the reality. A federal Highway Safety Program Standard purports to compel each state to set up a program "to ensure that persons involved in highway accidents receive prompt emergency medical care under the range of emergency conditions encountered." It mentions, among relevant minima, "training, licensing, and related requirements . . . for ambulance and rescue vehicle operators, attendants, drivers, and dispatchers"; standards for emergency vehicles, including supplies and equipment; and procedures for summoning and dispatching aid.[235] But a survey of state compliance with these standards, conducted by the National Highway Traffic Safety Administration, was unable to find a single jurisdiction meriting an "A" rating; thirty-one states received "B's," which denotes that programs "will conform substantially" to requirements *when implemented*; and twenty-one jurisdictions got "C's" for demonstrating "acceptable progress toward implementation."[236] A poverty lawyer's survey of twenty programs with reference to the emergency care standard showed "most to consist of little more than sketchy descriptions of present deficiencies and vaguely-worded proposals for the future."[237]

Private action. The problem in gross calls for increased legislative attention, but presently the situation may be ripe for private action to enforce the commands of existing combinations of statutes and regulations. There is a well-established body of cases imposing liability on hospitals for the failure to render emergency aid in individual cases.[238] Even private physicians face obligations expanded by federal law: the chairman of the Massachusetts medical licensure board and the state secretary of consumer affairs recently warned physicians that they could not deny treatment to Medicaid patients, after it was reported that a Cape Cod ophthalmologist had refused to treat a newborn infant with a viral infection affecting the eye.[239] Moreover, some judicial foundation already has begun to appear for more comprehensively focused citizen demands for adequate emergency care. A federal court in the District of Columbia, after finding that various facilities of the D.C. General Hospital—including the medical records department, the nursing staff, and the emergency room—fell "far short of recognized and acceptable standards in this community," required the institution to specify the resources it needed to rise to these standards and to submit detailed plans of corrective action, as well as to take "immediate steps to fill all budgeted positions now vacant."[240] The development of theory in this area is embryonic. But, although its course is uncertain, claimants can marshal a persuasive combination of factors: the total dependence of the victim, the state's virtually complete control over preparation for emergency, and the welfare expenditures that traumatic injuries now require.

Legislative rationales. More comprehensively, there is a strong basis for further congressional action, for example, through direct appropriation for the provision of emergency services or by conditioning federal largesse, such as highway construction funds, on effective state performance. The reasons supporting interstitial private enforcement, founded in reciprocities of power and dependence, replicate themselves with even greater force in favor of more adequate legislation. Traumatic injury presents a situation in which the citizen's dependence on government is not only complete but also desperate. The generally fortuitous nature of the events that cause such harm, and the lack of warning typical of them, results in the citizen's inability both to make preparation in advance for rescue services and to maneuver to secure them when they become necessary. The government's possession of financial resources and its ability to channel them into life-saving activities argue for significantly greater public commitments, especially in light of the commonwealth's general responsibility for the preservation of life. The case is bolstered by the potential savings in welfare costs of lost and ruined lives that could be saved or better preserved. But even in this summary application of the proposed analysis to trauma, I must note that serious problems will arise with respect to a variety of questions. Only illustrative is the issue of how much service should be provided to relatively unpopulated areas. It has been suggested that one solution to this problem would be a regulated monopoly, with requirements that the monopolist must service rural areas as well as heavily populated communities.[241] However, whatever the resolution of intermediate questions of this kind, the political case seems especially strong for generally improved rescue services for victims of trauma.

High-Risk Morbidity

Issues that arise with respect to public responsibility for trauma care recur throughout various areas of human suffering, requiring consideration of possible extensions of the analysis developed here. At its highest level of generality, the problem is no less broad than the obligation of government to provide medical services. My inquiry here is much more limited, centering on a few areas of recent concern from which broader principles may be developed. It is useful, first, as with our examination of the trauma problem, to expand the primarily judicial focus of this study to include some principally legislative possibilities of applying this analysis to advances in medical science.

The typical situation that I wish to consider here is one in which it is possible to save at considerable cost the lives of otherwise doomed patients, who are menaced by conditions relatively uncommon but hardly unique. The area of infant mortality, which is generally illustrative, offers a particularly interesting example in the development of treatments for hyaline membrane disease, the affliction that took the life of the infant son of President John F. Kennedy because his lungs lacked a surface fluid that would have allowed him to breathe. The tolerances in treatment of this deficiency are stringent: it takes three days for a baby so afflicted to produce enough surfactant to survive. During the preliminary assaults on the problem, heroic measures managed to decrease mortality; but until very recently even the best hospital treatment could save only one-third of the suffering infants. Now, the introduction of an ingenious technique of forcing air through a tube in the baby's lungs, which in effect blows them up like balloons, has raised survival rates to 80 or 90 percent. However, this heartening improvement requires round-the-clock care, an exemplar of the expense side of the medical progress account.[242] Comparable successes, with similar attendant cost features, are daily duplicated throughout the budding science of neonatology—the care of the newborn. A dramatic instance appears in a case, also involving infant breathing problems, in which a child was kept for ten days in a respirator until he developed oxygen poisoning, making it necessary for nurses to work double shifts for seventy-two hours to squeeze a bag that forced air into his lungs.[243] This kind of intensive care, with costs that run into hundreds of dollars a day, rendingly underlines the difficulties of the allocational question: to what extent is society under a duty to make preparations to deal with life-threatening medical problems that are fairly infrequent but still affect hundreds and thousands of people?

Long-term treatments. These difficulties become exacerbated when the condition is chronic and to stave off the constant threat of death requires expensive treatment throughout the patient's life. An adequate solution to any particular problem must necessarily be a political one in its inception. In a notable example of successful pressure from an ad hoc lobby, kidney disease patients achieved legislation conferring Medicare eligibility on persons with chronic renal failure.[244] Their most effective argument lay in the cause of their plaint—the staggering cost of treatment. Expenses run from $5,000 to $20,000 a year for patients who require dialysis, a mechanical treatment that does the work of kidneys in cleansing the body of impurities.[245] And dialysis itself does not ameliorate the deep psychic troubles of patients. Commentary on the isolated nature of medical specialties that work on this problem[246] is poignantly evocative of a theme sounded earlier, concerning the duty of ships' masters to treat drunken seamen with consideration and care.[247]

But with kidney patients advanced to the shelter of Medicare at least for their desperate physical requirements, other problems of great urgency have come to the fore. At this writing, the case of hemophilia posed some of the most difficult issues of social cost spreading. The plight of one child highlighted the problem: He required thirty-minute transfusions with a clotting factor, administered at a hemophilia center, to protect him from excessive bleeding for a two-day period. Each treatment cost $129. His total bill for one year climbed to $20,124,[248] and the costs of some other patients are double that.[249] A remark by the child's father embraces only the top of the iceberg but implies the financial chemistry of the rest: "I couldn't possibly pay for this treatment if I didn't have an excellent insurance company."[250] In cold theory, it is a simple application of the law of large numbers, thousands of rational calculations by isolated individuals coalescing in massed decisions to share risks. In a more practical perspective, the hemophilia case presents a special example of a problem that ranges across wide areas of illness into equally broad spheres of injury, reaching back to such questions as when there is a duty to pull unconscious sailors from fume-filled tanks.[251] What obligations does the commonwealth bear to citizens in life-threatening predicaments from which they cannot extricate themselves, and in which often they are enmeshed without any fault of their own? In the wake of the extension of Medicare to dialysis users came further efforts to extend the boundaries of political duty, with proposals to provide federal assistance to hemophiliacs, and with passage by at least two states of funding measures to help pay their bills.[252]

Policy factors. At the same time that the hemophilia problem churned legislative waters, it seemed inevitable that it should reach the courts, for example, in a suit seeking free medicine for hemophiliacs on the ground that this would provide equal protection with methadone maintenance of heroin addicts.[253] Constitutional doctrine would be stretched to the utmost by such a claim, perhaps beyond what it can safely accommodate. But whatever the proper judicial response to that particular problem, as one further pursues the implications of duties to act that stem from "tort" analysis, such cases require an effort to develop and confirm principles governing public obligations toward those in peril of their lives. And without essaying a full-scale examination of constitutional jurisprudence, my purpose here is to suggest how principles developed in this study may aid in that endeavor. Therefore, I will seek to identify several factors relevant to both political and judicial decision making on questions of this kind—policy elements that lie in the background of both equity and equal protection when a claim is made that government must act in the sense of rescue.

I shall use a claim for free hemophilia treatment as a vehicle, hypothesizing that the limits of charity have been exhausted. A suit of this kind confronts us immediately with the following factors: The risk of nontreatment is a fatal one for many sufferers. At the same time, since the population of afflicted persons is relatively small, the demands on the treasury made by such claims would not be crippling. Moreover, significant benefit would accrue to society from public provision of this kind of treatment. This is so not only from a rather sentimental standpoint but also from the viewpoint of encouraging participation in economic activity as well as in the general life of the community by persons with an affliction that otherwise would keep them from productive pursuits. To be sure, the element of control of the plaintiff by the defendant, often emphasized here, is lacking. And if there is entrustment, it is only in a very broad interpretation of the notion that citizens implicitly entrust their physical security to the state.

Yet that concept may provide the seed for a useful definition of the relationship between the imperiled individual and the commonwealth. This relationship is an on-going one in a profound sense, something considerably more than a child of the immediate circumstance. That is so because of the endangered person's status as a citizen and also because of the state's historic commitment to the preservation of life, manifested in one extreme aspect by anti-suicide statutes and in another, dramatic, context by judicial refusal to permit people to succumb voluntarily to life-threatening conditions.[254] Moreover, my intuition is that the hemophilia case presents the kind of situation in which a bystander study would yield a high percentage of positive individual responses. I hypothesize that there would be a clear majority for giving aid if one put to a random population the question of whether they would donate blood on the spot for a hemophilia victim lying in the road. And with respect to demands for needed preventive treatment, given that it is money rather than blood that would be required by ameliorating legislation—or by successful suits for "equal protection"—intuition further suggests that most people who understood the problem would find the case at least as convincing for either legislative or judicial action. A disposition to approve this line of argument seems implicit in a report of a temporary restraining order issued by a federal court, which prohibits a state vocational rehabilitation program from requiring that kidney patients must show an ability to pay for supplies.[255]

To be sure, there is a further twist in the hemophilia case which gives us pause because of its ramifications for state control of private lives. This is the fact that hemophilia occurs principally through genetic transmission, with the result that an increased survival rate in this generation entails more production of hemophiliacs in the next.[256] This suggests that when the political balance is struck social compassion may require a bargain. We may shudder at its Faustian implications, but eventually we must confront them. Without here pursuing these issues, which present a subject for independent and deep exploration, I conclude with these general remarks: Usually the duty to act arises over the term between half a minute—the time to effect a rescue in the most pressing circumstances—and ten years, a period exemplary of long-term research and development in the service of social planning and preparation. In its urgent aspects, the hemophilia problem falls within this area and, under the rationales of both humanitarianism and productivity mentioned above, summons various analogies of both private and public obligation. Although the case is a difficult one because of its potential genetic legacy, the balance appears to lie with the plea for legislative provision of treatment, and the weight of policy would seem to mandate judicial liberality to appeals that government respond to opportunities for life saving that arise in individual cases.

Judicial Harbingers of Public Duty

Cases already dotting the landscape provide occasional manifestations of the breadth of government's duty with respect to medical care, particularly as indicators that the dependence of its citizens deserves sympathetic response under existing statutes. Beyond that there is a spark of recognition, ready to jump the gap to legislation, of the political argument for fuller state intervention. At this point, one finds a kind of bending back of politics into an articulation by judges of a perceived community conscience, which concerns itself with duties to use available energies and abilities for the succor of those in serious need.

Defining "custodial" care. Evidence of judges' receptivity to statutorily based claims for medical services appears in a case involving an attempt to rehabilitate an elderly woman who had a nail inserted across the fracture line of a broken hip.[257] The question was whether the Department of Health, Education and Welfare properly denied Medicare benefits for a hospitalization period during which efforts were made to help the claimant to walk. This decision had ratified a hearing examiner's judgment that, "although claimant did require assistance in walking, such assistance does not come under the category of specialized physical therapy." The department based its denial of the claim on a provision of the Medicare legislation that excluded payment "where such expenses are for custodial care." The district judge, however, ruled that the benefits should have been paid. He rejected the argument that assistance in walking was not "specialized physical therapy," noting that "even trained medical personnel were having difficulty teaching the claimant to walk." Moreover, he said, "it is not the quantity of the care that is critical but it is the *quality* of care and the possible consequences of the lack of required services that is controlling in this case. If trained medical personnel had difficulty teaching her to walk is it feasible that this task should be entrusted to the unskilled?"[258] The judge also found it a "very significant factor" that an elderly frail person could not learn as fast as "a robust youthful person," pointing out that "a second fall could have been disastrous." He then combined arguments of efficiency and compassion in a brief paragraph: "Assuming *arguendo* that the government's economic argument is controlling it is clear that in this case more expense would be incurred by a fall caused by a premature discharge from the hospital. Moreover the Court cannot believe that such actions would be in keeping with the humanitarian aims of the Act which are of course controlling."[259]

The "humanitarian" argument is quite persuasive in this case, considering the initially helpless condition of the claimant and the fact that hospital personnel used their energy and skill to achieve the therapeutic result that the patient was able to walk when discharged. This is not to accuse the hearing examiner of perversity in his definition of custodial care to include care "designed essentially to assist the individual in meeting his activities of daily living."[260] It is, however, to say that to include in that category walking assistance with a training feature is a construction that seems insufficiently responsive to a legal situation in which there is room for interpretation, and inadequate to factual circumstances that suggest that a decision the other way would be demoralizing for the community as well as the patient. A thrust similar to the court's resolution of this problem appears in a recent report of a decision that rejects the placement of the "custodial" label on a patient hospitalized on the orders of a psychiatrist. In that case, the claimant received regular psychotherapy and required diagnostic tests as well as the administration of drugs that needed close professional supervision. The court placed substantial weight on the fact that the hospital's utilization review committee had found the patient's admission justified, and said it would frustrate the purpose of the Medicare statute to use a more stringent standard than that to test the necessity of extended-stay care.[261] Here again judicial interpretation simply provides a working realization of compassion already legislated.[262] It also parallels similar directions in medical thinking.[263]

Expansive concept of rights. Considerably more controversial is the issue of whether government has any obligation to assure med-

ical care beyond statutory mandates. This problem runs rather beyond the main current of legal thought, but there are some noteworthy instances of judicial hospitality to such pleas. In one case,
the claim was for $13,000 expenses incurred during an extended
hospital stay by one of eight children of a semi-itinerant miner
whose pay was $472 a month, as compared with the state welfare
department's indigency standards of $382.[264] Calling on a state
constitutional provision obligating counties to provide for those
"who, by reason of age, infirmity or misfortune may have claims
upon the sympathy and aid of society,"[265] the Montana Supreme
Court offered an exceptionally broad reading of a statutory concept
of medical indigency, saying, "[W]e believe the legislative intent
was to include those persons who do not have the present or future
hope of resources sufficient to pay for all the medical and hospital
services required in emergency instances."[266]

The court's repeated use of the term "emergency" serves to de-
limit its holding to situations defined in that way, but the definition is still an expansive one, going well beyond the peril of imminent threat to life. This interpretation of a combination of state
constitutional and statute law[267] reflects the court's view of the
realities of citizen dependence on state succor for medical necessities. It is true that the economic viability of the decision depends
partly on the court's characterization of the case as one of those
"infrequent emergency situations that confront one not on welfare." Several cases a year of that magnitude, signaling a never-
ending parade of working indigents lining up for judicial assistance,
might require a legislative reallocation responsive to prevailing
scarcities.[268] Yet it should be remembered that, on facts of this
kind, a considered political review of the matter well might cul-
minate in a decision to devote more resources to the problem
rather than to divide the existing pie into thinner slices. In any
event, the decision is an important indicator of what a court in a
relatively poor state considers to be the medical responsibilities
that attach to those who control the political energies of the commonwealth, with its attendant financial power.

No less remarkable, perhaps more so, is an unofficial account of
an equity judge's decision in Philadelphia, which reports that city
officials were preliminarily enjoined from eliminating several departments at the city's general hospital, including pediatrics, ob-
stetrics, and psychiatry. The report is not clear about the grounds
of decision. However, it says that the plaintiffs alleged not only
violations of state law and city charter provisions, but also the
threat of a public nuisance from danger to the community created

by lack of treatment of patients, as well as violations of equal protection because of distinctions based on race and wealth.[269]

Extrapolating these pleadings, there come together in this case the threads of several notions presented earlier. The deliberate withdrawal of support for particular services involves a kind of preparation-intent that blends aspects of intentional tort and negligence; and common law concepts of nuisance are alloyed with constitutional concepts of protecting vital personal interests to build a bridge over rights already created legislatively. The theme again is one of power: the control of knowledge and the dependence of ignorance; the ability to act and the dependence of indigence; power and reliance. And these elements meet in a most sensitive area of human welfare, in which anxieties born of neglect merge with the terrors of illness and the general deprivations of poverty. This combination of threads of both policy and doctrine may be too extended for appropriate and consistently effective judicial response, but even this informal report from a trial court firing line demands attention for the quest it embodies. Though the court's incursion into the sphere of legislative appropriation may seem intolerable under our conventional jurisprudence, it is at least useful as a probe, helping to delineate the judicial frontier of the duty to act. It also provides a triangulation point for marking the state of political advance.

MUNICIPAL SERVICES

On a broad intersecting canvas, a particularly interesting test of this analysis presents itself with respect to the provision of municipal services generally considered necessities.[270] In this area are met problems of duty, negligence, and discretion, in circumstances where a monopoly exists for government and the dependence of the citizen is great. These elements appear in sharp focus in the recent case of *Barney's Furniture Warehouse v. City of Newark*,[271] in which the court gives a negative answer to the question of whether the city must compensate persons injured by flooding that was the "result of a gradually increasing functional incapacity of the sewer system . . . because of urban development."

In the simple common law perspective from which we began, this would appear a classic case for the imposition of a duty. The city has definitely undertaken an obligation, creating not only a practical disincentive but also an effective legal bar to action by others as well as to self-help. Viewing the matter in light of basic negligence principles, it would seem that allegations of this kind of default present a case for the jury. In a case noted by the *Barney* court as the principal authority favoring municipal liability, a Kentucky decision found a litigable factual question on claims that the inadequacy of a sewer system was caused by "failure in the original construction to provide for subsequent development of the area."[272] Utilizing an "undertaking" rationale, the Kentucky court measured duty by reasonable expectations of metropolitan growth and said that "if the system thus inaugurated proves to be inadequate it must be changed to keep pace with . . . increasing demands."[273] This reasoning was not persuasive to the *Barney* court, however. Besides finding no support in New Jersey law for the creation of a duty, it declared that "too much of the official decision-making process in dealing with such a problem at the various phases of its development was grounded in governmental judgment and discretion to permit the sanction of an imposition of damages for the results of its exercise."[274] In this regard, the court referred to the increasing costs of remedying the sewer problem and, generally, "the competing needs of the city in other directions and its intervening fiscal deterioration."[275]

Limits of discretion as shield. Given the evocations of Newark in the national consciousness, this answer has some bite, but it also is double-edged. Presumably, the local government has the option of prohibiting further development in this kind of situation. As the Kentucky court suggested, there should be no bar to recovery because the "house moved to the sewer."[276] In the practical theory of governmental duty developed here, to deny liability is to permit an evasion of a primary municipal responsibility—one quite as basic, by analogy, as the duty of employers to care for employees who become ill on the job.[277] A clearer view of the problem emerges from the mundane principle that a municipality must compensate for mishaps caused by faulty construction and repair of sewers. Long ago the Supreme Court announced this rule by dictum in a case in which it denied municipal liability on grounds that "judgment and discretion" were exercised in the making of a drainage plan.[278] Given the baseline requirement of this dictum, I would suggest the desirability of a more liberal approach to duty than that taken in *Barney*. In light of the view this study has begun to develop about the nature of public duty, one may doubt both the necessity and the wisdom of drawing sharp lines between default in preparation and carelessness in maneuver—and between judgment in the selection of plans and in their execution. Indeed, the

Barney court itself appends to its decision a foreshadowing of obligation: "[T]he city should be aware that a point could well be reached when continued inattention to serious and progressive injury to private interests might have to be adjudged such an arbitrary failure to act as to compel judicial relief."[279]

Governmental choice and private misfortune. The signal for the future that seems to manifest itself in such language, and which is explicitly suggested by the present analysis, is this: in a world of scarcity, governments cannot evade responsibilities that have come to be regarded as traditional for them; nor may they fall short of the standards that generally have been placed on individuals by private law. When scarcities are such that they must be visited on all equally, the judiciary should not intervene. But when the effect of government decisions, taken deliberately, is to visit disaster on particular households, discretion seems a flimsy immunizer if those decisions are quite analogous to resource choices for which the common law often penalizes private persons. To allow a default of the *Barney* kind to pass unremedied is inefficient. If government creates a situation in which the humdrum routine of normality masks substandard planning for predictable fortuities, citizens must make a major purchase deprived of a clearcut presentation of material facts; and the engine of a free market thus lacks the drive toward alternative housing arrangements that this would exert at the margin of their choice. At the same time, community morale falls because of the disappointment of expectations regarding a service implicitly considered the obligation of the commonwealth. In contrast, to impose liability in this kind of case is to put pressure on decentralized units for rational behavior, both in physical planning and in communication to citizens so that they themselves may plan more rationally. And in broad, normative terms, to hold government responsible is simply to respond to the gathering of power in the public sector, both in resources themselves and in the sole legal ability to direct them in particular channels. Correlatively, when the citizen practically entrusts his security to government, the judiciary becomes the repository and enforcer of that trust.

EDUCATIONAL STANDARDS

Numerous other problems stand at the theoretical frontier of governmental duty. Presently quite at the edge, and involving strongly competing views of legal and social policy, is the question of what role courts should play in the setting of educational standards. Inevitably, as with many other emerging efforts to expand tortlike conceptions, this issue twists in and out of mighty clashes of contending forces in the area of constitutional development—particularly litigations dealing with school financing[280] and those concerned with the overlapping issue of public school integration.[281] But the reduction of the problem to one of allegedly unfulfilled duty for which compensation is sought provides a sharp focus for analysis, which may illuminate larger issues as well as drawing out the implications of the theory developed here.

Hypothetical visions of suits at common law for failure to educate[282] are now attaining reality.[283] Useful as points of departure for examination of the general problem are specific allegations offered in one commentary as possible bases for such a complaint: negligent selection of inappropriate, obsolete, and ineffective instructional materials and procedures; employment of teachers with inadequate certification, experience, or training; and use of inadequate learning environments, including deficiencies in lighting and acoustics.[284] Let us begin *arguendo* from the viewpoint that these allegations present only a complex example of the kind of duty that I have been suggesting should be imposed on governmental units, in areas of activity in which they specialize, which they effectively monopolize, and in which historically they have set standards. In broad terms, suits for deficient education would ask courts to give full recognition to the implications of the conglomeration of power in public school systems, in light of the educational requirements of social success. Certainly, in the case of low-income families, the monopoly element in education is an inescapable fact of life, and the argument for the creation of a duty becomes strengthened by the force of law that compels school attendance. In this sense the case analogizes readily to that of failure to protect children from physical attacks, a category that I have argued should definitely give rise to a duty.[285]

Problems of proof, philosophy, and politics. There are several practical and theoretical hurdles, however, to the attempt to develop the analogue. In a suit for deficient education, one confronts the overall provision of a comprehensive service over a period of years rather than the typical single miscarriage in the exercise of power. In practice, there frequently would be insuperable difficulties in the effort to pinpoint negligent acts or omissions. Moreover, the task of proving causation would often be virtually impossible. The less able the pupil, the more difficult the proof might be, as intuitive generalizations of jurors would be likely to associate aptness with accomplishment. Collaterally, serious normative questions —sometimes of constitutional dimensions—would arise about the propriety of separating students on the basis of intellectual ability, concentrating with the less promising on only the most rudimentary reading and calculating skills and emphasizing low-level vocational training for them from young ages. Moreover, courts would be drawn into complex questions that arise from the multiple missions that parents demand of school systems. Could a high school senior who had exhibited early signs of a genius that went undeveloped sue for inadequate nurture, on a basis comparable to that on which his duller cousin won damages because he read at only fifth-grade level after twelve years of school?[286]

Other broad policy questions would surround any attempt to seek compensation for inadequate education. The fears of Judge Breitel in *Riss* about unpredictable consequences of judicial resource allocation would come to the fore, as would the general argument that the question is one for political resolution of conflicting claims on the fisc. In this regard, litigation involving educational achievement would require much more judicial caution —and would present more difficult problems of financing court-imposed obligations—than would suits for deficient physical protection of children in school corridors or on playgrounds. Here the judgment has more raw political character, and this discussion is proportionally more speculative. There is power in the argument that it is entirely outside the judicial province to effectively require an increase in school tax millages to pay for better instruction, whereas the question of liability for inadequate physical protection of pupils seems clearly within the purview of judges.[287] Yet, although the case has a multilayered complexity compared with the prevention of schoolroom assaults—in some specific cases a matter of some legal difficulty itself—one also should note how it differs from the problem of general failures in police response. By the nature of the individual needs of the student, it differs in the same particularized and poignant way that Ms. Riss's case contrasts with that of the ordinary mugging victim—a distinction which I have suggested should have supported her claim. Indeed, in some respects the claim for seriously substandard education presents a more persuasive case. For in the realm of public education the relationship between commonwealth and citizen arises from an initial compulsion on the side of government; it originates in the implementation of a consensus that the confinement in school walls produces results beneficial for both the individual and society. In Ms. Riss's case, the monopoly was there, and she came begging to it. In the case of deficient education, the monopoly brings the child in, mewing and puking, and kicking if necessary.

Public conception of school. These realities of power provide strong arguments for a broad view of governmental duty, and they are joined by a point that derives from a culturally embedded conception of school, which presents a less obvious but important perspective on the relation of control and dependence between public education and its charges. By widespread agreement, the traditional idea of school has been that it teaches certain fundamental skills and communicates certain basic information. Certification for promotion or graduation strongly implies that these minima have been met. The private school that gave inaccurate certifications of that kind theoretically might open itself to fraud suits. And, at least in theory, perhaps substantially in practice, it would be much at risk from negative advertising by disappointed customers. Because the vulnerability of public schools in this regard is significantly less, force is lent to the argument that a duty exists—by virtue of compulsion, dependence, and general social agreement about institutional role, bolstered by the representation inherent in certifications.[288]

To elaborate an earlier caveat, it is true that proof of culpability would be quite difficult because of the very fact of the suffusion of children's lives with the process of public education. Moreover, to pursue a theoretical vein opened above, school officials could mount a legal defense on communicated disclaimers, collaterally emphasizing financing woes, to undercut a representational theory of action. Or, with respect to cases of serious learning problems, they could base excuses on proof of an incorrigibility that prevented the fulfillment of the educational mission. Generally, as a practical matter, the problem is more likely to be reachable politically. But the seeds of duty are there. Perhaps knowledgeable parents, by parity with administrators fearing litigation, would independently be able to document a record of preventable failures; and the law occasionally might impose liability on their behalf, incidentally producing salutary social by-products. More often, in the case of the parent who is unequipped to understand the deficiencies in the training of an educable child, a requirement of compensation for default on pedagogical obligations would emphasize to the school that it must be prepared to measure up to the general public conception of its role.

Governmental choices and individual deprivations. At a more abstract level, it is well to add some general observations that relate to the broader potential applications of this analysis. Given finite public resources, any existing governmental allocations may be characterized as transfers of wealth that help one person at the expense of another. Yet it is true that in practice it would usually be impractical for a party allegedly deprived by an existing allocation to identify a particular account as one credited with benefits to which he lays claim, and thus impossible to prove in litigation that any particular allocation has caused him injury. Moreover, claims for better minimum levels of public services will meet analogical opposition in authority holding that government need not compensate for the consequences of decisions that impinge on vital individual interests, so long as it is exercising police power. But the fact that arguably deprived individuals cannot identify the pockets which receive the benefits they desire should not mandate a finding that government need do no more, when it has established standards that not only are generally honored but concerning which citizen expectations are well established. And, to reiterate a point made earlier,[289] characterizations of "police power" should not provide facile conceptual bars against the imposition of government obligations, when they are simple analogues of duties already quietly developed on a broad front of the law dealing with misuse and defaults in the use of power.[290]

The trust in government inculcated in individuals with the growth of government's role, and their submission to the exercise of its vast powers, should produce a correlative increase in duty, proportional to citizens' justifiable reliance. Compensation should be required for harm caused by control of power by government officials, including the refusal to take corrective measures in situations in which serious risks apparently outweigh the savings from nonaction, when warnings cannot effectively be brought home to affected persons, and self-help will not suffice to prevent injury. In these situations and also in circumstances beyond the province of formal determinations of economic efficiency, judicially administrable, minimum standards of decency should be imposed on activities in which government is involved and concerning which it has created general expectations of safe conditions or competent service.[291] This is not a plea for further government involvement in social life, but rather an argument for recognition of obligations already undertaken. Figuratively, the disappearance of the frontier[292] has placed us all in the same boat,[293] and, by analogy with the relations on shipboard to which I have occasionally referred, the government has become its master in the fullest metaphorical sense in the areas of our lives where it already has intruded. A twentieth-century view of the duty of government must be matched with its power and its control.

LINKING PUBLIC AND PRIVATE OBLIGATION: POLICE DUTY AND INDIVIDUAL WELFARE

Finally, I shall essay a tentative beginning in the endeavor to close the circle between private and public duties. I shall focus on a homely situation removed from the social tensions of education, the political cross-currents that wash around the provision of municipal services, and the emergent problems and vexing choices involved in the allocation of medical care. The vehicle is a case[294] in which a police officer failed to make good on his promise to an injured motorcyclist to get the name and number of the driver who hit him. The plaintiff claimed that while he was lying on the ground in pain he asked the policeman to get the information, and that the officer said, "All right, don't worry about anything. . . . I'll take care of everything." Although the plaintiff then observed the policeman talking with the driver, the officer did not get the information. Replicating a taxi passenger's earlier effort to recover for default on a private duty to act,[295] the cyclist sought damages on the ground that the police officer's failure had precluded his institution of a negligence action. But, echoing the Pennsylvania Supreme Court in the taxi case, New York's answer was negative. The appellate division, which wrote the only full opinion,[296] relied on *Riss* and the *Motyka* case,[297] which dealt with a failure to follow up on correcting a dangerous condition. In familiar language, the court declared that the city had no duty of care to particular persons or classes situated like the plaintiff.

Power, public role, and trust. This seems too stiff an approach to the administration of justice. I have rehearsed previously the reasons for imposing liability on private parties in comparable situations. And when a public servant defaults in the execution of a task so easily within his ability and so well within his general role, it would seem that the argument for liability is even stronger. In the case described, this is so given the relationship of power and dependence that existed not only in fact, but practically in law. The literal physical helplessness of the plaintiff makes the case more legally compelling for governmental obligation, as well as more emotively appealing. The policeman's informal promise sets up a relationship of trust in words as well as circumstances. To say that his municipal employer owes no duty to this particular citizen is to deny the most basic tort principles requiring aid from superior parties in sharply defined relationships. It is true that one may conceive situations so frantic that a well-trained officer might reasonably fail to get the data that policemen usually acquire on such occasions.[298] But the opportunity to secure the necessary information in these circumstances argues strongly against dismissal of these allegations. An alternate basis for demurrer to such an action would be to characterize it as a claim for "economic loss,"[299] but this would meet quite as strong an objection under the view offered here of governmental obligation. Granting that loss of a chance to maintain a personal injury action does not involve facts as desperate as those in a claim for failure to provide emergency medical care, the case still involves weighty considerations of welfare as well as justice. It is especially galling, as well as ironic, to deny compensation when a government default leads to an inability to use the legal process.

Summary

This study has surveyed issues of government obligation in a number of areas of social activity, principally from a perspective of tort duty theory with particular attention to the duty to act; it also has summoned analogies from neighboring areas of the law, in particular from civil rights litigation. I have presented the idea that it is useful to view duty as arising from the possession of energy, ability, and information. From this perspective, I have noted how elements of situational control and dependence appear as crucial factors both in decided cases and with respect to hypothesized claims for legal relief, sometimes expressly and often implicitly. The development of this analysis has led me to suggest that a more satisfactory theory of governmental duty might evolve from increased attention to these and associated elements of citizen trust and reliance on the commonwealth. This almost fiduciary approach to governmental obligation has some bases in the goal of increasing the measurable social product; but often its predominant rationale is one of justice, with an associated emphasis on a fostering of morale that is traceable to efficiency considerations only at a most theoretical level of utilitarianism. It is important to note that the coincidence of several of the elements mentioned here will not necessarily call forth judicial impositions of obligation. In some areas of the greatest social tension and economic conflict, considerations of policy and polity would make judicial action ultimately counterproductive and thus ill-advised. But I have offered a twofold approach: First, I have argued that, with Brandeis, judges must let their minds be bold. And, second, in areas where judicial activism would outrun the boldest reason, I have tried to provide a point of departure for further discussion of legislative agendas that thrust toward a juster society.

Notes

INTRODUCTION

1. Heaven v. Pender, 11 Q.B.D. 503, 509 (1883) (Brett, M.R.).
2. Palsgraf v. Long Island R. Co., 248 N.Y. 339, 344, 162 N.E. 99, 100, 59 A.L.R. 1253, 1256–1257 (1928).
3. Green, The Duty Problem in Negligence Cases (pts. 1–2), 28 Colum. L. Rev. 1014, 29 Colum. L. Rev. 255 (1929).
4. I. de S. et ux. v. W. de S., Y.B., Lib. Assis. f.99, pl. 60 (1348).
5. *Cf.* High Voltage Engineering Corp. v. Pierce, 359 F.2d 33, 21 A.L.R.3d 1345 (10th Cir. 1966).
6. This is Cardozo's phrase in a fraud case, Ultramares v. Touche, Niven and Co., 255 N.Y. 170, 181, 174 N.E. 441, 445, 74 A.L.R. 1139, 1146 (1931).
7. Shapo, A Representational Theory of Consumer Protection: Doctrine, Function and Legal Liability for Product Disappointment, 60 Va. L. Rev. 1109 (1974).
8. *See, e.g.,* Crisci v. Security Ins. Co., 66 Cal. 2d 425, 426 P.2d 173, 58 Cal. Rptr. 13 (1967).
9. *See, e.g.,* Pino v. Trans-Atlantic Marine, 348 Mass. 498, 265 N.E.2d 583 (1970), L'Orange v. Medical Protective Co., 394 F.2d 57 (6th Cir. 1968).
10. See, most comprehensively, G. Calabresi, The Costs of Accidents (1970). For later elaboration, see Calabresi & Hirschoff, Toward a Test for Strict Liability in Torts, 81 Yale L.J. 1055 (1972). *See also* Calabresi & Melamed, Property Rules, Liability Rules and Inalienability: One View of the Cathedral, 85 Harv. L. Rev. 1089 (1972).
11. *See* Calabresi & Hirschoff, *supra* note 10.
12. Coase, The Problem of Social Cost, 3 J. L. & Econ. 1 (1960).
13. Posner, A Theory of Negligence, 1 J. Leg. Studies 29 (1973). *See also* Posner, Strict Liability: A Comment, 2 J. Leg. Studies 205 (1973).
14. Fletcher, Fairness & Utility in Tort Theory, 85 Harv. L. Rev. 537 (1972).
15. See especially Epstein, A Theory of Strict Liability, 2 J. Leg. Studies 151 (1973).
16. *Compare* Calabresi & Hirschoff, *supra* note 10, *with* Epstein, *supra* note 15; and *compare* Restatement (Second) of Torts § 402A (1965) *with* Restatement (Second) of Torts §§ 519–520 (Tent. Draft No. 10, 1964).
17. *See, e.g.,* Calabresi, The Decision for Accidents: An Approach to Non-fault Allocation of Costs, 78 Harv. L. Rev. 713 (1965).
18. Laurence Eldredge, in Restatement (Second) of Torts, Notes to § 893, at 73–74 (Tent. Draft No. 9, 1963).

19. State v. Massey, 229 N.C. 734, 51 S.E.2d 179 (1949), *appeal dismissed,*
    sub nom. Bunn v. North Carolina, 336 U.S. 942 (1949).
20. Bisenius v. Karns, 42 Wis. 2d 42, 165 N.W.2d 377 (1969), *appeal dis-*
    missed, 395 U.S. 709 (1969).
21. Thomas v. Housing Authority of City of Bremerton, 71 Wash. 2d 69,
    426 P.2d 836 (1967).
22. Henningsen v. Bloomfield Motors, 32 N.J. 358, 161 A.2d 69, 75
    A.L.R.2d 1 (1960).
23. Horne v. Patton, 291 Ala. 701, 287 So. 2d 824 (1973).
24. *Id.*

PART ONE: PRIVATE DUTIES TO ACT

1. *Cf.* Snyder, Liability for Negative Conduct, 35 Va. L. Rev. 446, 456–467
   (1949), on "mixed acts."
2. I diverge here somewhat from classifications that other analysts of the
   problem have used. For example, Honoré divides his categories by
   cases involving "professionals" and quasi-professionals, those involving "special ties," and those involving no professional obligation or "special links" at all. Honoré, Law, Morals and Rescue in The
   Good Samaritan & the Law 225, 230–231 (J. Ratcliffe, ed. 1966). As
   will appear, I suggest that each category of relation deserves a separate analysis based on the particular factors that distinguish it. Thus,
   the fact that a case involved a professional will often be a crucial
   factor, but given the rather fluid movement of concepts of profes-
   sionalism across occupational lines, I do not think that the classification "professionals" should be set off from other categories that
   involve "special ties."
3. 132 N.J.L. 331, 40 A.2d 562 (1945).
4. 131 N.J.L. 238, 239, 36 A.2d 8, 9 (1944).
5. 132 N.J.L. at 332, 333, 40 A.2d at 563.
6. 287 U.S. 367 (1932).
7. *Id.* at 372.
8. *Id.* at 377.
9. *See, e.g.,* the elliptical reference by Epstein, in A Theory of Strict Liability, 2 J. Leg. Studies 151, 168 n.48 (1973), to Green, Foreseeability in
   Negligence Law, 61 Colum. L. Rev. 1401, 1412 (1961).
10. For illustrative examples of these problems, see M. Shapo, Tort and
    Compensation Law 500–524 (1976).
11. *Cf.* G. Calabresi, The Costs of Accidents 55–57 (1970).
12. *Cf.* the reference to the requirement that sailors be "treated with, at
    least, decent humanity," in Rice v. Polly & Kitty, 20 Fed. Cas. 666
    (D. Pa. 1789), for which I am grateful to Stephen Presser.
13. Central Gulf S.S. Corp. v. Sambula, 405 F.2d 291, 16 A.L.R.F. 70
    (5th Cir. 1968). By analogy, the failure of a vessel to have rudimen-

tary radio communication devices supports a finding of "unseaworthiness and negligence" in favor of an injured seaman who suffered prolonged pain without sedation. Stevens v. Seacoast Co., 414 F.2d 1032 (5th Cir. 1969).

14. MacQueen v. Nat'l Gypsum Co., 287 F. Supp. 778, 782 (E.D. Mich. 1968).

15. Dantzler v. Defender Shipping Co., 285 F. Supp. 541 (E.D. Pa. 1968), *aff'd*, 411 F.2d 792 (3d Cir. 1969).

16. As confirmation that the key question revolves around the master's duty rather than technical classifications of tort theory, it may be noted that the plaintiff in *Dantzler, supra*, pleaded only negligence and not false imprisonment.

17. *Compare Dantzler, supra* note 15, in which the court emphasizes that "negligence was the only theory of liability presented to the jury," *with Cortes, supra* note 6 (characterizing issue as "whether death resulting from the negligent omission to furnish care or cure is death from personal injury" under the Jones Act), *and* Central Gulf S.S. Corp. v. Sambula, *supra* note 13 (summarizing maintenance and cure doctrine in its discussion of Jones Act claim).

18. Indeed, the foreman testified that he did not want Szabo to walk to the tool shed in the heat, so he got an employee who had a car to take him to his residence. *See* 131 N.J.L. at 239, 36 A.2d at 9.

19. I exclude from this discussion the situation in which the job by definition is linked tightly to exceptional risk, as in the case of stunt riding.

20. *See* 131 N.J.L. at 239, 36 A.2d at 9.

21. Compare Fried, The Value of Life, 82 Harv. L. Rev. 1415 (1969).

22. Epigrammatically, it may be said that *Szabo* concerns misdirection of power rather than abuse of it, and the approach the law takes to this difficult case should signal directions for legal response to less responsible manipulations.

23. *Cf.* Budd v. Erie Lackawanna R.R., 93 N.J. Super. 166, 225 A.2d 171 (1966), *aff'd*, 98 N.J. Super. 47, 236 A.2d 143 (1967) (railroad union contract saying that employees who become ill "shall be given medical treatment as soon as possible," held admissible in FELA action as relevant to issue of negligence, in a decision that poses the question of whether the employer fulfilled its duty "to render medical aid under the 'humane instincts' doctrine" of *Szabo*).

24. Waldron v. Moore-McCormack Lines, 386 U.S. 724 (1967).

25. *Id.* at 727, 728.

26. *See* Fields v. Burlison Packing Co., 405 S.W.2d 105 (Tex. Civ. App. 1966) (upholding defendant's verdict against female employee who did not request assistance, but citing the general rule that employer must furnish "an adequate force of competent workmen").

27. Wohlgemuth v. Meyer, 139 Cal. App. 2d 326, 293 P.2d 816 (1956).

28. *See generally* Shapo, A Representational Theory of Consumer Protec-

tion: Doctrine, Function and Legal Liability for Product Disappointment, 60 Va. L. Rev. 1109 (1974) [hereinafter cited as Shapo, "Representational Theory"]. The court in *Wohlgemuth, supra* note 27, declares that "[w]ithholding information would in a sense amount to misrepresentation," and says that the patient "is entitled to rely on the doctor's assurances." 139 Cal. App. 2d at 331, 293 P.2d at 820.

29. Lopez v. Swyer, 115 N.J. Super. 237, 279 A.2d 116 (1971), *modified*, 62 N.J. 267, 300 A.2d 563 (1973).

30. 115 N.J. Super. at 251, 279 A.2d at 124.

31. Symbolic of the problems in uncovering evidence of medical malpractice is the testimony of this plaintiff about her accidental discovery of how her case came to be a cause célèbre in the local medical community. After being shown to a group of surgeons while in the hospital, she heard through an open door the statement, "And there you see, gentlemen, what happens when the radiologist puts a patient on the table and goes out and has a cup of coffee." *Id*. at 245, 279 A.2d at 120–121.

32. Hofmann v. Blackmon, 241 So. 2d 752, 753 (Fla. App. 1970), *cert. denied*, 245 So. 2d 257 (1971). *Cf.* Hungerford v. United States, 307 F.2d 99 (9th Cir. 1962) (communicated misdiagnosis as "misrepresentation" under Federal Tort Claims Act exclusion, but court holds that there was also independent negligence, not excluded by FTCA, in examination and diagnostic tests).

33. 8 Cal. 3d 551, 105 Cal. Rptr. 358, 503 P.2d 1366 (1972).

34. *Cf.* Betesh v. United States, 400 F. Supp. 238 (D. D.C. 1974) (failure of Selective Service physicians to advise plaintiff of abnormal X-ray; liability based on both army regulation and several common law formulas). *See also* Patterson v. Norfolk & W. Ry. Co., 489 F.2d 303 (6th Cir. 1973) (failure to discover tuberculosis in plaintiff's fellow employee, who had exhibited signs of the illness for a considerable time); Derrick v. Ontario Community Hosp., 47 Cal. App. 3d 145, 120 Cal. Rptr. 566 (1975) (duty based in statute, though not common law, to report contagious disease afflicting third party, which was communicated to plaintiff).

35. Williams v. City of Baton Rouge, 252 La. 770, 214 So. 2d 138 (1968).

36. *Id*. at 782, 214 So. 2d at 143.

37. *See* Murray v. Boston & Me. R.R., 107 N.H. 367, 224 A.2d 66 (1966) (affirming jury verdict against woman who claimed violation of duty to help her onto train, with argument by dissenter that instruction on applicability of company rule requiring assistance in boarding was diluted by emphasis on whether necessity was subjectively apparent to employees).

38. 437 Pa. 509, 264 A.2d 373 (1970).

39. The first report of the case appears in 260 A.2d 759 (1970), and the opinions are identical to those in the report cited in note 38 *supra*, except that in the earlier volume the opinion of Justice Jones appears first, and the opinion of Justice Cohen appears second and is listed

as a concurrence. The only differences in language are changes conforming to the new order of the opinions.

40. A fact question could be raised, however, about whether the cab driver's act in getting out to talk to the colliding motorist effectively created the impression in the plaintiff that he would secure the information usually acquired in such conversations.

41. *See* Tubbs v. Argus, 140 Ind. App. 695, 225 N.E.2d 841, 33 A.L.R.3d 295 (1967).

42. Traudt v. City of Chicago, 98 Ill. App. 2d 417, 240 N.E.2d 188, 34 A.L.R.3d 1440 (1968); Bishop v. City of Chicago, 121 Ill. App. 2d 33, 257 N.E.2d 152 (1970).

43. *Traudt, supra* note 42.

44. *Bishop, supra* note 42.

45. *See Bishop, supra* note 42, 121 Ill. App. 2d at 38, 35–36, 257 N.E.2d at 154, 153.

46. *See Bishop, supra* note 42, 121 Ill. App. 2d at 38, 35–36, 257 N.E.2d at 154, 153.

47. *See Bishop, supra* note 42, 121 Ill. App. 2d at 38, 257 N.E.2d at 154.

48. *See Bishop, supra* note 42, 121 Ill. App. 2d at 35, 257 N.E.2d at 154.

49. After writing this paragraph, I came upon a decision in a case involving the negligence of air traffic controllers that gives powerful emphasis to the "control of the controllers." *See* the passage following Roman numeral II in Yates v. United States, 497 F.2d 878, 882–883 (10th Cir. 1974).

50. L.S. Ayres & Co. v. Hicks, 220 Ind. 86, 40 N.E.2d 334 (1942).

51. Lee v. Peerless Ins. Co., 175 So. 2d 381 (La. App. 1965), *aff'd*, 248 La. 982, 183 So. 2d 328 (1966).

52. 175 So. 2d at 384. The Louisiana Supreme Court, affirming, approved the idea that the "proximate cause" of the injury was "the act of the purchaser in drinking the liquor" and rejected the argument that a statute prohibiting sale of alcoholic beverages to intoxicated persons abrogated the defense of contributory negligence. *See* 248 La. 982, 987–994, 183 So. 2d 328, 330–332.

53. 175 So. 2d at 385.

54. *See* the dissenting opinion of Sanders, J., in the Supreme Court decision, 248 La. at 1015–1017, 183 So. 2d at 340, using a "last clear chance" concept. For an imposition of duty, *see* Black v. N.Y., N.H. & H. R. Co., 193 Mass. 448, 79 N.E. 797 (1907). *See also* Slavitt v. Kauhi, 384 F.2d 530 (9th Cir. 1967) (duty of care imposed by affirmative action of leading a patron to the head of a stairs, knowing of his intoxication).

55. *See* Guss v. Jack Tar Management Co., 407 F.2d 859 (5th Cir. 1969).

56. The opinion is *per curiam* and sketchy concerning the facts.

57. *Cf.* text with note 123 *infra*.

58. Mick v. Kroger Co., 37 Ill. 2d 148, 224 N.E.2d 859, 21 A.L.R.3d 926 (1967).

59. The plaintiff complainingly shouldered a package that she said she felt

was too heavy for her, and carried it outside. The injury occurred after she had rested the bag on a car while waiting for her husband's return, on which occasion she picked up the bag and fell when she stepped off the sidewalk.

60. *Cf.* Shapo, "Representational Theory," *supra* note 28, 60 Va. L. Rev., *e.g.* at 1304.

61. 397 Pa. 316, 155 A.2d 343 (1959).

62. There is established precedent that one whose conduct contributes to placing another in an endangered and powerless position has a duty to do what he can to help the other. A gory Texas case makes this clear, both as an obligation under a statute that requires drivers involved in accidents to render reasonable assistance to injured persons and as a matter of common law. In this case the defendant's employee, operating a large piece of road machinery, collided with the car of the plaintiff's decedent. Despite his knowledge that the plaintiff's decedent was suffocating from his own blood, accented by the pleas of others at the scene, the operator refused to move his machine on the grounds that he could not do it until law enforcement officers came or his foreman told him to move it. Rains v. Heldenfels Brothers, 443 S.W.2d 280 (Tex. Civ. App. 1969).

63. *See* Tubbs v. Argus, *supra* note 41.

64. *See, e.g.,* Schwartz v. Helms Bakery Ltd., 67 Cal. 2d 232, 60 Cal. Rptr. 510, 430 P.2d 68 (1967).

65. Seavey, I Am Not My Guest's Keeper, 13 Vand. L. Rev. 699, 702 (1960).

66. Restatement (Second) of Torts § 339 (1965).

67. Pridgen v. Boston Housing Authority, 364 Mass. 696, 711, 308 N.E.2d 467, 476, 70 A.L.R.3d 1106, 1118 (1974).

68. Appling v. Stuck, 164 N.W.2d 810, 814 (Iowa 1969).

69. McClure v. United States Lines Co., 247 F. Supp. 272 (E.D. Va. 1964).

70. *Id.,* 368 F.2d 197, 67 Marit. Cas. 948 (4th Cir. 1966).

71. There seems an implicit recognition of this point in Brennan v. Matson Navigation Co., 345 F. Supp. 1179 (N.D. Calif. 1972), allowing a negligence award for a ship's failure to have a safety net, which would have cushioned the fall of a sailor who was trying to help a drunken crew member up the gangway.

72. See note 78 *infra* and accompanying text.

73. *See* Maltman v. Sauer, 84 Wash. 2d 975, 979, 530 P.2d 254, 257 (1975).

74. D.O.T. News–Fed. R.R. Admin. Release FRA-1172 (March 31, 1972).

75. Grigsby v. Coastal Marine Service of Texas, Inc., 412 F.2d 1011, 1021–1022 (5th Cir. 1969), *cert. denied,* 396 U.S. 1033 (1970).

76. *Cf.* Theodories v. Hercules Navigation Co., 448 F.2d 701, 704 n.8 (5th Cir. 1971), questioning on assumed facts whether an injury allegedly caused by lack of good lighting was the "proximate cause" of the heart attack death of a rescuer maneuvering "on a well-lighted main deck."

77. *See* Grigsby, *supra* note 75, 412 F.2d at 1021.

78. However, Britt v. Magnum, 261 N.C. 250, 134 S.E.2d 235, 4 A.L.R.3d

551 (1964), allowing recovery against a rescued person who negligently endangered herself, says that it makes no difference whether the defendant is the rescued person or a third party. *But cf.* Saylor v. Parsons, 122 Iowa 679, 98 N.W. 500 (1904) (no liability against rescued person, who even if he was careless was not negligent "as to" the plaintiff).

79. *See* Dawson, Rewards for the Rescue of Human Life? in The Good Samaritan & The Law 63, 73–74 (J. Ratcliffe, ed. 1966) (citing German decision holding that rescuer had managed the "affair" of both rescued person and her husband, that his action conformed to the interest and [possible] will of both, and that both were therefore jointly liable to reimburse for the rescuer's "expenditure"). *Cf. id.* at 86 (citing "dilemma" that, although as claim of rescuer or dependents appears more appealing the greater the rescuer's sacrifice, it becomes the more unjust in the same degree to put the whole loss on a victim who was not at fault).

80. *See, e.g.,* 15 How. L.J. 672, 676–681 (1969).

81. *See id.*

82. *See* Holland, The Good Samaritan Laws: A Reappraisal, 16 J. Pub. L. 128, 134 (1967).

83. *See id.* at 132–134.

84. Presumably such statutes would not excuse one whose efforts to aid another created an increased probability of harm to third persons. *Cf., e.g.,* Cuppy v. Bunch, 214 N.W.2d 786 (S.D. 1974), refusing to impose liability on an auto driver who was leading the auto of a "hung over" friend, but emphasizing that the lead driver was not exercising and was not shown to be capable of exercising control over his friend, and that there was no showing that he "undertook to assist" him.

85. Lee v. State, 490 P.2d 1206 (Alaska 1971).

86. *See generally* Shapo, "Representational Theory," *supra* note 28.

87. *Cf.* Henningsen v. Bloomfield Motors, 32 N.J. 258, 161 A.2d 69, 75 A.L.R.2d 1 (1960).

88. *See, e.g.,* Kassarjian & Cohen, Cognitive Dissonance and Consumer Behavior, 8 Calif. Mgt. Rev. No. 1 at 55 (1965).

89. *See* Ward v. Morehead City Sea Food Co., 171 N.C. 33, 87 S.E. 958 (1916) (defendant wrote letters to warn of fish that were making people sick, instead of sending telegrams, which might have averted death of plaintiff's decedent).

90. *See, e.g.,* 15 U.S.C. § 1411 (1976), providing for notification to auto purchasers of safety-related defects. Exemplary of the problem, in the case of automobile recalls, is the question of whether a manufacturer must respond in tort for accidents that happen during protracted negotiations with the National Highway and Traffic Safety Administration over whether the firm must issue a public warning. A seedbed example appears in the saga of defective motor mounts on a number of General Motors cars. An investigation by the

NHTSA went on for more than a year before the agency issued a "Consumer Protection Bulletin," alerting motorists to "specific use risks in connection with the highway operation of certain General Motors Corporation vehicles which may be subject to front engine mount failure, and *inviting reports from motorists who experience such failures.*" GM finally recalled 6,686,000 Chevrolets because of the motor mount problem, after it became evident that the Department of Transportation was ready to rule that the vehicles had a "safety-related defect." *See* Irvin, "Chevy Engine-Mount Complaints Rise," Wash. Post, Oct. 12, 1971, at D9; NHTSA Consumer Protection Bulletin No. 2-71 (D.O.T. News, Oct. 15, 1971); Mintz, "GM Recalls 6.6 Million Chevrolets," Wash. Post, Dec. 5, 1971, at A1. For an analogue in the area of prescription drugs, *see, e.g.,* Roginsky v. Richardson-Merrell, 378 F.2d 832 (2d Cir. 1967), with its report of fierce defensive tactics by a manufacturer under FDA pressure as news mounted of serious side effects.

91. Bryant v. International Union, U.M.W. of America, 467 F.2d 1 (6th Cir. 1972), *cert. denied,* 410 U.S. 930 (1973).

92. Burgess v. Charlottesville Savings & Loan Ass'n, 349 F. Supp. 133 (W.D. Va. 1972).

93. The appellate court found that these common law theories predominated and that a pleading under the Truth in Lending Act was unfounded and thus remanded to the state court. Burgess v. Charlottesville S & L Ass'n, 477 F.2d 40 (4th Cir. 1973). The discussion here is unconcerned with this problem of jurisdiction, but rather focuses on the case from the point of view of state substantive law.

94. 349 F. Supp. at 137.

95. McCune v. Grimaldi Buick-Opel Inc., 45 Mich. App. 472, 206 N.W.2d 742 (1973).

96. *Id.* at 475, 206 N.W.2d at 743. *See also* Scheuer v. Central States Pension Fund, 394 F. Supp. 193 (E.D. Wis. 1975) (reasonable for plaintiff to believe that union representative could promise pension coverage because of "the manner of defendant's administration of the fund").

97. *Cf.* Tcherepnin v. Franz, 393 F. Supp. 1197 (N.D. Ill. 1975), for an articulated emphasis on fiduciary obligation to act, in a case involving the failure of the director of a state department of financial institutions to investigate a collapsing savings and loan association and his acquiescence in fraudulent representations.

98. International Terminal Operating Co. v. N.V. Nederl. Amerik Stoomv. Maats., 393 U.S. 74, 75 (1968).

99. *See, e.g.,* McCrossin v. Hicks Chevrolet, Inc., 248 A.2d 917 (D.C. App. 1969). *See also* Anthony v. General Motors Corp., 33 Cal. App. 3d 699, 109 Cal. Rptr. 254 (1973), and background in Keeton and Shapo, Products and the Consumer: Defective and Dangerous Products 635–636 (1970).

100. *See* Lacey v. United States, 98 F. Supp. 219, 220 (D. Mass. 1951) (dictum).

101. Schwartz v. Helms Bakery Ltd., 67 Cal. 2d 232, 60 Cal. Rptr. 510, 430 P.2d 68 (1967).
102. *Cf.* Mendoza v. White Stores, 488 P.2d 90 (Colo. App. 1971) (once one takes charge of a blind pedestrian, there is a duty to exercise reasonable care in guiding him, but this was not breached with respect to the possibility that the blind man would fall on a flat piece of cardboard lying on the sidewalk 25 to 40 feet from where defendant's employee released him).
103. Nelson v. Union Wire Rope Corp., 31 Ill. 2d 69, 199 N.E.2d 769 (1964).
104. *Cf.* Bahamas Agr. Indus. Ltd. v. Riley Stoker Corp. 526 F.2d 1174 (6th Cir. 1975) (duty of service representative, monitoring boiler controls, is not fulfilled by "idly standing by" while knowing of conditions that could lead to an explosion).
105. An index to the seriousness with which potential liability of this kind is taken is the articulation of concern about litigation against safety engineers, industrial officials, and others connected with the field of occupational safety and health. *See, e.g.,* Safety Professionals' Liability Increasing, Hygienists Are Told, 5 OSHR 1833 (1976); Safety Professionals May Be Sued, Krikorian Tells ASSE Washington Meeting, 4 OSHR 564 (1974). *See also* Amer. Ass'n for Advancement of Science, *Scientific Freedom and Responsibility* 29 (1975), criticizing "abdication" by industrial physicians reportedly opposing upgraded standards of health protection.
106. Stacy v. Aetna Casualty & Surety Co., 484 F.2d 289 (5th Cir. 1973).
107. Mann v. Highlands Ins. Co., 461 F.2d 541, 543 (5th Cir. 1972).
108. Johnson v. Aetna Casualty & Surety Co., 339 F. Supp. 1178 (M.D. Fla. 1972).
109. Johnson v. Aetna Cas. & Surety Co., 348 F. Supp. 627 (M.D. Fla. 1972).
110. *See supra,* text preceding note 103.
111. 338 F. Supp. 999 (S.D. N.Y. 1972), *aff'd,* 478 F.2d 235 (2d Cir. 1973).
112. *See generally* the authorities collected at Keeton and Shapo, Products and the Consumer: Defective and Dangerous Products 518–525 (1970).
113. *Cf.* Great American Ins. Co. v. Bureau Veritas, 388 F. Supp. at 1013, citing precedent.
114. Mogabgab v. Orleans Parish School Board, 239 So. 2d 456 (La. App. 1970), *writ refused,* 256 La. 1152, 241 So. 2d 253 (1970).
115. *See* 239 So. 2d at 459.
116. Randolph v. Arizona Board of Regents, 19 Ariz. App. 121, 123, 505 P.2d 559, 561 (1973), *cert. denied,* 414 U.S. 863 (1973).
117. Hegel v. Langsam, 29 Ohio Misc. 147, 55 Ohio Op. 2d 476, 477, 273 N.E.2d 351, 352 (1971).
118. *Cf., e.g.,* Schultz v. Gould Academy, 332 A.2d 368 (Me. 1975) (dereliction of dormitory watchman at boarding school in following up on evidence of intruder; court refers to academy's "dual role of teacher and family to its students").
119. It may be noted that a strictly economic analysis presumably would

reach the result of compensating the student in the Valley Fever case only if the printing of a cautionary entry would be cheaper than the costs of the illness. In this connection, it should be pointed out that from the standpoint of acquiring information the position of the student is completely disadvantaged–the problem is one whose existence he apparently did not even know about and therefore he could not even formulate the relevant question. This is a profile common to many tort cases, and this reference is not limited to this application. In such cases the characterization of the problem as one involving information costs is perhaps not as meaningful as one that emphasizes the factor of control over the circumstances of life. In any event, under the point of view advanced here, even if it would be more costly to print the warning, the law might justly require compensation if this were not done. This is so because of not only the university's advertising and recruiting but also the control inherent in its status as an institution catering to young persons.

120. 150 Mich. 206, 113 N.W. 1128 (1907).
121. *See* text with note 35 *supra.*
122. *But cf.* Lancaster v. Montesi, 216 Tenn. 50, 390 S.W.2d 217 (1965) ("proximate cause" of suicide of woman, sadistically treated by man with whom she had illicit relationship, as her "voluntary and free act").
123. Nordmann v. National Hotel Co., 425 F.2d 1103 (5th Cir. 1970).
124. *See* Kline v. 1500 Mass. Ave. Apt. Corp., 439 F.2d 477, 43 A.L.R.3d 311 (D.C. Cir. 1970) (apartment management reduced number of personnel in security jobs, despite increasing crime perpetrated on tenants). Of particular interest is a passage in which the court declares that "the most analogous relationship to that of the modern day urban apartment house dweller is not that of a landlord and tenant, but that of innkeeper and guest." *Id.* at 485. An analogous recent holding appears in Samson v. Saginaw Professional Building, Inc., 393 Mich. 393, 224 N.W.2d 843 (1975) (landlord's negligence in protecting persons in common area of its building from assaults by visitors to mental clinic to which it leased space).
125. La Sota v. Philadelphia Transp. Co., 421 Pa. 386, 219 A.2d 296 (1966).
126. F.W. Woolworth v. Kirby, 293 Ala. 248, 302 So. 2d 67 (1974).
127. Stark v. Penn Central Co., 32 App. Div. 2d 910, 302 N.Y.S.2d 38 (1969), *aff'd without opin.,* 26 N.Y.2d 761, 309 N.Y.S.2d 203, 257 N.E.2d 651 (1970).
128. 32 App. Div. 2d at 911, 302 N.Y.S.2d at 38–39 (Steuer, J., dissenting).
129. Goggin v. New State Ballroom, 355 Mass. 718, 719, 247 N.E.2d 350, 351 (1969).
130. Lillie v. Thompson, 332 U.S. 459, 461–462 (1947).
131. McCann v. Smith, 370 F.2d 323 (2d Cir. 1966).
132. Hartel v. Long Island R.R. Co., 476 F.2d 462, 466 (2nd Cir. 1973), *cert. denied,* 414 U.S. 980 (1973). *Cf.* Comer v. Texaco Inc., 514 F.2d 1243

(5th Cir. 1975) (employee who knew the gas station where he worked was in a high crime area "was free to quit").

133. 476 F.2d at 464.

134. 414 U.S. at 982 (Douglas, J., dissenting).

135. *Cf.* Bryant v. United Mine Workers, summarized *supra* text with note 91.

136. Martin v. Erie-Lackawanna R.R. Co., 388 F.2d 802 (6th Cir. 1968).

137. 8 Ill. App. 3d 140, 146, 289 N.E.2d 218, 222 (1972).

138. 56 Ill. 2d 95, 306 N.E.2d 39 (1973). *Cf.* Nigido v. First Nat'l Bank of Baltimore, 264 Md. 702, 288 A.2d 127, 51 A.L.R.3d 704 (1972) (failure to provide armed guards may be good judgment rather than negligence, given that their presence might tend to provoke gunplay). *See also* Laidlaw v. Sage, 158 N.Y. 73, 52 N.E. 679 (1899).

139. *See* Helms v. Harris, 281 S.W.2d 770 (Tex. Civ. App. 1955). *But cf.* Kelly v. Kroger Co., 484 F.2d 1362 (10th Cir. 1973).

140. The plaintiff alternatively complained that the defendant had negligently failed to inform its customers that it had a policy to defend its money even at that price. *See* 8 Ill. App. 3d at 143, 289 N.E.2d at 220.

141. *Cf. Helms, supra* note 139, in which the court in a dictum on the problem of the merchant grappling with the bandit articulates a requirement of "unreasonable risk of grave harm to innocent third persons" as a standard for recovery. 281 S.W.2d at 773.

142. *See* G. Calabresi, The Costs of Accidents 56–57 (1970).

143. Smith v. 601 Liquors, 101 Ill. App. 2d 306, 243 N.E.2d 367 (1968).

144. Gorby v. Yeomans, 4 Mich. App. 339, 144 N.W.2d 837 (1966).

145. Sparks v. Ober, 192 So. 2d 81 (Fla. App. 1966).

146. The list ranged from "call the police" and "warn patrons . . . of the impending affray" to "conduct the patrons to a place of safety" and "comply with Florida statutes and applicable ordinances prohibiting dueling, public affrays, and use of deadly weapons." *Id.* at 82.

147. *See* Overocker v. Retoff, 93 Ill. App. 2d 11, 16, 234 N.E.2d 820, 822 (1968), imposing liability under the liberally interpreted Illinois Dram Shop Act.

148. *See* Morris, Compensation & the Good Samaritan, in The Good Samaritan & the Law 135, 137 (J. Ratcliffe, ed. 1966).

149. *See* Lindsay v. Hartog, 76 N.M. 122, 412 P.2d 552 (1966).

150. *Cf., e.g.,* Jacobsma v. Goldberg's Fashion Forum, 14 Ill. App. 3d 710, 303 N.E.2d 226 (1973) (store manager's apparent signaled request to plaintiff customer to stop fleeing shoplifter, known for previous theft attempts).

151. *Cf.* McNiece and Thornton, Affirmative Duties in Torts, 58 Yale L.J. 1272 (1949), viewing the "binding thread" in the imposition of duties to act as a "benefit principle." For these authors, the law imposes affirmative duties only when "the one under a duty to act has voluntarily brought himself into a certain relationship with others from

which he obtains or expects benefits." *Id.* at 1282–1283. In their
view, the question of whether there is a benefit draws "the basic
distinction between moral and legal duty." *Id.* at 1287.

152. Mike v. Lebanon Miridites League, 421 Pa. 217, 220, 218 A.2d 814,
815 (1966).

153. *See* summary in Dawson, *Negotiorum Gestio*: The Altruistic Inter-
meddler (pt. 2), 74 Harv. L. Rev. 1073, 1099–1100 (1961).

154. *See, e.g.,* Overocker, *supra* note 147.

155. Of course, it might be argued that an obligation arises from the suppo-
sition that if the question had surfaced explicitly the owner would
have offered compensation in advance of the attack. *Cf.* Dawson,
Rewards for the Rescue of Human Life? in The Good Samaritan &
the Law 65, 73–74 (J. Ratcliffe, ed. 1966) (summarizing German decision that concludes that rescuer's deed conformed to the interest
and possible will of the rescued person and her husband).

156. Taylor v. Centennial Bowl, Inc., 65 Cal. 2d 114, 123, 52 Cal. Rptr. 561,
567, 416 P.2d 793, 799 (1966).

157. Boss v. Prince's Drive-Ins, 401 S.W.2d 140 (Tex. Civ. App. 1966).

158. *Id.* at 142.

159. As I shall subsequently argue, the possession of a license to practice
medicine would appear to place analogous obligations upon physicians whose patients appear to be dangerous to others. *See* text with
note 179 *infra*.

160. An intriguing analogy in a rather quirky case appears in a libel action
by a person who felt defamed by graffiti on an exterior wall and sued
the owner of the wall for failure to remove the offending words. The
court gave short shrift to the claim, quoting secondary authorities
that require an act to support a defamation claim, and concluding
that "nonfeasance . . . is not a predicate for liability." Scott v. Hull,
22 Ohio App. 2d 141, 144, 51 Ohio Op. 2d 289, 291, 259 N.E.2d 160,
162 (1970). This is a rule logically deduced from conventional notions of defamation, but given the analysis developed here it is not
necessarily persuasive against requiring compensation for allowing
the continuance of such a condition on one's property. Presumably
a local government could order a landowner to remove an obscene
picture painted on his building by another, even if the landowner
took no part in the deed and did not countenance it. Similarly, legal
rules on nonfeasance in a graffiti kind of case should follow the law
as it develops generally for cases in which one person could prevent
serious harm to another with little risk to himself. The case is fairly
analogous to that of someone's failure at least to publicize the imperiled position of another; and if the point of view advanced here
should take further hold in common law development in the settings
discussed in the text, it should apply in this area as well. A duty in
a case like this might be derived by analogy from the principle that
property ownership imposes certain basic obligations to abate nuis-

ances, but quite as fundamentally from a legally enforced minimum of humanitarian concern.

161. 81 Vt. 471, 71 Atl. 188, 20 L.R.A. (N.S.) 152 (1908).
162. 109 Minn. 456, 124 N.W. 221 (1910).
163. 7 Cal. 3d 64, 101 Cal. Rptr. 768, 496 P.2d 840 (1972), *appeal dismissed for want of a substantial federal question* 409 U.S. 1121 (1973).
164. *Id.* at 84–85, 101 Cal. Rptr. at 781, 496 P.2d at 853.
165. *Id.* at 98, 101 Cal. Rptr. at 784, 496 P.2d at 856 (Mosk, J., concurring and dissenting).
166. *See* La Fave & Scott, Handbook on Criminal Law 190 (1972).
167. *Id.* at 184–185.
168. *See id.* at 185–186.
169. *See, e.g.,* Linden, Tort Liability for Criminal Nonfeasance, 44 Canad. Bar Rev. 25, 42 (1966).
170. *Id.* at 64.
171. *See* text with note 148 *supra.*
172. Stevens, The "Rat Packs" of New York, N.Y. Times Magazine, Nov. 28, 1971, at 29, 93–94.
173. "Death of a Stranger on Rain-Swept Street," captioning front page picture in Houston Post, Dec. 16, 1966.
174. The respected journalist Tom Wicker, speaking of the bloody riot at Attica prison, is quoted as saying that although he is "not a petition signer, I've never believed a photographer ought to take a picture of a dying man instead of trying to save him. I think there do come times when you've got to be a human being first and a reporter second." —Book of the Month Club News, April 1975, at 4. I am grateful to Harvey Perlman for calling to my attention the coincidence of this quotation with the argument in the text.
175. Wash. Post, July 15, 1974, at A11.
176. "Cellblock Hostages Flee While One Captor Sleeps," in jump story, Wash. Post, July 15, 1974, at A10.
177. Indeed the nature of such cases serves to underline the undesirability of making a rigid distinction between action and inaction when what is at issue is how power should be wielded over the life-or-death destiny of particular individuals. Analogously, if an officer responsible for the handling of such a situation felt it necessary to communicate something on the air so that the convicts could hear it, it is equally arguable that he could legally commandeer the microphone, in default of the commentator's refusal to convey the message himself.
178. At the very moment when the hostages escaped, a reporter was pursuing with one of the prisoner-captors a line of telephone questioning that began with the inquiry, "What do you see as being the major problem, Bobby?" "'Hey, Get Away from that Door,'" Wash. Post, July 15, 1974, at A1.
179. Tarasoff v. Regents of Univ. of California, 13 Cal. 3d 177 (opinion

omitted), 118 Cal. Rptr. 129, 529 P.2d 553 (1974), *vacated*, 17 Cal. 3d 425, 131 Cal. Rptr. 14, 551 P.2d 334 (1976). *See also* Semler v. Psychiatric Institute of Washington, D.C., 538 F.2d 121 (D.C. Cir. 1976), *cert. denied*, —— U.S. ——, 45 U.S. L.W. 3250 (1976) (liability against psychiatric institute, physician, and probation officer for transfer of patient from day care to outpatient status without judicial approval).

180. 17 Cal. 3d at 436, 131 Cal. Rptr. at 24, 551 P.2d at 344.

181. Hernandez v. Toney, 289 So. 2d 318 (La. App. 1973).

182. *Id.* at 321.

183. *See* Lee v. Peerless Ins. Co., discussed text *supra* with notes 51–54.

184. *See* text with notes 15–16 *supra*.

185. Cruz v. American Export Isbrandtsen Lines Inc., 310 F. Supp. 1364, 1368 (S.D.N.Y. 1970).

186. Ship's Medicine Chest and First Aid at Sea 10, quoted *id.* at 1368.

187. Simonsen v. Thorin, 120 Neb. 684, 234 N.W. 628, 81 A.L.R. 1000 (1931).

188. *See* text *supra* with notes 61–65.

189. *See* Note, The Failure to Rescue: A Comparative Study, 52 Colum. L. Rev. 631, 641–647 (1952).

190. There is considerable variation in continental statutes with respect to the quantum of danger that will excuse a potential rescuer from performing his duty, ranging from a stringent requirement of risk to life to a standard that excuses persons from rescue attempts that would cause "the violation of one's own important obligations." *See* Rudzinski, The Duty to Rescue: A Comparative Analysis, in The Good Samaritan & the Law 91, 105–106 (J. Ratcliffe, ed. 1966).

191. Nothing in this analysis would preclude the imposition of a fee on the rescued person, on grounds akin to restitution, with the law deeming the rescue a bargain that requires the post hoc application of a schedule to save the personal and social costs of haggling about the worth of one's life to himself.

192. *Cf.* Bohlen's eloquent statement more than a half century ago that "all ethical and moral conceptions, which are not of the mere temporary manifestations of a passing wave of sentimentalism or puritanism, but on the contrary, find a real and permanent place in the settled convictions of a race and become part of the normal habit of thought thereof, of necessity do in time color the judicial conception of legal obligation." The Moral Duty to Aid Others as a Basis of Tort Liability (pt. 2), 56 U. Pa. L. Rev. 316, 334–335 (1908). *See also* Waller, Rescue & the Common Law: England and Australia, in The Good Samaritan & the Law 141 (J. Ratcliffe, ed. 1966) ("whether or not the law leads to direct, individual changes of heart, it at least continues to serve as a *public enunciation* of what ought to be done and a *public denunciation* of what is considered reprehensible"); *and* Barth, The Scope of Law: Man, Morals, or Money? 1967 Wis. L. Rev. 961. The latter essay is a theologian's

argument that social recognition of citizens' duties "to live up to their neighbors' and their own humanity" is so important that it requires a constitutional amendment that would both protect voluntary rescuers "from later penalty" and provide for community aid to injured rescuers. *Id.* at 968.

193. Depue v. Flateau, 100 Minn. 299, 111 N.W. 1 (1907) (liability imposed for turning ill invitee–dinner guest out into cold).

194. *See* text preceding note 160 *supra.*

195. *Cf.* French Penal Code section discussed *supra* text with note 69.

196. The summary below comes from Bystander "Apathy," 57 Am. Sci. 244 (1969). Direct inspiration for these studies was provided by the widely reported incident in which Kitty Genovese was murdered in front of her Kew Gardens residence as thirty-eight onlooking neighbors did nothing to help her, none even calling the police. The incident is summarized *id.* at 244. Incidents of this sort have continued to recur: in a recent Chicago occurrence, for example, a 74-year-old man was stabbed twelve times by three attackers while a score of people watched. "20 Stand By as Man Fights for Life," Wash. Post, Nov. 19, 1974, at A2.

197. Duty to Aid the Endangered Act, Vt. Stat. Ann. tit. 12, § 551 (1973).

198. *Compare* Rudzinski, The Duty to Rescue: A Comparative Analysis, in The Good Samaritan & the Law 122 (J. Ratcliffe, ed. 1966) (if legal demands are not excessive, law "quite successfully modifies human attitudes, reinforces moral impulses, and awakens the indifferent and the passive"), *and* Note, Stalking the Good Samaritan: Communists, Capitalists and the Duty to Rescue, 1976 Utah L. Rev. 529, 541–542 ("added impetus of a legal duty with immediate and direct sanctions could tip the balance"), *with* Zeisel, An International Experiment on the Effects of a Good Samaritan Law, in The Good Samaritan & the Law 209 (J. Ratcliffe, ed. 1966), reporting that the presence or absence of a law requiring aid is not dispositive on people's attitudes about what the law should be, although those interviewed were rather accurate in their description of what their nation's law was on the subject.

199. *Cf., e.g.,* H.L.A. Hart, The Concept of Law 84–85 (1961).

200. Note, The Duty to Rescue, 47 Ind. L.J. 321, 325 (1972). *Cf.* Rudzinski, The Duty to Rescue: A Comparative Analysis, in The Good Samaritan & the Law 121 (J. Ratcliffe, ed. 1966), suggesting that an obligation to rescue may be "unjust" to persons "with a timid disposition."

201. Note, The Duty to Rescue, 47 Ind. L.J. at 327.

202. An eloquent statement of an individual's response to the starved condition of a two-month-old girl in Juárez appears in Bode, "You Should Have Been There," Tex. Observer, Dec. 27, 1968, at 1–2:

> Well, what would you have done? You would have perhaps taken charge in a more effective way, would have managed the situation better; . . .

Me? I just did things in the usual American way: I took out my wallet and gave the boys some money. Sure I was troubled, concerned. I explained to the boys that the mother must go to the doctor and that she must do exactly what he said and the boys gave the money to the woman and she slowly gathered up the child and the three of them started off toward a doctor's office two blocks away. I stood there on the street corner and watched until she went through the doctor's door.

What I want to know is: Who is to blame? Do you blame Mexico as a country? God as a Creator? Juárez as a poverty-filled town? The man sitting on the curb? The shoeshine boy? The father? The mother; should you blame her for being poor and perhaps ignorant and out of work? Or the child: maybe it for not being born stronger? Or blame me, for not staying there and doing more? *Nobody?* Just say, Well you know that's life . . . ?

203. It follows that I shall not consider questions of what might be called political duties to act — obligations of conscience. *Cf., e.g.,* Duff, "Bearing the Burden of the Berrigan Brothers," New Republic, March 6, 1971, at 18.

204. *Compare* Nipper v. California Automobile Assigned Risk Plan, 58 Cal. App. 3d 752, 130 Cal. Rptr. 100 (1976) *with* the California Supreme Court's opinion vacating that decision, 19 Cal. 3d 35, 136 Cal. Rptr. 854, 560 P.2d 743 (1977). This litigation was brought by a motorist injured in a collision with a 79-year-old driver. The defendants were an insurance broker and an unincorporated association of insurance companies, administering a legislatively created assigned risk plan. The suit alleged that the broker knew and that the Plan should have discovered the incompetence of the elderly driver. In the portion of its opinion holding that a cause of action was stated against the Plan, the appellate court refers to the Plan's "special relationship with appellant as a member of the motoring public," arising out of "the quasi-public nature of the insurance industry," and characterizes the statute as contemplating that the Plan will reject incompetent drivers. 130 Cal. Rptr. at 107.

However, the Supreme Court held to the contrary, rejecting the attempt to impose either statutory or common law obligations on the Plan. Replying to the plaintiff's argument that the statute's reporting requirement was designed to weed out unsafe drivers, the court said that its primary purpose was to extend coverage to drivers who were otherwise unacceptable, and said that to impose liability would force the Plan to an "almost irresistible compulsion to reject doubtful or borderline applicants." 19 Cal. 3d at 46, 136 Cal. Rptr. at 859, 560 P.2d at 748. The court also refused to find a common law duty, noting that no precedent had been adduced for the proposition that an insurer stood "in a special relationship with the applicant or his potential victims, or alternatively owes any affirmative duty of inquiry or disclosure regarding the applicant." 19 Cal. 3d at 47, 136 Cal. Rptr. at 860, 560 P.2d at 749.

205. I must emphasize that this is offered only analogically as a guide for testing the actions of private power holders and does not suggest that their obligations are qualitatively identical to those of governments or officials.

I should also take note of the observations of some helpful critics who have questioned whether this monograph evinces proper recognition of the individualistic tradition in America. I believe that a careful consideration of the results for which I contend in specific cases, together with my general emphasis on relationships, will indicate that I intend no violence to that tradition. However, in connection with the arguments here advanced for a broad formulation of private duties, it is well to note that there are competing strains of thought in our national psyche. A recent opinion survey is reported to have found a fear that the nation is "trending toward a psychology of self-interest so all-embracing that no room is left for commitment to national and community interests." This fear is characterized as being that "in their pursuit of their organizational goals, the politicians and the businessmen and the unions and the professions have lost sight of any larger obligation to the public and are indifferent or worse to anything that does not benefit–immediately and directly–themselves or their institutions. They fear that the very meaning of the public good is disappearing in a sea of self-seeking." *Public Agenda* report, quoted in Reston, "Debates: What's the Question," N.Y. Times, News of the Week in Review, Sept. 19, 1976, at 15.

One can easily recognize that it is central to our notions of freedom that "self-seeking" produces an overall "public good" and, moreover, that private duties are not qualitatively the same as public ones; yet one can also perceive that the concerns reflected by these survey results might simultaneously tend to support an expansion of certain private obligations.

206. *Compare* Coase, The Problem of Social Cost, 3 J. L. & Econ. 1 (1960), *and* Posner, A Theory of Negligence, 1 J. Leg. Studies 29 (1972); *cf.* G. Calabresi, The Costs of Accidents (1970); *see also* Calabresi & Hirschoff, Toward a Test for Strict Liability in Torts, 81 Yale L.J. 1055 (1972).

207. See Fletcher, Fairness and Utility in Tort Theory, 85 Harv. L. Rev. 537 (1972).

208. *See* Epstein, A Theory of Strict Liability, 2 J. Leg. Studies 151 (1973).

209. For specific explication in the case law, *see infra* Part Two, text with note 104.

PART TWO: PUBLIC DUTIES TO ACT

1. I believe that this area, some phenomena of which are discussed in this inquiry, and the recent spectacular growth of which already has occasioned much commentary, merits further, separate treatment in the perspective offered here. For examples of the scholarship of the last decade from a variety of perspectives, *see, e.g.*, Developments in the Law: Section 1983 and Federalism, 90 Harv. L. Rev. 1133 (1977); Nahmod, Section 1983 and the "Background" of Tort Liability, 50 Ind. L.J. 5 (1974); Chevigny, Section 1983 Jurisdiction: A Reply, 83 Harv. L. Rev. 1352 (1970); Krier, Civil Rights and State Authority: Toward the Production of a Just Equilibrium, 1966 Wis. L. Rev. 831; Shapo, Constitutional Tort: *Monroe v. Pape*, and the Frontiers Beyond, 60 Nw. U. L. Rev. 277 (1965). *Cf.* Hill, Constitutional Remedies, 69 Colum. L. Rev. 1109 (1969).
2. *See generally* National Traffic and Motor Vehicle Safety Act, 15 U.S.C.A. §§ 1381–1431 (1974).
3. *See* City of Austin v. Daniels, 160 Tex. 628, 335 S.W.2d 753, 81 A.L.R.2d 1180 (1960).
4. *See* Murphy v. De Revere, 279 App. Div. 929, 111 N.Y.S.2d 2 (1952), *aff'd without opin.*, 304 N.Y. 922, 110 N.E.2d 740 (1953).
5. Martin v. City of Winchester, 278 Ky. 200, 206, 128 S.W.2d 543, 545 (1939).
6. City of Russellville v. Greer, 440 S.W.2d 269 (Ky. 1968).
7. Emphasis in original.
8. City of Tampa v. Davis, 226 So. 2d 450 (Fla. App. 1969).
9. Hargrove v. Town of Cocoa Beach, 96 So. 2d 130, 60 A.L.R.2d 1193 (Fla. 1957).
10. Emphasis in original.
11. Emphasis in original.
12. As in *Hargrove, supra* note 9.
13. Board of Comm'rs of Delaware County v. Briggs, 337 N.E.2d 852 (Ind. App. 1975).
14. See text with note 187, Part One.
15. The case also emphasizes the blurriness of the boundaries between the conventional classifications of "intent," a subject of which full discussion would require a long excursion but which at least deserves mention here. If a vandal had broken the stop sign in the *Davis* case, discussed *supra* text with note 8, his conduct would be characterized as an intentional tort, in contrast to that of the policeman, which would be labeled "negligent." But it would seem appropriate to divide responsibility between them equally, on the basis of the realities of life if not the usual use of legal terminology. Although the policeman was only "negligent" in the traditional locution, he did act deliberately and chose the method of propping up the sign; and apparently he, or those to whom he reported, elected not to take

other action immediately. These elements of choice and deliberation, in the context of the facts that attending to traffic control is
the city's job and that the populace practically places considerable
trust in municipal performance of that task, argue that the city
should be at least partly responsible for accidents resulting from
this default in the use of its power.

16. Fankhauser v. City of Mansfield, 19 Ohio St. 2d 102, 108, 48 Ohio Opin.
2d 103, 106, 249 N.E.2d 789, 792 (1969).

17. Bergen v. Koppenal, 52 N.J. 478, 480, 246 A.2d 442, 444 (1968).

18. *Id.* at 480, 246 A.2d at 444.

19. *Id.* at 480, 246 A.2d at 444. *See also* Freeport Transport Inc. v. Commonwealth Dept. of Highways, 408 S.W.2d 193 (Ky. App. 1966)
(dangerously slippery conditions created by flaking of surfacing material on sharp curve, in existence for eight months; failure to discover and take protective action held negligent against dissent who
asks, "When it rains how often must the Department inspect for
slick spots the road up Chicken Gizzard Ridge and over to Possum
Trot?").

20. Miehl v. Darpino, 53 N.J. 49, 247 A.2d 878 (1968).

21. For example "government" as against "transportation."

22. Holdings of this kind properly govern cases in a variety of contexts in
which imposition of a duty would be "completely disproportionate
to the dangers presented," *see, e.g.,* Alesi v. City of New York, 9 App.
Div. 2d 236, 192 N.Y.S.2d 929 (1959), *aff'd without opin.,* 12 N.Y.2d
703, 233 N.Y.S.2d 481, 185 N.E.2d 916 (1962).

23. Compare a report of McCurley v. Louisiana, a trial court decision holding the state liable for negligent highway maintenance because it
permitted clover to grow to a height that obstructed motorists'
views. 11 Personal Injury Newsletter No. 22 at 256 (1968). This is a
case of governmental default in a situation in which the state has
acted to the substantial benefit of the public in the broad activity
of highway building, but thereby creates expectations in citizens
who have no choice but to entrust their lives to proper maintenance.

24. *See, e.g.,* Yates v. United States, 497 F.2d 878 (10th Cir. 1974). But by
parity with my discussion of Miehl v. Darpino, *supra* text with note
20, I should note that foolish utilization of information given will
bar a claim. *See* Somlo v. United States, 274 F. Supp. 827 (N.D. Ill.
1967), *aff'd,* 416 F.2d 640 (7th Cir. 1969).

25. Rindfleisch v. State, 27 N.Y.2d 762, 315 N.Y.S.2d 297, 263 N.E.2d 663
(1970).

26. *Id.,* 59 Misc. 2d 1074, 301 N.Y.S.2d 830 (Ct. Cl. 1968), *aff'd without
opin.,* 32 App. Div. 889, 302 N.Y.S.2d 1016 (1969), *aff'd mem.* 27
N.Y.2d 762, 315 N.Y.S.2d 297, 263 N.E.2d 663 (1970).

27. *See* 27 N.Y.2d at 766–767, 315 N.Y.S.2d at 300–301, 263 N.E.2d at
664–666.

28. *Cf.* Flores v. Norton & Ramsey Lines Inc., 352 F. Supp. 150 (W.D. Tex.

1972) (licensing and weighing officer's direction to plaintiff to stop, resulting in rear-end collision, held "use" of public roadway, supporting liability under state tort claims act).

29. *Compare generally* the Court of Claims opinion, *supra* note 26, and the per curiam opinion of the Court of Appeals, *supra* note 25, *with* the Court of Appeals dissent.

30. Burchard, "Perilous Beltway," Wash. Post, Nov. 28, 1971, at A1 and A10.

31. D.O.T. News–Fed. Highway Admin. FHWA Release 2-72 (Jan. 7, 1972).

32. *See, e.g.*, Thedie and Abraham, Economic Aspect of Road Accidents, 2 Traffic & Engineering Control No. 10 at 589 (Feb. 1961).

33. *See id.* at 593.

34. Hughes v. County of Burlington, 99 N.J. Super. 405, 414, 240 A.2d 177, 181–182 (1968), *petition for certification denied* 51 N.J. 575, 242 A.2d 379 (1968).

35. *See* Hughes, *supra* note 34, 99 N.J. Super. at 413, 240 A.2d at 181, quoting Fitzgerald v. Palmer, 47 N.J. 106, 109–110, 219 A.2d 512, 514 (1969).

36. Emphasis in original.

37. Hughes, *supra* note 34, 99 N.J. Super. at 413, 240 A.2d at 181, quoting Fitzgerald v. Palmer, 47 N.J. at 109–110, 219 A.2d at 514.

38. Park v. Village of Waverly, 457 F.2d 1139, 1140 (2d Cir. 1972).

39. Stuart-Bullock v. State, 38 App. Div. 2d 626, 627, 326 N.Y.S.2d 909, 912 (1971).

40. *Id.*, 33 N.Y.2d 418, 421, 353 N.Y.S.2d 953, 955, 309 N.E.2d 419, 420 (1974).

41. Bolm v. Triumph Corp., 33 N.Y.2d 151, 350 N.Y.S.2d 644, 305 N.E.2d 769 (1973) (motorcycle design).

42. Pickering v. Washington, 260 So. 2d 340 (La. App. 1972), *cert. denied* 261 La. 1062, 262 So. 2d 43 (1972).

43. *Id.* at 342.

44. *Id.*

45. *See, e.g.*, Underwood v. United States, 356 F.2d 92 (5th Cir. 1966).

46. 350 U.S. 61 (1955).

47. Exemplifying the possibilities for mandamus-type enforcement of governmental obligations when they have a statutory basis is Natural Resources Defense Council, Inc. v. Train, 411 F. Supp. 864 (S.D.N.Y. 1976), *aff'd*, 545 F.2d 320 (2d Cir. 1976) (requiring listing of pollutant found to have "adverse effect on public health or welfare").

48. *Cf.* Franklin, Replacing the Negligence Lottery: Compensation and Selective Reimbursement, 53 Va. L. Rev. 774, 803 (1967).

49. *See infra*, text with note 166.

50. *In re* M/T Alva Cape, 405 F.2d 962 (2d Cir. 1969).

51. "Firemen Let It Burn: 'No Tag, No Service,'" undated and unidentified clipping (Austin American Statesman c. 1968?).

52. In line with the views developed above concerning the duties of private parties, it could be argued that the commonwealth's contributions to the sustenance and enrichment of the lives of all individuals

impose obligations toward imperiled fellows on those who possess special strength or expertise. See, *e.g.*, text *supra*, p. 70. However, even if this contention proved persuasive, in practice it would be difficult to impose liability in a case of this kind because of the necessary qualification that risk to the defendant must be insignificant. This being said, it is worth remarking from a standpoint of mores that the chief engineer of the department was quoted as saying that the firemen had "made certain there were no persons in the house," and that "if there had been someone inside we would have saved his life."

53. H.R. Moch Co. v. Rensselaer Water Co., 247 N.Y. 160, 159 N.E. 896, 62 A.L.R. 1199 (1928).

54. Tuthill v. City of Rochester, 32 App. Div. 2d 873, 301 N.Y.S.2d 648 (1969).

55. *Id.*, 27 N.Y.2d 558, 313 N.Y.S.2d 127, 261 N.E.2d 267 (1970).

56. 295 N.Y. 51, 64 N.E.2d 704, 163 A.L.R. 342 (1945).

57. Reynolds Boat Co. v. City of Haverhill, 357 Mass. 668, 260 N.E.2d 176 (1970).

58. I am grateful to Mr. Randolph J. Haines for his comments in this connection.

59. Among the various competing definitions of fairness, perhaps the most practical one for these purposes is Michelman's gloss on Rawls, specifically applied to losses suffered as a result of the kind of governmental activity usually classified as eminent domain: "A decision not to compensate is not unfair as long as the disappointed claimant ought to be able to appreciate how such decisions might fit into a consistent practice which holds forth a lesser long-run risk to people like him than would any consistent practice which is naturally suggested by the opposite decision."–Michelman, Property, Utility and Fairness: Comments on the Ethical Foundations of "Just Compensation" Law, 80 Harv. L. Rev. 1165, 1223 (1967).

60. *Cf.* Broeder, Torts and Just Compensation: Some Personal Reflections, 17 Hastings L.J. 217, *e.g.* at 250 (1965); *compare generally* Sax, Takings and the Police Power, 74 Yale L.J. 36 (1964), *with* Michelman, *supra* note 59.

61. Dutton v. Bognor Regis Urban Dist. Council [1972] 1 Q.B. 373, [1972] 2 W.L.R. 299, [1972] 1 All E.R. 462 (C.A.).

62. [1972] 1 Q.B. at 392, [1972] 1 All E.R. at 470.

63. Setting limits at one perimeter of the problem is Gercey v. United States, 540 F.2d 536 (1st Cir. 1976), *cert. denied* 430 U.S. 954 (1977) (refusal to impose liability on Coast Guard for failure to set up a program to protect passengers from the dangers of ships whose certificates it had revoked). Other judicially imposed boundaries appear in Copeland v. United States, 347 F. Supp. 247 (M.D. Ala. 1972) (refusing liability under the Federal Tort Claims Act for deaths and injuries caused by defective heater in public housing project, allegedly attributable to inspector's negligent approval of installation;

no showing of undertaking to inspect heating systems, or of reliance; all approvals of work to be given only by the local housing authority); Davis v. United States, 395 F. Supp. 793 (D. Neb. 1975), *aff'd per curiam* 536 F.2d 758 (8th Cir. 1976) (failure of federal OSHA inspector to issue citation or make followup inspection; officer "not in control, either actually, contractually, or otherwise").

64. Which would turn around the result, *inter alia*, in Jeffries v. United States, 477 F.2d 52 (9th Cir. 1973). Adoption of this view likely would also produce a decision contrary to the one in the particularly outrageous fact situation in Roberson v. United States, 382 F.2d 714 (9th Cir. 1967), favorably cited in *Jeffries*. In *Roberson*, the plaintiffs fell when a large scaffold called a "jumbo" slipped, in circumstances in which a government construction engineer who inspected the jumbo's rigging had said he did not use it himself because it was "too dangerous." In confirmation of the engineer's judgment, several safety devices were installed after the accident. The court denies liability because it views as inapplicable Restatement Second 324A, which requires compensation for the careless rendition of services to another that should be recognized as necessary for the protection of third persons, saying that the government in this case did not undertake to render services but only "to protect its own interest." This may be correct technical parsing but, if that is so, it would simply demonstrate the need for an expansion of the concept retailed in the Restatement. From whatever motives, including that of self-protection against liability and that of the humanitarian concern which might reasonably be imputed to the United States because of its reservation of inspection rights and its creation of a comprehensive safety inspection program, the government had in fact acted with one of its goals as the protection of those who used the jumbo. That it should escape liability in such a situation seems an odd result, even by the analogical light of the palmiest articulations of the "right-privilege" distinction.

65. Motyka v. City of Amsterdam, 15 N.Y.2d 134, 256 N.Y.S.2d 595, 204 N.E.2d 635 (1965). *Compare*, for a galling result in a case involving only economic harm, Redmond v. United States, 518 F.2d 811 (7th Cir. 1975), in which the plaintiff is pincered between the misrepresentation exception of the Federal Tort Claims Act—which is used to bar a claim that government agents were involved in the dissemination of misleading information about securities—and the general principle that there is no duty to warn or compensate victims of crime, *see, e.g.*, text *infra*, pp. 98–104.

66. *But cf.* a much later New York precedent, holding a city liable for the death of an excavation workman in a cave-in that occurred shortly after an inspector opined, "It is pretty solid there" and "I don't think it needs to be shored." Smullen v. City of New York, 28 N.Y.2d 66, 320 N.Y.S.2d 19, 268 N.E.2d 763 (1971).

67. Griffin v. United States, 500 F.2d 1059, 24 A.L.R. Fed. 441 (3d Cir. 1974).

68. Clemente v. United States, 422 F. Supp. 564 (D.P.R. 1976), *motion for reconsideration denied*, 426 F. Supp. 1 (D.P.R. 1977).
69. Brown v. MacPherson's, Inc., 86 Wash. 2d 293, 302, 545 P.2d 13, 19 (1975).
70. See text with notes 223–241, *infra*.
71. General Assembly Resolution No. 2345 (XXII), U.N. General Assembly, 22nd Sess., Official Records, Suppl. 16 at 5 (1968).
72. Agreement on the Rescue of Astronauts, the Return of Astronauts and the Return of Objects Launched into Outer Space, Art. 1, *id.* at 6.
73. Agreement on the Rescue of Astronauts, *supra* note 72, Art. 2, *id.*
74. Dembling & Arons, The Treaty on Rescue and Return of Astronauts and Space Objects, 9 Wm. & Mary L. Rev. 630, 657.
75. United States v. Sandra & Dennis Fishing Corp., 372 F.2d 189 (1st Cir. 1967), *cert. denied* 389 U.S. 836 (1967), explaining at 197 n.16 that "interdum prudens" means "sometimes careful."
76. Petition of United States of America, as owner of the United States Coast Guard Vessel CG-95321, 255 F. Supp. 737, 748–749 (D. Mass. 1966).
77. 372 F.2d at 197; *see also* 255 F. Supp. at 748–749.
78. *See* 372 F.2d at 198.
79. *See id.*
80. 22 N.Y.2d 579, 293 N.Y.S.2d 897, 240 N.E.2d 860 (1968).
81. *Id.* at 581, 293 N.Y.S.2d at 898, 240 N.E.2d at 860.
82. *Id.* at 582, 293 N.Y.S.2d at 898, 240 N.E.2d at 861.
83. *Id.* at 586, 293 N.Y.S.2d at 901, 240 N.E.2d at 863.
84. This language now appears in Local Governmental and Governmental Employees Tort Immunity Act, Smith-Hurd Ill. Ann. Stat. ch. 85, § 4–102 (1966).
85. LeMenager v. Fitzgerald, 1 Ill. App. 3d 803, 274 N.E.2d 913 (1971).
86. Simpson's Food Fair, Inc. v. City of Evansville, 149 Ind. App. 387, 272 N.E.2d 871, 46 A.L.R.3d 1077 (1971).
87. *See* text sentence with note 85 *supra*.
88. Huey v. Town of Cicero, 41 Ill. 2d 361, 363–364, 243 N.E.2d 214, 216 (1968).
89. Huey v. Barloga, 277 F. Supp. 864, 870 (N.D. Ill. 1967).
90. *Id.* at 872–873.
91. *Id. Cf.* Chestnut v. City of Quincy, 513 F.2d 91 (5th Cir. 1975) (confirming "affirmative duty to preserve law and order" of police chief but finding that there was no breach of duty in assignments of officer who shot plaintiff, when claim of failure to supervise rested on alleged shooting incident several years before).
92. 38 App. Div. 2d 407, 330 N.Y.S.2d 569 (1972), *aff'd without opin.*, 32 N.Y.2d 894, 346 N.Y.S.2d 814, 300 N.E.2d 154 (1973).
93. 38 App. Div. 2d at 415, 330 N.Y.S.2d at 577.
94. *Steitz, supra* text with note 56.
95. *Motyka, supra* text with note 65.
96. *See* dissenting opinion, 38 App. Div. 2d at 418, 330 N.Y.S.2d at 580.

97. Bass v. City of New York, 61 Misc. 2d 465, 468, 305 N.Y.S.2d 801, 805 (1969).

98. 68 Misc. 2d at 468, 305 N.Y.S.2d at 805.

99. Keane v. City of Chicago, 98 Ill. App. 2d 460, 240 N.E.2d 321 (1968).

100. Evers v. Westerburg, 38 App. Div. 2d 751, 329 N.Y.S.2d 615 (1972), *aff'd without opin.*, 32 N.Y.2d 684, 343 N.Y.S.2d 361, 296 N.E.2d 257 (1973).

101. 38 App. Div. 2d at 751, 329 N.Y.S.2d at 618. (Emphasis in original.)

102. Massengill v. Yuma County, 104 Ariz. 518, 523, 456 P.2d 376, 381, 41 A.L.R.3d 692 (1969).

103. Veach v. City of Phoenix, 102 Ariz. 195, 197, 427 P.2d 335, 337 (1967).

104. Massengill v. Yuma County, 9 Ariz. App. 281, 286–287, 451 P.2d 639, 644–645 (1969).

105. 9 Ariz. App. at 287, 451 P.2d at 645.

106. Full recognition of this monopoly appears in a decision refusing to dismiss a claim that various state and federal law enforcement agencies had made only a "token" investigation of the shooting of a black man by a white state trooper, accompanied by various other charges of laxity and abdication in investigating violations of constitutional rights. NAACP v. Levi, 418 F. Supp. 1109 (D.D.C. 1976). *See also* McKee v. Breier, 417 F. Supp. 189 (E.D. Wis. 1976), denying motion to dismiss of police chief accused of "negligent" supervision of officers investigating the murder of policemen.

107. Wasserstein v. State, 32 App. Div. 2d 119, 300 N.Y.S.2d 263 (1969), *aff'd without opin.*, 27 N.Y.2d 627, 313 N.Y.S.2d 759, 261 N.E.2d 665 (1970).

108. These facts appear in the contrary lower court decision, 56 Misc. 2d 225, 288 N.Y.S.2d 274 (1968).

109. *Compare* 32 App. Div. 2d at 120 ("no previous acts of physical violence"), 300 N.Y.S.2d at 264, *with* 56 Misc. 2d at 277 (officer's testimony that he knew the three youths by sight and evidence that witnesses' descriptions had connected them with crimes), 288 N.Y.S.2d at 276.

110. *See* 32 App. Div. 2d at 121, 300 N.Y.S.2d at 265, appearing to imply that a record of violence might have imposed a higher duty on the parole officer, but also citing *Riss* as a case in which "the factual situation was more favorable to the claimant than presently."

111. Hansen v. City of Saint Paul, 298 Minn. 205, 210, 214 N.W.2d 346, 350 (Minn. 1974).

112. *Id.* at 209 n.3, 214 N.W.2d at 349 n.3.

113. These figures are from Remarks by Secretary of Transportation Volpe, Announcing Air Transport Security Program, in D.O.T. Release DOT 103-72 (Dec. 5, 1972).

114. This is so as to abusive acts since the 1974 amendment to the Federal Tort Claims Act, which removes the government's exemption from liability for the kinds of intentional torts usually alleged in claims for police misconduct. *See* 28 U.S.C.A. §2680(h) (Supp. 1977).

115. *Cf.* Rosman v. Trans World Airlines, Inc., 34 N.Y.2d 385, 358 N.Y.S.2d 97, 314 N.E.2d 848, 72 A.L.R.3d 1282 (1974) (absolute liability under Warsaw Convention for physical consequences of psychic trauma caused by hijacking).

116. Eastman v. Williams, 124 Vt. 445, 207 A.2d 146 (1965).

117. *Id.* at 447, 207 A.2d at 148.

118. *Id.* at 448, 207 A.2d at 148.

119. Ranging across legal categories, one may note analogically that the law provides severe remedies for the abuse of even the basic power, in the form of statutes that take custody away from parents of "dependent and neglected" children.

120. Butler v. District of Columbia, 417 F.2d 1150 (D.C. Cir. 1969).

121. Cioffi v. Board of Education, 27 App. Div. 2d 826, 827, 278 N.Y.S.2d 249, 250, 36 A.L.R.3d 326 (1967).

122. Both opinions claim support from a court of appeals decision that denies recovery for failure to police snowball throwing, in which the court says that "a parent of ordinary prudence," although he would not discourage the throwing of snowballs, "would stop dangerous throwing, if he learned hard frozen snow or ice had come into play." Lawes v. Board of Education, 16 N.Y.2d 302, 305, 266 N.Y.S.2d 364, 366, 213 N.E.2d 667, 668 (1965).

123. This duty thrusts in a different direction as well, requiring school officials to prevent excessive punishments. *See* Bramlet v. Wilson, 495 F.2d 714 (8th Cir. 1974), in which the majority says that proof of excessive past corporal punishment and of a threat of future injury would support injunctive relief on a complaint characterized by a dissenter as centering on the defendant officials' "failure to provide regulations."

124. *See, e.g.,* text *supra,* pp. 7–8, 10–13, 47.

125. *See, e.g.,* text *supra,* pp. 8–10, 27, 62.

126. Susman v. City of Los Angeles, 269 Cal. App. 2d 803, 75 Cal. Rptr. 240 (1969).

127. Cal. Gov't Code § 845 (West 1966).

128. 237 So. 2d 132 (Fla. 1970).

129. 229 So. 2d 659 (Fla. App. 1969).

130. 237 So. 2d at 134.

131. 229 So. 2d at 662–663 (dissenting opinion of Carroll, J.). It is on this ground that a New York trial court distinguishes *Riss* and *Bass* to hold a cause of action stated by store owners whose property was vandalized. Bloom v. City of New York, 78 Misc. 2d 1077, 357 N.Y.S.2d 979 (1974).

132. *Compare* Susman v. City of Los Angeles, 269 Cal. App. 2d 803, 75 Cal. Rptr. 240 (1969), in which this view is advanced, *with* Scheuer v. Rhodes, 416 U.S. 232 (1974).

133. *See* Silver v. City of Minneapolis, 284 Minn. 266, 170 N.W.2d 206 (1969).

134. *See* Silver, *supra* note 133, 284 Minn. at 271, 170 N.W.2d at 209.

135. Jahnke v. Incorporated City of Des Moines, 191 N.W.2d 780 (Iowa 1971).
136. *See id.* at 794 (dissenting opinion).
137. *Cf.* Shelton v. City of Chicago, 42 Ill. 2d 468, 248 N.E.2d 121 (1969), *cert. denied* 396 U.S. 906 (1969) (opposing strict liability to bystanders, one of whom was hurt by police action attempting to suppress mob, and another injured by the mob itself).
138. *Cf.* Epstein, A Theory of Strict Liability, 2 J. Legal Studies 151, 203 (1973).
139. *See, e.g.*, Van Alstyne, Governmental Tort Liability: A Decade of Change, 1966 U. Ill. L.F. 919.
140. City of Chicago v. Sturges, 222 U.S. 313 (1911).
141. *Id.* at 322.
142. *Id.* at 324.
143. *See* Note, Riot Insurance, 77 Yale L.J. 541, 554 (1968).
144. Direct attack on the argument that making the entire community responsible for riot damages will stimulate preventive measures appears in Interstate Fire & Casualty Co. v. City of Milwaukee, 45 Wis. 2d 331, 173 N.W.2d 187 (1970), in which the court says that "in this era of 'confrontation politics,' 'protest marches' and 'civil disobedience' it is naive to think that riot statutes such as that before the court will retard such occurrences or keep them from developing into damaging riots, especially considering the spontaneity with which they occur." *Id.* at 337, 173 N.W.2d at 191.
145. *See, e.g.*, Manzo v. City of Plainfield, 107 N.J. Super. 303, 308, 258 A.2d 149, 152 (1969) ("the obligation of government to protect life, liberty and property against the conduct of the indifferent, the careless and the evil-minded" as "lying at the very foundation of the social compact"), *modified, affirmed, and remanded*, 59 N.J. 30, 279 A.2d 706 (1971). *See also* A & B Auto Stores of Jones Street, Inc. v. City of Newark, 59 N.J. 5, 279 A.2d 693 (1971) (within "reasonable discretion" of legislature to decide what group of taxpayers shall bear the burden of riots).
146. *See* Note, Municipal Liability for Riot Damage, 81 Harv. L. Rev. 653, 654 (1968).
147. *See id.* at 654–655.
148. Jackson v. Kansas City, Kansas, 448 F.2d 518 (10th Cir. 1971).
149. Shake v. Board of Commissioners, 210 Ind. 61, 67, 1 N.E.2d 132, 134 (1936).
150. Sturges, text with notes 140–142 *supra*.
151. Berberick v. City of Topeka, 119 Kan. 552, 240 Pac. 968, 44 A.L.R. 1135 (1925).
152. Berberick, *supra, id.* at 554, 240 Pac. at 969, characterizing Blakeman v. City of Wichita, 93 Kan. 444, 144 Pac. 816 (1914).
153. Blakeman, *supra*, 93 Kan. at 448, 144 Pac. at 817.
154. Earle v. Greenville County, 215 S.C. 539, 56 S.E.2d 348 (1949) (Thurgood Marshall, co-counsel for the plaintiff).

155. Comment, The Aftermath of the Riot: Balancing the Budget, 116 U. Pa. L. Rev. 649, 683 (1968). (Emphasis in original.)

156. It should be emphasized that the scope of largesse is not infinite under this analysis, rather being limited by the rationales for compensation. For example, an insurer should not be able to recover for its compensation of insureds for damage sustained in a riot, under a statute that imposes municipal liability to persons whose property is destroyed or injured. Holding this way, a court says that to rule otherwise would be to allow recoupment by the insurer of losses from the insureds because the city would have to pass on its burden to residents in the form of increased taxes. Interstate Fire & Casualty Co. v. City of Milwaukee, 45 Wis. 2d 331, 173 N.W.2d 187 (1970).

157. Williams v. State, 308 N.Y. 548, 127 N.E.2d 545 (1955).

158. *See, e.g.*, Bannon v. United States, 293 F. Supp. 1050 (D.R.I. 1968) (citing the problem of handling suicidal potential as "the most perplexing prediction in a psychiatrist's entire clinical practice").

159. Williams v. State, 30 App. Div. 2d 611, 290 N.Y.S.2d 263 (1968).

160. *See* 30 App. Div. 2d at 612, 290 N.Y.S.2d at 265, saying that the decision to place a patient in an open ward is a "medical judgment," for which liability would not arise if it "was, in fact, erroneous."

161. *See id.* at 612, 290 N.Y.S.2d at 265–266.

162. An excellent journalistic essay captures the reason in its quotation of a district attorney's statement about the attitude of a mental hospital administrator who had pioneered open wards: "Dr. Sedberry tells me she's got 300 patients out there. About ten of them jump every month. . . . Dr. Sedberry says she'll be darned if she'll let me ruin the treatment and progress of her 290 other patients just because ten of 'em jump. She says those open wards are the first step toward getting past the Dark Ages in mental care. But I sure do wish we had some place to keep those 10. They cause me a bunch of trouble." Ivins, "I'm sorry, lady, there's nothing we can do," Tex. Observer, Dec. 15, 1972, 11 at 13 (recording stories of various crimes by escaped patients, including murder of author's dog).

163. This view would not require the government to compensate when it can show that the contribution of a release decision to the plaintiff's injury is insignificant. *Cf., e.g.*, Tilden v. United States, 365 F.2d 148 (7th Cir. 1966) (suit for failure to confine drunken serviceman over two-day period, in alleged violation of agreement with civil policeman, when likelihood was that civil authorities would have let him go anyway).

164. *Cf.* Mulberg v. State, 35 App. Div. 2d 856, 315 N.Y.S.2d 176 (1970), in which there is disagreement within the court over whether one attendant is enough for "30 mentally ill, active and unruly children," when the attendant himself has requested extra help. In view of this plea, although a decision for the state is affirmed without opinion in 29 N.Y.2d 916, 329 N.Y.S.2d 97, 279 N.E.2d 854 (1972), it rings a bit hollow for the appellate division majority to say that "the degree of

reasonable care is measured by the physical and mental infirmities of the patients as the hospital officials and employees know them." 35 App. Div. 2d at 856, 315 N.Y.S.2d at 177.
165. 69 Cal. 2d 782, 73 Cal. Rptr. 240, 447 P.2d 352 (1968).
166. *Id*. at 797–798, 73 Cal. Rptr. at 251, 447 P.2d at 363.
167. *Cf*. Dalehite v. United States, 346 U.S. 15, 57 (1953) ("not a tort for government to govern") (Jackson, J., dissenting).
168. Although a distinction might be made between governmental liability and the immunity of individual officials. For a decision immunizing parole officials on the ground that this will encourage independent judgment, *see* Pate v. Alabama Board of Pardons and Paroles, 409 F. Supp. 478 (D. Ala. 1976). *See also* Reiff v. Commonwealth, 397 F. Supp. 345 (E.D. Pa. 1975) (immunity for parole officials and parole officer as performing "discretionary duties within the framework of a quasi-judicial process").
169. *See* text with note 179, Part One.
170. *See, e.g.*, Daniels v. Andersen, 195 Neb. 95, 237 N.W.2d 397 (1975) (affirming recovery for drunk tank prisoner badly beaten by another prisoner who was an ex-boxer and mental institution escapee, on grounds of insufficient monitoring of the "tank").
171. Wheeler v. Glass, 473 F.2d 983 (7th Cir. 1973).
172. Sinclair v. Henderson, 331 F. Supp. 1123 (E.D. La. 1971).
173. *See* Landman v. Royster, 333 F. Supp. 621, 634 (E.D. Va. 1971), 354 F. Supp. 1302, 1305–1307 (E.D. Va. 1973).
174. *See* Sostre v. McGinnis, 442 F.2d 178, 202–204 (2nd Cir. 1971), *cert. denied sub nom*. Sostre v. Oswald, 404 U.S. 1049 (1972), Oswald v. Sostre, 405 U.S. 978 (1972).
175. *See Landman, supra* note 173, 354 F. Supp. at 1307.
176. "Va. Prison Workers Insured," Wash. Post, Feb. 22, 1974 at C1 and C4.
177. *See, e.g.*, Kaimowitz v. Department of Mental Health, 2 Prison L. Rep. 433 (Cir. Ct. Wayne County, Mich. 1973) (edited).
178. *Cf*. Comment, 4 N.Y.U. Rev. of Law & Soc. Change 207, 215–216 (1974).
179. Holt v. Sarver, 309 F. Supp. 362, 375 (E.D. Ark. 1970), *aff'd* 442 F.2d 304 (8th Cir. 1971).
180. The plaintiff in Matthews v. Brown, 362 F. Supp. 622 (E.D. Va. 1973), tried to present a constitutional claim because of conditions in the shop, which manufactured auto tags, arguing that he was knowingly subjected to constant and imminent danger and fear of loss of limb. The court found no credible evidence of negligence. But it added that even if there were "it could not be seriously contended that there was a continued disregard for safety and knowing and conscious refusal by defendants to provide readily available safety equipment." 362 F. Supp. at 626. The decision thus seems to imply that the knowing creation of an especially high risk of physical injury, resulting in desperate levels of fear, could be grounds for an Eighth Amendment claim under section 1983.

181. *See Holt, supra* note 179, 309 F. Supp. at 377.
182. *Id.* at 378. For an imposition of liability against a state for specific failures to protect prisoners, see Breaux v. State, 326 So. 2d 481 (La. 1976). In this case, the decedent was an older prisoner who attempted to help carry out a plan to transfer a newly imprisoned young convict from a dormitory where he was threatened with homosexual subjugation. He was stabbed to death by a homosexual convict who was trying to prevent the transfer. The court found that there was negligence on the part of the security officers, both in not taking reasonable safeguards to protect the process of moving and in falling below the standard of care in stopping the attack when it took place. Interestingly, the court distinguishes the "legal fault" of the prison guards, which it suggests is not the occasion for "moral blame or serious professional defect," from the state's responsibility for "the undermanned and harassed conditions in which these employees must perform their most important duties." 326 So. 2d at 484. Compare Morris, Compensation and the Good Samaritan, in The Good Samaritan & the Law 135, 137 (J. Ratcliffe, ed. 1966), arguing for legislative compensation of rescuers of crime victims. Though eschewing as unrealistic the rationale that crime represents a failure of social organization, Morris contends that a society so organized that crime is endemic should bear this burden, particularly given the factors of chance in the occurrence of victims and rescuers and of high moral qualities in the rescuer.
183. *See* 442 F.2d at 308.
184. Quoted in American Medical News, March 11, 1974, at 11.
185. 334 F. Supp. 1341 (M.D. Ala. 1971); 344 F. Supp. 373 (M.D. Ala. 1972); 344 F. Supp. 387 (M.D. Ala. 1972).
186. *See* 334 F. Supp. at 1343 (M.D. Ala. 1971).
187. *See* "2 Psychiatrists Differ in Court on Needs in Staffing Hospitals," N.Y. Times, Feb. 6, 1972, at 49.
188. 344 F. Supp. at 379.
189. *Id.* at 395.
190. *See id.* at 384–386, 397–399.
191. Wyatt v. Aderholt, 503 F.2d 1305, 1316 (5th Cir. 1974).
192. *Id.* at 1319.
193. *Cf.* O'Connor v. Donaldson, 422 U.S. 563 (1975), in which the Court held that "a finding of 'mental illness' alone" would not justify indefinite, "simple custodial confinement," *id.* at 575, but explicitly refused to deal with the right-to-treatment question.
194. For Judge Johnson's subsequent finding that Alabama prison conditions constituted "cruel and unusual punishment," *see* Pugh v. Locke, 406 F. Supp. 318 (M.D. Ala. 1976). *See also* McCray v. Sullivan, 413 F. Supp. 444 (S.D. Ala. 1976), refusing to make a "definitive order" on what would "meet Constitutional muster," but declaring that "it is and should be the province and burden of the State . . . to undertake corrective action to provide the minimum

requirements of a system that does not impose cruel and unusual punishment." 413 F. Supp. at 446.

195. For an important essay in this direction, labeled "preliminary" by its author, see Chayes, The Role of the Judge in Public Law Litigation, 89 Harv. L. Rev. 1281 (1976).

196. *See, e.g.*, Hyde, "If Prisoners Could Talk to Judges," 51 Judicature 256 (1968) (written by the Dean of the National College of State Trial Judges, who says, "I left the prison . . . wondering how I had ever gotten the notion that spending a year locked up, or three years, or twenty years, might improve a man's character and make him a better citizen"); "Judges Must Look at What They Have Done," 20 Crime and Delinquency 425 (Oct. 1974) (news item reporting that an administrative rule of the New York State Judicial Conference requires judges to make intermittent visits to jails, prisons, drug-addiction centers, and training schools). *See also* Feature, "If you must do time . . ." in "White-Collar Justice" supplement to U.S.L.W. April 1974 at 4–5. This item quotes the director of the Bureau of Prisons about the Bureau's "obligation" to protect white-collar criminals by putting them in prison camps instead of "in an eight-man cell in Leavenworth with a bunch of rapists and armed robbers," where they "might well be abused sexually and every other way." As revealing in another sense is one white-collar convict's statement that the prison camp in which he is serving his term is "not a country club . . . The punishment is deprivation of liberty."

197. Martinez v. Mancusi, 443 F.2d 921, 924 (2d Cir. 1970), *cert. denied* 401 U.S. 983 (1971).

198. *Id.* at 924.

199. Coleman v. Johnson, 247 F.2d 273 (7th Cir. 1957).

200. 365 U.S. 167 (1961).

201. Sawyer v. Sigler, 320 F. Supp. 690, 696–697 (D. Neb. 1970) (petitioner Becker), *aff'd* 445 F.2d 818 (8th Cir. 1971) (much leeway should be left to prison administrators with respect to "day-to-day treatment and disciplining of individual inmates").

202. 320 F. Supp. at 696.

203. Sloan v. Zelker, 362 F. Supp. 83 (S.D.N.Y. 1973) (request for specialist because of belief that warts are cancerous).

204. Matthews v. Brown, 362 F. Supp. 622 (E.D. Va. 1973). The existence of pain, along with more objective guaranteeing symptoms, has been a distinguishing factor in cases allowing relief. *Compare, e.g.*, West-lake v. Lucas, 537 F.2d 857 (6th Cir. 1976) (bleeding ulcer, with several days of pain followed by vomiting of blood, after which the only relief for at least two more days was the provision of a mild antacid).

205. Estelle v. Gamble, 429 U.S. 97 (1976).

206. In line with the Court's analysis, the court of appeals subsequently upheld the dismissal of the plaintiff's claims against the director of

the state department of corrections and the prison warden. Gamble
v. Estelle, 554 F.2d 653 (5th Cir. 1977). *Cf.* Harris v. Chanclor, 537
F.2d 203 (5th Cir. 1976) (jailer stood by and watched beating without attempting to intervene and made no effort tc get medical aid).
207. 429 U.S. at 110.
208. *Id.* at 104.
209. *Id.* at 107.
210. "Medical care behind bars–a horror story," American Medical News,
March 11, 1974, at 11.
211. *See, e.g.,* Goodchild v. Schmidt, 279 F. Supp. 149, 150 (E.D. Wis. 1968)
(citing cases).
212. Haskew v. Wainwright, 429 F.2d 525, 526 (5th Cir. 1970).
213. *See Sloan, supra* note 203.
214. Robinson v. Jordan, 355 F. Supp. 1228 (N.D. Tex. 1973), *vacated*, 494
F.2d 793 (5th Cir. 1974).
215. Justice Marshall's opinion in Estelle v. Gamble, 429 U.S. 97 (1976),
is consistent with this analysis.
216. This element is made articulate, inter alia, in Fitzke v. Shappell, 468
F.2d 1072, 1076 (6th Cir. 1972).
217. *Cf.* discussion of Holt v. Sarver, *supra* text with note 179 and following.
218. See Standards Relating to the Legal Status of Prisoners § 6.10 (Tent.
Draft), 14 Am. Crim. L. Rev. 377, 402 (1977), and comments *id.* at
547–551.   .
219. *Accord,* Estelle v. Gamble, 429 U.S. 97, 106 (1976) ("Medical malpractice does not become a constitutional violation merely because the
victim is a prisoner").
220. This is so because of the possibility of punitive damages under some
theories.
221. I would here emphasize the view that the fact the government is
exercising "police power" should not alone bar claims for improper
use of that power either in its governmental capacity or its role as
a controller of medical knowledge. *See also supra,* text with note 60,
Part One.
222. *See supra* text with notes 6–17, Part One.
223. National Academy of Sciences–National Research Council, Accidental Death and Disability 5 (1966).
224. Freese, Trauma: The Neglected Epidemic, Saturday Review, May 13,
1972, at 58.
225. Freese, *supra* note 224, at 59.
226. "Emergency Proficiency Goal of New Specialty," American Medical
News, April 5, 1971, at 8.
227. "Emergency Care Guidelines Set," American Medical News, April 5,
1971, at 3.
228. Scharff, "Ambulance Firm Ailing," Wash. Evening Star, Oct. 28, 1971,
at D7 ("you're always having to deal with the sick and the elderly,
and often they are hard to get along with").

229. Levey, "Ambulances: 'Hardest Job,'" Wash. Post, Jan. 16, 1972, at D1 (describing 14-hour day of ambulance crew members who dealt, among other cases, with elderly man who said he had been drinking to kill a pain in his leg and "appeared to be suffering more from the whisky than the pain," and who were bled on twice – by a seriously ill old man and by a child whose sister had smashed a punch bowl across his forehead).

230. "City's New Ambulance Service Wins Admirers," American Medical News, June 21, 1971, at 8.

231. Zimmerman, "When It's a Matter of Life and Death," N.Y. Times, Nov. 5, 1972, § 4 (The Week in Review) at 11.

232. Note, Ambulance Service in the State of Utah, 1970 Utah L. Rev. 570, 577.

233. *Id.* at 582.

234. *See* 23 U.S.C.A. § 402 (Supp. 1977).

235. Highway Safety Program Standard #11: Emergency Medical Services, 23 C.F.R. § 1204.4 (1977).

236. Alexander, The State of Emergency Medical Services under the Highway Safety Act, or Don't Be Caught Dead in an Ambulance, 5 Clearinghouse Review No. 2, 72 at 73 (1971) (the total of 52 jurisdictions includes the District of Columbia and Puerto Rico).

237. *Id.* at 73.

238. *See, e.g.,* Guerrero v. Copper Queen Hospital, 112 Ariz. 104, 537 P.2d 1329 (1975) (granting leave to amend complaint to nonresident alien plaintiffs who crossed Mexican border to seek emergency treatment; emphasis on "statutes and regulations" as "the actual basis for the requirement to provide emergency services"); Stanturf v. Sipes, 447 S.W.2d 558, 35 A.L.R.3d 834 (Mo. 1969).

239. "MD refusals hit by state," American Medical News, Jan. 31, 1977, at 12.

240. Greater Washington D.C. Area Council of Senior Citizens v. District of Columbia Government, 406 F. Supp. 768, 776 (D.D.C. 1975). *Cf.* Penn v. San Juan Hospital Inc., 528 F.2d 1181 (10th Cir. 1975) (claim that hospital utilizing federal funds denied request for emergency care by Indians on racial grounds; class action for permanent injunction maintainable).

241. 1970 Utah L. Rev., *supra* note 232, at 599.

242. Zimmerman, "Hope for a Defense against a Baby-Killer," N.Y. Times, Jan. 16, 1972, § 4 (The Week in Review) at 7.

243. Auerbach, "Care of Newborn Infants: 'A Great Revolution,'" Wash. Post, Feb. 1, 1971, A1 at A13.

244. *See* 42 U.S.C.A. §§ 426(e)–(g) (1974 & Supp. 1977). Subsection (f) provides: "Medicare eligibility on the basis of chronic kidney failure shall begin with the third month after the month in which a course of renal dialysis is initiated and would end with the twelfth month after the month in which the person has a renal transplant or such course of dialysis is terminated."

245. Lyons, "When a Disastrous Illness Strikes," N.Y. Times, Oct. 22, 1972, § 4 (The Week in Review) at 7.
246. A physician who has had dialysis and five kidney transplants finds himself "distressed by the controversial dialogue that separates the nephrologist from the transplant surgeon, so that, in the end, it is the patient who is given short shrift. I have observed that both nephrologist and transplant surgeon work alone in their own separate fields, and that the patient becomes lost in a morass of professional role playing and physician self-justification. As legitimate as their altruistic but differing opinions may be, the nephrologist and the transplant surgeon must work together for the patient, so that therapy is tailored to suit the individual patient, his circumstances, his needs and the quality of his life." Calland, Iatrogenic Problems in End-Stage Renal Failure, 287 New Eng. J. Med. 334 (1972).
247. *See* text with notes 184–186 *supra*, Part One.
248. Whitaker, "The High Cost of Treating Hemophilia," Wash. Post, March 3, 1974, A1 at A3.
249. Schwartz, "Money Is Part of the Treatment," N.Y. Times, Dec. 31, 1972, § 4 (The Week in Review) at 10.
250. *See* Wash. Post article, *supra* note 248.
251. *See supra* text with notes 75–77, Part One.
252. *See* N.Y. Times article, *supra* note 249. The politics of hemophilia in Britain has been complex. Though it was Oxford researchers who developed a blood factor that effectively speeded clotting for sufferers, and though other European countries had been making the product, the national Department of Health licensed its import only on condition that hard-pressed regional health authorities would pay for it. The inability of these agencies to do so led to re-exportation of the extract. After an ensuing furor, the national department began buying up stocks of the factor—for sale to the regional authorities at the normal commercial price. "The cure is ready but Jon's suffering goes on," Sunday Times, Feb. 16, 1975, at 3.
253. *See* N.Y. Times article, *supra* note 249.
254. *See* Application of President and Directors of Georgetown College, Inc., 331 F.2d 1000, 9 A.L.R.3d 1367; 331 F.2d 1010 (D.C. Cir. 1964), *cert. denied* 377 U.S. 978 (1964).
255. Butler v. Jones, 3 Clearinghouse Review No. 11 at 305 (E.D. Pa. 1969), reported before the extension of Medicare coverage to kidney patients.
256. *See* I.H. Porter, Heredity & Disease 212–214 (1968).
257. Bremer v. Richardson, 347 F. Supp. 465 (D. Neb. 1972).
258. *Id.* at 469. (Emphasis in original.)
259. *Id. Accord, e.g.*, Sheeran v. Weinberger, 392 F. Supp. 106 (S.D. Ohio 1975) (construing regulatory language "skilled nursing services").
260. 347 F. Supp. at 468.
261. Tylka v. Weinberger, 7 Clearinghouse Review No. 4 at 216 (N.D. Ohio 1973) (summary).

262. *Cf.* Bennett v. Butz, 386 F. Supp. 1059 (D. Minn. 1974) (requiring compliance with "outreach" requirements of Food Stamp Act). *See also* Williams v. Wohlgemuth, 540 F.2d 163 (3d Cir. 1976) (utilizing the supremacy clause to invalidate Pennsylvania regulations limiting emergency assistance program to emergencies caused by civil disorder or natural disaster, while citing legislative history indicating a concern for "the emergency needs of all children approaching destitution"); Burrell v. Norton, 381 F. Supp. 339 (D. Conn. 1974) (invalidating state limitation of "catastrophic event" aid to fire and flood, in case where practically all family's property was stolen); Lombard v. Staszak, 83 Misc. 2d 1050, 373 N.Y.S.2d 967 (1975) (relief ordered for "bureaucratically engendered catastrophe" caused by social services department's failure to notify petitioner that it would no longer pay utility bills).

263. *Cf.* Gillum & Barsky, Diagnosis and Management of Patient Noncompliance, 228 J.A.M.A. 1563 (1974), emphasizing importance of attention to physician-patient communication as element in overcoming psychological and social hindrances to compliance with therapeutic regimes. *See also* Calland quotation, *supra* note 246.

264. St. Patrick Hosp. v. Powell County, 156 Mont. 153, 477 P.2d 340 (1970).

265. 156 Mont. at 157–158, 477 P.2d at 342.

266. 156 Mont. at 160, 477 P.2d at 343.

267. For a suggestion of strategies using this kind of attack, see Carey, A Constitutional Right to Health Care: An Unlikely Development, 23 Cath. U.L. Rev. 492 (1974).

268. And once a legislative decision is taken to devote a certain amount of resources to medical care, it has been held that courts cannot require that massive efforts to identify and treat the eligible population must be even more massive. *See* Woodruff v. Lavine, 417 F. Supp. 824 (S.D.N.Y. 1976). *But cf.* Bennett v. Butz, note 262 *supra*.

269. Boone v. Tate, CCH Pov. L. Rep. ¶12,653 (Pa. Com. Pl. 1970) (summary).

270. I can here only suggest a basic application of the analysis to this problem, which has provoked much recent litigation. Further exploration is merited on a wide range of specific issues, including summary terminations of utilities and substandard preparation in the operation of a variety of services.

271. 62 N.J. 456, 303 A.2d 76 (1973).

272. City of Louisville v. Cope, 296 Ky. 207, 208, 176 S.W.2d 390, 391 (1943).

273. 296 Ky. at 209, 176 S.W.2d at 391.

274. 62 N.J. at 469, 303 A.2d at 83.

275. *Id.* at 469–470, 303 A.2d at 83.

276. 296 Ky. at 209, 176 S.W.2d at 391. It should be noted that the defense

of contributory negligence is available when the plaintiff possesses the ability to avoid particular hazards that have become apparent to him. *See id.* at 210, 176 S.W.2d at 392.

277. See text with notes 3–23 *supra*, Part One.

278. Johnston v. District of Columbia, 118 U.S. 19, 21 (1886).

279. 62 N.J. at 470–471, 303 A.2d at 84. Previsions of this view had filtered through the decision of a New York trial court in a case involving garbage services, according to a summary of its opinion. *See* Serina v. Lindsay, CCH Pov. L. Rep. ¶12,095 (N.Y. Sup. Ct., Spec. T. 1970) (summary).

280. *Cf.* San Antonio Independent School District v. Rodriguez, 411 U.S. 1 (1973).

281. *Compare, e.g.*, Milliken v. Bradley, 418 U.S. 717 (1974) *and* Milliken v. Bradley, ——— U.S. ———, 97 S. Ct. 2749 (1977) *with* Note, The Affirmative Duty to Integrate in Higher Education, 79 Yale L.J. 666 (1970).

282. *See* Saretsky & Mecklenburger, "See You in Court?" Saturday Review, Oct. 14, 1972, at 50.

283. A brief summary of a lawsuit by a San Francisco high school graduate describes claims for $500,000 general damages and $500,000 punitive damages, as well as for the cost of a private tutor to bring the plaintiff's fifth-grade reading capacity up to a proper level. "Poor Reader Sues School," Trial Magazine, Jan.–Feb. 1973, at 3.

284. *See* Saretsky & Mecklenburger, *supra* note 282, at 55.

285. *See* text with notes 120–125 *supra*.

286. *See* note 283 *supra*.

287. Compare *supra*, text following note 125.

288. The next frontier—indeed in many ways an even more sympathetic case—has already been reached with a suit by a foster child for psychological injury caused by official acceptance of an allegedly mistaken diagnosis of mental retardation, coupled with placements in sixteen foster homes in seventeen years. "Youth Sues Over Foster Homes," Wash. Post, Nov. 17, 1976, at A3.

289. *See* text *supra* with note 60.

290. *Cf.*, generally, Justice Jackson's reference to a "dependent society," effectively linking both governmental duty and the obligation of private manufacturers, in Dalehite v. United States, 346 U.S. 15, 51 (1953) (dissenting opinion).

291. *Cf.* Tribe, Unraveling *National League of Cities*: The New Federalism and Affirmative Rights to Essential Government Services, 90 Harv. L. Rev. 1065 (1977). Reading Professor Tribe's essay after the completion of this manuscript, I found some intriguing parallels in his very differently focused analysis, to which it is particularly appropriate to refer in these paragraphs.

292. *See, e.g.*, F.J. Turner, The Frontier in American History 219–221 (1920).

293. *Cf.* Whittaker v. Sandford, 110 Me. 77, 85 Atl. 399 (1912).
294. Falco v. City of New York, 34 App. Div. 2d 673, 310 N.Y.S.2d 524 (1970), *aff'd without opin.*, 29 N.Y.2d 918, 329 N.Y.S.2d 97, 279 N.E.2d 854 (1972).
295. *See* Stupka v. Peoples Cab Co., 437 Pa. 509, 264 A.2d 373 (1970), discussed text with notes 38–40 *supra*, Part One.
296. *See* note 294 *supra*.
297. *See* text with note 65 *supra*.
298. *Cf.* Levey, "Ambulances: 'Hardest Job,'" Wash. Post, Jan. 16, 1972, at D1 (reporting earthy complaint of one victim that she was whisked away from the accident scene so quickly that she had no time to get the offending driver's number herself). Clearly to be distinguished is the case in which a full-scale investigation is undertaken but is unsuccessful, *e.g.*, Jackson v. Heymann, 126 N.J. Super, 281, 314 A.2d 82 (1973) (no cause of action on allegations that police failed to make sufficient investigation of accident, on facts which included preliminary investigation, survey of trucking firms, and interviewing of several witnesses).
299. *Cf.* Stupka v. Peoples Cab. Co., *supra* note 295, 437 Pa. at 512–513, 264 A.2d at 374 (opinion of Cohen, J.).

Index